People and Communication

Communication in Organisations

Desmond W Evans

Contents

Acknowledgments

The author and publishers have made every effort to trace the
ownership of all copyright material and to obtain permission from
the owners of copyright.
Thanks are due to the following for permission to reprint the
material indicated:

West Sussex County Council for the organisation chart, p 12

PITMAN EDUCATION LIMITED
39 Parker Street, London WC2B 5PB

Associated Companies
Pitman Publishing Pty Ltd, Melbourne
Pitman Publishing New Zealand Ltd, Wellington

© Desmond W Evans 1978

First published in Great Britain 1978
Reprinted 1979, 1980

Text set in 10/12pt Sabon
printed and bound in Great Britain
at The Pitman Press, Bath

ISBN 0 273 01246 0 (bound book)
     0 273 01247 9 (module pack)

Introduction

'I've always believed in calling a spade a spade. . . .'

'I don't believe in beating about the bush. . . .'

'Always speak my mind. . . .'

'I fancy I'm pretty clear-minded . . .'

'Communication? No problem – it's the other people round here. . . .'

It's a fact of life that we all consider ourselves to be good communicators. After all, by the time we start work we've been at it for at least sixteen years, and we manage to get what we want. Or do we? Part of our self-esteem, that image of ourselves which acts as a kind of defence-mechanism in the face of the bruisings of this world, requires that we see ourselves as straight-talking, level-headed, able, honest, and above all, effective communicators.

Yet how often do we fail to see ourselves as others see us?

'Trouble with Harry, he always calls a spade a shovel. . . .'

'Like a bull in a china shop at the last meeting. . . .'

'Every time she opens her mouth, she puts her foot in it. . . .'

'Janet's all right, she just has a talent for rubbing people up the wrong way. . . .'

All too often there is a difference between what we say and what we think we have said, and between how we feel we have handled people and how they think they have been treated. When such 'gaps' occur between the intent and the action often it is stated that there has been 'a break-down in communication'. Sometimes the breakdown is allowed to become so serious that the gap becomes a chasm – relatives in families ceasing to speak to one another, managements and trade unions refusing to meet and governments recalling ambassadors when relations between states reach a low ebb.

In fact, whenever people communicate, either as individuals or within groups, problems inevitably occur – instructions may be impossible to carry out, offence is taken at a particular remark, a directive is ambiguously phrased, or people's attitudes are coloured by jealousy, resentment or frustration.

'Communications are pretty straightforward here – the Old Man tells us what to do and we do it! . . .'

During the past fifty years, industrial, commercial and public service organisations have grown prodigiously to meet the needs of advanced technological societies. Sometimes as many as 10 000 people work on one site, or one company employs more than 50 000 people. Clearly, good communications are essential to the efficient operation of any organisation, and vital to the fulfilment of all those who commit their working lives to it.

For this reason, management specialists and behavioural scientists have devoted much thought and energy over recent years to analysing the problems caused by bad communication practices, and to creating good communication climates, and systems.

As a result of the current structure of societies and economies, most of us will spend our working lives in an organisation – for many of us it will be a large one. If we are to understand our working environment it is essential that we become good communicators with social skills.

Theory and process

When communication specialists began to study the theory and process of communication methodically, they developed an approach to the mechanics of communicating which is, perhaps, best expressed as a cycle. Essentially, 'messages' are 'sent' and 'received' and confirmation of their receipt and interpretation is returned by a 'receiver' to a 'sender'; effective communication is always a two-way process.

As a result of carefully performed experiments and the patient compilation of case-histories of various communication practices, management specialists and behavioural scientists came to appreciate that what appeared on the surface to be a simple and straightforward process was, in fact, both involved and subtle. After all, if the workings of one human mind are complex, how much more so must be the various inter-actions and relationships of two, or even many minds, in the process of communication!

Simply expressed the cycle of communicating proceeds through a number of stages during which a message is conceived by a sender, encoded and relayed via a particular route to a receiver who then decodes and interprets it and finally confirms to the sender that it has been understood. This process is set out in more detail in the diagram.

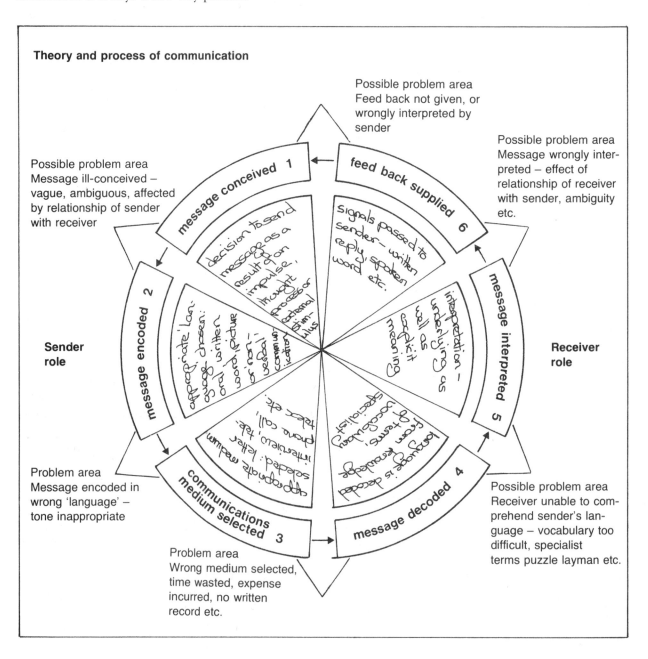

Theory and process of communication

Possible problem area
Feed back not given, or wrongly interpreted by sender

Possible problem area
Message wrongly interpreted – effect of relationship of receiver with sender, ambiguity etc.

Possible problem area
Message ill-conceived – vague, ambiguous, affected by relationship of sender with receiver

Sender role

Receiver role

Problem area
Message encoded in wrong 'language' – tone inappropriate

Possible problem area
Receiver unable to comprehend sender's language – vocabulary too difficult, specialist terms puzzle layman etc.

Problem area
Wrong medium selected, time wasted, expense incurred, no written record etc.

message conceived 1
feed back supplied 6
message encoded 2
message interpreted 5
communications medium selected 3
message decoded 4

decision to send message as a result of an impulse, thought or mental process of internal communication

signals passed to sender – written reply, spoken word etc.

interpretation – underlying as well as explicit meaning

appropriate language chosen: written or oral; good or poor; verbal or non-verbal communication

language is decoded from knowledge of terms, specialist vocabulary etc.

appropriate medium selected: letter, interview, tel. phone call, telex etc.

Stage one: conceiving the message

The first stage in the communication process is the decision made by a sender to communicate a message. Some messages are sent involuntarily – such as a scream of fright or gasp of pain. Others are the result of an impulse which occurs so quickly that the sender is barely conscious of having decided to say or do anything. Yet others may be the result of a careful process of reasoning. Some messages are the product of an internal reasoning or emotional process and some of an external stimulus.

The very act of articulating an idea in words, expressions or gestures is in itself a development of originating the idea itself. Even so, it is not uncommon for people to conceive ideas which when uttered are regarded as 'half-baked', or for someone to regret at the moment of speaking a conceived message:

'I really put my foot in it!'

Stage two: encoding the message

Before a message may be sent to its recipient, the sender needs to encode it in an appropriate language. The language may take the form of a sympathetic grunt, an abrupt gesture of impatience or a carefully written letter or report. It may also take the form of a picture, symbol or non-verbal expression or gesture.

The languages of communication include the following:

the spoken word
the written word
the number
the picture, drawing or symbol
the non-verbal communication: expression, gesture, posture

The eventual success of the message depends in no small part upon the choice of an appropriate language. At a sales conference, for example, a chart may express instantly what a long, spoken address may fail to impart.

Stage three: selecting the communications medium

Once the appropriate language has been chosen, the sender needs to select the right medium through which to transmit the message. The choice of a medium depends upon a number of, sometimes, quite complicated factors. The proximity and availability of a colleague in a neighbouring office may suggest a head round a door and a spoken word. If the message is disciplinary, however, then a formal, private interview may be required.

Some messages need to be written – contracts are an obvious example – and geographical distance may require that the message is transmitted in letter-form. Sometimes the very complexity of a message dictates that it is produced as a written report which may be composed and studied in stages. Alternatively, the need for a quick exchange of attitudes and opinions may suggest a meeting as the best medium.

The likely effect of a message upon its receiver will also influence the choice of medium. Bad news, for example, is much better broken in a private interview than more impersonally in a letter.

Some major factors influencing the choice of the communications medium are:

potential effectiveness
need for tact
simultaneous reception of information by recipients
need for a written record
confidentiality
need for instant feedback
complexity of message
time
cost

Stage four: decoding the message

Before a message can be absorbed or acted upon it first needs to be understood. Many messages are ineffective because the sender failed to realise that the language he had chosen was beyond the ability of his receiver to comprehend. Terms like 'officialese' and 'jargon' are frequently employed when someone has used inappropriate language. Some of the reasons for a failure by a receiver to decode a message successfully are:

The receiver does not share the sender's language (e.g. he cannot read a graph).

The sender's vocabulary (words or phrases) is unknown to the receiver.

The sender's sentence structure and use of English are too difficult for the receiver to grasp.

The sender is a specialist and the receiver is a layman.

Education, cultural pursuits and outlooks create a language block between sender and receiver.

The sender uses over-simple language and thus condescends to the receiver causing resentment to create a block.

Stage five: interpreting the message

As well as comprehending the language of the message, the receiver also needs to be able to interpret it correctly. The underlying import of a message may be rather different from the words actually spoken:

'Sorry about old Jonesy. Liked him a lot. I daresay they'll be looking for someone with experience of marketing to head up the division pretty soon now.'

It doesn't need a crystal-ball gazer to 'read between the lines' of the above message and to determine that the sympathy for 'old Jonesy' does not run very deep and that the speaker perhaps 'fancies his chances' for the arising post! In point of fact, many messages are capable of more than one interpretation – the apparent meaning and the underlying one. Often we speak sarcastically, with innuendo or *double-entendre*. Sometimes we reveal innermost thoughts unconsciously. Also, the context in which a message is sent affects the way in which it may be interpreted. 'Have a bit of a clean up' may mean one thing on a routine Friday afternoon, but quite another on the day before the managing director's visit! Problems of interpretation also arise when there is 'bad blood' between the sender and receiver:

'Get on with it right away, would you!'

may be interpreted by a receiver who dislikes the sender as a deliberate attempt to 'needle', and may result in a task being deliberately left as a means of passive retaliation. In this situation, however, it must not be forgotten that the sender may also be at fault for having 'encoded' the message in a provocative way.

Stage six: providing feedback

All the stages so far outlined are important, yet the need for feedback is perhaps the most essential. Feedback provides a means of reassuring a sender that:

A message has been received
It has been comprehended
It has been correctly interpreted
The receiver is ready for the next part.

Such feedback, when positive, may be signalled by a nod, smile, a written acceptance of an invitation or a series of agreeing murmurs at the other end of a telephone line. Alternatively, it may be negative – a stifled yawn, a restless fidgeting, an angry silence or vociferous clamour.

Either way, such a feedback is essential for a successful communication process, since it serves to confirm to a sender that he is on the one hand 'pitching' the message successfully, or on the other that an alternative language, medium or totally different approach is called for. Whether positive or negative, if correctly interpreted, feedback is always productive to the alert and sensitive sender.

It is therefore important to be able to recognise the signals and read them correctly.

Using the process effectively

Research has proved that, with effort and application, communication techniques may be improved out of all recognition! The first step in becoming a more efficient communicator is to be more aware – of what you are trying to achieve and of the abilities, outlooks and interests of other people with whom you communicate. Next it is important to remember the circumstances in which the receiver is likely to receive your message – the telephone line may be bad, the receiver may be busy, he may have 'got out of the wrong side of the bed', he may be preoccupied or he may be prejudiced.

The following guide-lines and approaches are intended to help you to think more consciously about developing good techniques and avoiding pitfalls during the communication process:

As a sender

1 When composing the message decide carefully what sort of action or response you desire from the receiver.

2 Choose a language or combination of languages – spoken or written word, picture or symbol, non-verbal expression – most suitable for your needs and the situation.

3 When encoding the message take time to structure your ideas logically. Give thought not only to the choice of language but also to the way you use it.

4 Select the most appropriate medium – letter, telephone-call, meeting, telex message or interview etc. Think carefully about which medium (or combination of media) is most likely to help you to achieve your aim.

5 Ensure that your chosen language is fully comprehensible to the receiver. Put yourself in his or her position. Try to ascertain your receiver's abilities and limitations.

6 Take care that your message is not capable of being misinterpreted. Avoid vagueness, ambiguity, sarcasm, pettiness or innuendo.

7 Check that you are receiving the desired feedback – answers, confirmations, indications of attitudes.

As a receiver

1 Give an in-coming message all your attention. Avoid being side-tracked or distracted. Read, look or listen positively and with concentration.

2 Check that the sender's chosen communication medium is meeting your needs. Don't settle for a bad line, an interminable wait for a letter or incoherence in a speaker. Help the sender to put his message across effectively by letting him know tactfully if the medium is inappropriate.

3 Ensure that you comprehend the message fully. Take the trouble if part of the message's language is unfamiliar to check a reference, word or concept. Seek confirming feedback from the sender if the message is unintelligible by asking for explanations or repeats.

4 Take care to interpret the message correctly. Check whether there is any underlying or implied meaning in the message. Think carefully about what its implications might be before you act upon or divulge its contents. Learn to attend to *how* something is said as well as what is said.

5 Avoid the temptation deliberately to misinterpret a message as a means of retaliating against its sender. If you are not on good terms, endeavour to thrash the matter out with goodwill. Try to realise when you are being hostile to a message and why.

6 Provide the sender with sufficient feedback, so as to reassure him that you have received the message, understood and interpreted it in the way the sender intends.

The media of communication

The electronic revolution, following its mechanical predecessor has brought profound changes to the way that organisations communicate. The 'communications explosion' is still resounding through the second half of the twentieth century. The developments in telecommunications, computers and solid state electronics have revolutionised the business world. Executives speak of 'drowning in a sea of bumf', the shrill of telephone bells punctuates some offices incessantly and computer print-out has the capacity to paper the walls of many an office tower block! The world of Victorian copper-plate, hand-written invoicing already seems centuries old.

The sheer range of communications media, their sophistication and the technology which makes instant communicating possible place heavy demands upon those who communicate within organisations. The manager must control and direct the flow of communication which he generates and receives; the secretary must become proficient in the use of a wide range of business systems and pieces of business equipment; he or she needs to have mastered often very complex record storage and retrieval systems. The following diagram illustrates the broad extent of the manager's and secretary's business activities and the range of communications media available, together with some of the communicating 'tools'. Every employee within an organisation is making constant value-judgments about what to communicate, how to do it, what medium to choose, and what 'tool' or equipment to employ. Moreover, being successful in one's job means mastering the media and equipment rather than allowing them to master you!

Communication: the functions, the media, the tools

The manager		The secretary
reads speaks listens drafts	**Written communication** letters, memoranda, reports, minutes, press-releases etc.	reads speaks listens
informs explains persuades	telegrams, telex messages, abstracts etc.	takes shorthand transcribes types
decides delegates consults proposes suggests organises	**Oral communication** conversations, interviews, meetings, conferences, public addresses telephone-calls, intercom, video link-ups	proof-reads edits disseminates filters informs explains consults
classifies analyses evaluates	**Non-verbal communication** reinforcing expressions, gestures, postures	records files
selects summarises appraises assesses plans thinks	**Communication tools:** voice, face, body, dictaphone, audio tape-recorder, video tape-recorder, typewriter, telephone, intercom, film, public-address system, pocket calculator, computer, business accounting and duplicating machines, overhead projectors, poster, noticeboard, house journal, micro-film, micro-fiche equipment etc.	classifies evaluates confirms arranges assists

Talking point: Behind every communicator stands a technician

Advantages and disadvantages of principal media

	ADVANTAGES	DISADVANTAGES

Written communication

LETTER MEMORANDUM REPORT ABSTRACT MINUTES ARTICLE PRESS-RELEASE etc	Provides written record and evidence of despatch and receipt; capable of relaying complex ideas; provides analysis, evaluation and summary; disseminates information to dispersed receivers; can confirm, interpret and clarify oral communications; forms basis of contract or agreement.	Can take time to produce, can be expensive; communication tends to be more formal and distant; can cause problems of interpretation; instant feedback is not possible; once despatched, difficult to modify message; does not allow for exchange of opinion, views or attitudes except over period of time.

Oral communication

FACE-TO-FACE CONVERSATION INTERVIEW MEETING ORAL BRIEFING PUBLIC ADDRESS ORAL PRESENTATION TELEPHONE-CALL CONFERENCE TRAINING SESSION etc.	Direct medium of communication; advantages of physical proximity and, usually, both sight and sound of sender and receiver; allows for instant interchange of opinion, views attitudes – instantaneous feedback; easier to convince or persuade; allows for contribution and participation from all present.	More difficult to hold ground in face of opposition; more difficult to control when a number of people take part; lack of time to think things out – quality of decision-making may be inferior; often no written record of what has been said; sometimes disputes result over what was agreed.

Visual communication

NON-VERBAL
  COMMUNICATION
  – EXPRESSION,
  GESTURE, POSTURE
DIAGRAM
CHART
TABLE
GRAPH
PHOTOGRAPH
FILM SLIDE
FILM
VIDEO-TAPE
MODEL
MOCK-UP
etc.
	Reinforces oral communication; provides additional visual stimulus; simplifies written or spoken word; quantifies – provides ideas in number form; provides simulations of situations; illustrates techniques and procedures; provides visual record.	May be difficult to interpret without reinforcing written or spoken word; requires additional skills of comprehension and interpretation; can be costly and expensive in time to produce; may be costly to disseminate or distribute; storage may be more expensive; does not always allow time for evaluation.

Talking point: Effective communication is usually the result of a careful selection of the appropriate medium, or combination of media available

Organisational structures

The structure of any organisation is very much the product of 'what it was, what it is and what it would like to be'. That is to say that structures are not static but constantly evolving.

In industry and commerce, organisations are continually alert to the 'needs of the market-place'. The development of a new technology or manufacturing process may have far-reaching consequences for a manufacturing company. Changes in the purchasing behaviour of consumers may radically alter the pattern of trading of a retailing organisation – for example supermarkets and hypermarkets have mushroomed over recent years. In the public sector changes in society are mirrored in, say, the restructuring of local government and the integration of some central government departments.

The form of commercial organisations depends very much upon the scope of their activities. For example, some companies carry out the entire process of manufacturing goods, marketing them, and distributing them to their own retail outlets:

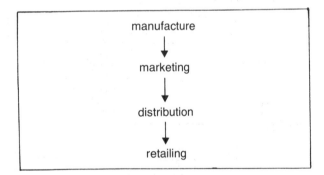

When the whole operation is undertaken within one company, it is said to be 'vertically integrated'.

Other companies specialise in one activity only – manufacturing or distribution or retailing. In such instances a company either makes for others to distribute and retail, acts as a distributing 'middleman', or buys in for retailing goods which a distributor or wholesaler has purchased from a manufacturer. The advantages of vertical integration stem from extensive control and the potential for greater profits, whereas the specialist is able to concentrate expertise and experience within a specific part of the trading area.

Such differences of approach affect the shape of a company's organisational structure. A manufacturing company may look like this:

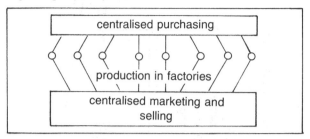

A retailing company, however, may be structured differently:

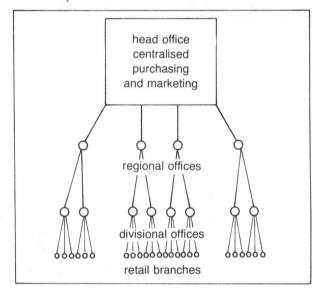

And a distributing company may take this form:

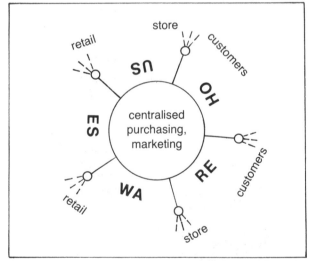

Thus the manufacturer may not need a dispersed sales force, and the distributor avoids the complexities of the manufacturing process, while the retailer concentrates on direct selling to the consumer.

In this way, very different communication needs and climates are established, ranging from the maintenance of good shop-floor industrial relations to keeping the retail customer satisfied.

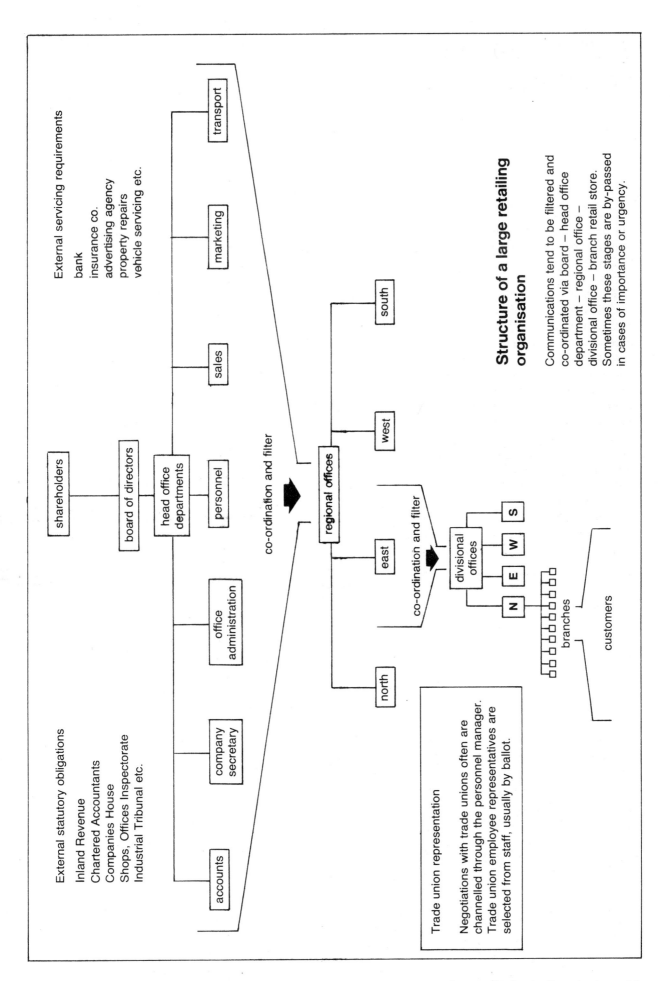

External statutory obligations

Inland Revenue
Chartered Accountants
Companies House
Shops, Offices Inspectorate
Industrial Tribunal etc.

External servicing requirements

bank
insurance co.
advertising agency
property repairs
vehicle servicing etc.

shareholders

board of directors

head office departments

accounts — company secretary — office administration — personnel — sales — marketing — transport

co-ordination and filter

regional offices

north — east — west — south

co-ordination and filter

divisional offices

N — E — W — S

branches

customers

Trade union representation

Negotiations with trade unions often are
channelled through the personnel manager.
Trade union employee representatives are
selected from staff, usually by ballot.

Structure of a large retailing organisation

Communications tend to be filtered and
co-ordinated via board – head office
department – regional office –
divisional office – branch retail store.
Sometimes these stages are by-passed
in cases of importance or urgency.

STRUCTURE OF A COUNTY COUNCIL

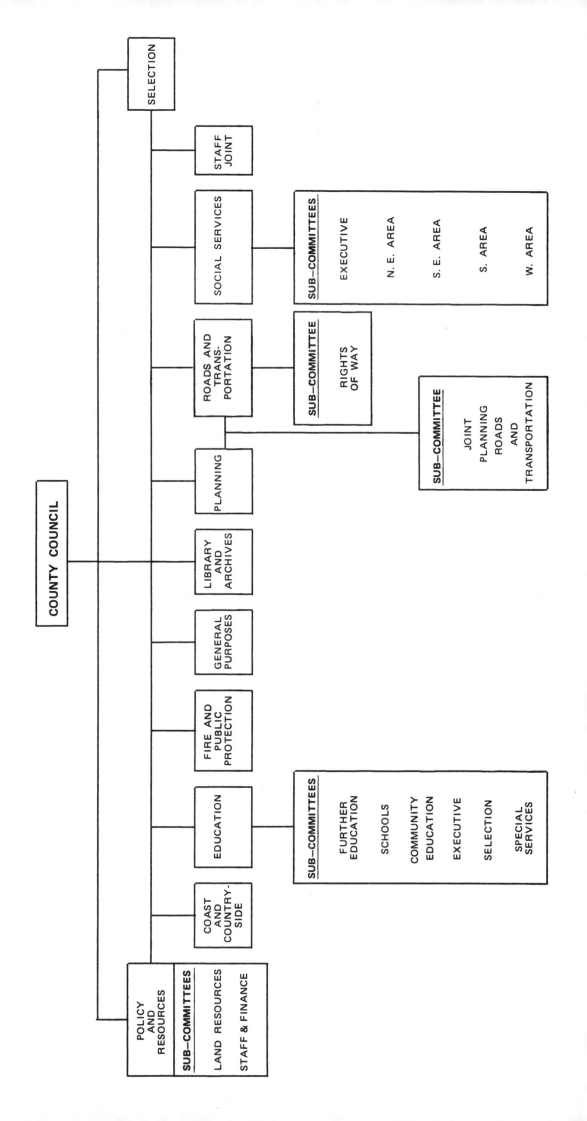

Organisations tend, therefore, to become 'product intensive' or 'people intensive'; that is to say that the constraints imposed upon them come from making things, where assembly-line flow, quality-control and the meeting of deadlines and output targets are crucial, or from dealing with people, servicing their needs, where selling techniques, customer satisfaction and consumer behaviour are central to the activity.

Of course, whether the organisation concentrates on manufacturing or sells to consumers in the High Street, it will need to care about people's needs, about its own employees and its customers.

Hierarchies

Apart from the structures which are determined by an organisation's general activities – whether in the private or public sector, whether selling goods or services – most organisations are internally structured.

Perhaps the most significant aspect of organising people into groups which have specific aims and functions is that either intentionally or unconsciously a 'pecking-order' is established. Few groups operate successfully without leaders and followers. Organisations are no exception. When organisations are composed of 'layers' or gradings of personnel they are termed hierarchies. A popular way of expressing this concept is the organisational pyramid.

The structuring of organisations into hierarchies is in many ways inevitable – although some organisations are evolving other structures, such as the franchise system. The need for important decisions to be made by people with expertise and experience, in consultation very often with those affected, together with the need to provide a person with sufficient authority to execute a decision, results in the 'pyramid effect'; by this means a small number of senior managers or officials are given the responsibility of directing an organisation's activities. It should be pointed out, however, that they are also, by dint of office, made accountable for its success or failure!

Specialist divisions

The other source of the pyramid effect in organisations is the division of the total operation into specialist departments, all of which are answerable to a more senior co-ordinator.

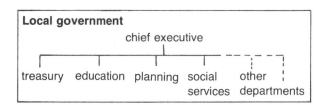

There are problems – in communication, administration and effectiveness – which are attributable to the size and the complicated grading of authority in some hierarchic structures. To avoid such complications many organisations deliberately limit size and grant extensive independence to departments.

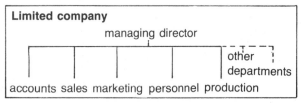

Each department will have its own pyramid structure of head, senior, middle and junior staff, and career hopes and expectations will cause employees to seek to climb the pyramid.

'I've called you in because I'm not too happy about the way things have been going here lately. . . .'

There are problems – in communication, administration and effectiveness – which are attributable to the size and the complicated grading of authority in some hierarchic structures. To avoid such complications many organisations deliberately limit size and grant extensive independence to departments.

A structure evolves

First, it is necessary to examine how communication paths and systems are established in organisations. For a model, let us consider the story of Fred Parkins, greengrocer. Fred started out by selling fruit and vegetables in a small shop he rented. Though he had other worries, his communication paths were straightforward, in that he dealt directly with everybody:

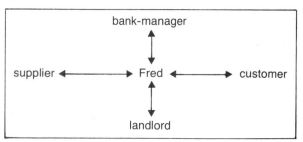

As a result of his hard work and enthusiasm, Fred's business prospered – he took on Harry, a sales assistant. This one act transformed Fred's communication system. He had become an employer, and soon found that he was no longer able to see to the needs of each customer personally – frequently he had to delegate, and communicate his requirements to Harry.

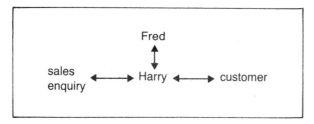

And Harry now first handled some of the sales enquiries. Clearly, Fred's business success now very much depended upon Harry as well, and it became important for both to communicate effectively.

Fred's business prospered further, and he decided to open another shop. Harry was put in to manage it, and Fred, meanwhile had trained another assistant, Jack, to manage the founding shop. His organisational structure looked like this:

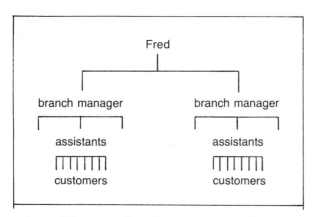

Part of the price of Fred's success was that he could no longer manage all the administration himself. He found it necessary in the end to appoint a number of administrative personnel. His organisation had become more complex.

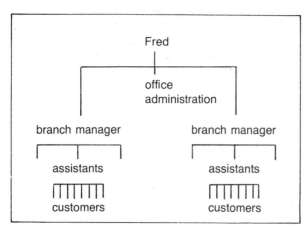

Fred found that he had generated a number of new problems with his extra business:
- In some ways he felt he had 'lost control' and missed serving his customers.
- He did not always get to know about customers' complaints until events had taken a serious turn.
- His two branch managers did not always like it if any of the assistants approached him directly about problems.
- Relations were not always good between the shop and office staffs.
- There was a certain amount of unproductive rivalry between the branch managers – for example when one branch was re-fitted.
- His instructions had a way of becoming distorted and misinterpreted by the time they reached the assistants.

In other words, Fred, in building up his organisation, encountered many of the communication problems common to most organisations. His problems stemmed from his having to learn to achieve his aims and objectives *through* his employees and overcoming many of the problems which occur when people work in groups which are structured as hierarchies.

Routes

In developed organisations, communications flow down, up and across, from board-room to shop-floor and back, between departmental managers or between sales assistants. They also move diagonally between different levels of different departments:

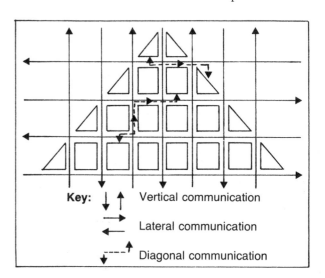

Vertical communication

This term is used to describe the principal channel for routing directives, instructions and policies from top decision makers down through the organisation to the people who, at various levels, will implement them.

Correspondingly, the term describes those upward channels through which flow ideas, suggestions, criticisms and queries from the retail branch, factory floor or middle management.

To an organisation, an upward communication flow is just as important as a downward one. When downward communication becomes an avalanche and upward communication a tremble, then, sooner or later, an organisation will suffer from poor morale, low productivity and potentially explosive frustration in its employees.

The downward flow of communication is most frequently channelled through an organisation's 'line of authority', from manager to subordinate in a 'reports to' relationship.

Lateral communication

The most frequent and routine communication occurs between people who operate at the same or similar levels. For example, sales assistants behind a counter may share an on-going dialogue as part of the daily serving of customers. Similarly, clerical staff in a large county council office need to interact constantly in the course of their business. Lateral communication occurs at all levels of an organisation and is generally marked by the increased frankness and ease with which groups at similar levels – peer groups – communicate. The reason is that they are less affected or inhibited by the 'chain-of-command' situation which employees tend to experience when communicating with superiors.

Sometimes, however, lateral communication between peer groups may be adversely affected by attitudes of rivalry or jealousy. At other times remote geographical location prevents frequent communication. For this reason, among others, the relatively lonely sales representative is brought to meet his fellow at the Annual Sales Conference.

Diagonal communication

Frequently tasks arise in organisations which span departments. In this situation there may be no obvious line of authority through which a middle-manager, for example may 'require' a service or a job to be performed. He may be dealing with a colleague more senior to him in another department, and if the colleague is junior to him, he or she still will not report to him, and may therefore feel under less of an obligation.

Diagonal communication, therefore relies heavily on reservoirs of cooperation and good-will which the proficient communicator will have been careful to nurture by way of the friendly greeting or brief chat to this and that colleague on his journeys through the company's offices.

Summary

One of the most demanding tasks in any organisation lies in keeping all communication routes as open as possible. They are the veins and arteries carrying the organisation's life-blood.

The routes or channels along which communication flows may be classified in another way:

formal
informal
grapevine
bypassing

Formal

This description is applied to those communications which are routed through what have been called 'official channels'. For instance, a written memorandum from a managing director to his departmental heads to call a meeting, or a written report from a regional manager to his sales manager are termed 'formal communications'.

This route, understandably, is used to disseminate an organisation's directives and instructions for execution, since it is reinforced by the authority of those executives who act as 'staging-posts' in relaying such requirements.

Informal

A surprising amount of communicating is done in organisations informally even when it is official. That is to say that much information is passed on by word of mouth among interested colleagues who have received it from various sources – briefings, memoranda, visits, reports and so on. Spontaneous gatherings around a desk may spark off the exchange of such informal information. Informal meetings act in the same way. Usually, however, even when staff communicate informally there is an underlying presence of line authority in that they may share a restricted access to certain types of information, and unwritten rules exist to ensure that it does not leave a particular set of people.

Grapevine

Every organisation has its grapevine. The term describes the interleaving branches of a totally unofficial communication system which has been constructed informally and which is constantly changing.

Users and distributors of grapevine sources of information find their material in the form of confidential letters left unattended on desks, accidental, careless remarks, loud voices coming from behind closed doors or sudden changes in established

'Hello, Grapevine? I'd like to scotch a rumour. . . .'

routines and practices. The basis of the grapevine is gossip and rumour. It is often the cause of misplaced resentments or unfounded fears. It flourishes more particularly in organisations in which communication channels are more closed than open. Like the real grapevine, it is extremely hardy, and flourishes on many different types of soil. Unlike the real grape, however, its fruit is seldom sweet!

Bypassing

Sometimes the urgency or importance of a communication requires that its sender, perhaps a managing director or sales manager chooses a route which bypasses any intermediate management or supervisory stages. For example, the managing director may wish to send an individual letter to all company employees regarding rumours of a proposed merger, or a sales manager may wish to relay direct to all sales staff details of a new bonus scheme.

Most middle managers are mindful of their authority, which is sometimes uneasy in between top management and junior staff. Too frequent bypassing of them in the communication process tends to lead to resentment. This route, therefore, is used judiciously.

The job

Starting a new job in an organisation is invariably a taxing experience. The work may be unfamiliar, faces almost all strange and the geography of a building or territory unexplored. Also, if the job is to be carried out successfully, then its extent and boundaries need to be clearly signposted to avoid duplication or overlap – the stepping on someone else's toes, which causes friction and tension.

For this reason, organisations take pains to define jobs and to establish lines of authority, so that work-loads are equitably distributed and tasks achieved effectively. In view of the complexity of an organisation's total operation, work is directed by delegation and concentrated within specialisms. More particularly, it is often done by inter-acting and cooperating teams. If the new employee, then, is to make a good start, and function effectively, he or she needs to be given straightforward answers to a number of pertinent questions:

What do I do?

Implicit in this question is the desire to know the extent of one's responsibilities. Performance forms the basis of measurement for pay-rises or promotion and if a job has not been adequately defined, then its holder will be unable to execute it and will feel uneasy. In manufacturing, jobs are carefully described and analysed as part of efficient production and arriving at the 'rate for the job'. In offices, however, it is much more difficult to give a precise and total definition to a job; at the more junior levels work is directed closely by more senior managers, but as staff are given more responsible posts, often their responsibilities are more loosely defined and they generate more of their work on their own initiative.

Many organisations produce a 'job specification', a kind of check-list of the qualities needed by a person to perform a job, and the detailed components of the job are often recorded in a 'job description' which may become a working manual for the employee. Some organisations also evaluate different jobs which are then graded in terms of pay.

Who directs my work? To whom do I report?

If the process of delegation is to work effectively then employees need to know who their immediate superior or boss is. This person will act as a focal point or filter for the subordinate, allocating work to be done, assessing work performed, developing the potentials of the employee and generally supervising his or her activities. In some jobs different people will sometimes require work of an individual – a secretary may do work for two or more executives – but unless it is clear where a 'reports to' allegiance lies, problems occur. They may stem from conflicting priorities, unduly imposed work-loads or countermanded instructions. Moreover, the employee needs to know to whom he or she is accountable for any work done, and who will provide him or her with an authority to carry out a particular task as, for example, when a private secretary phones a regional manager:

'*The Sales Manager has asked me* to remind you about your overdue sales report. . . .'

Whose work do I direct?

By the same token, it is unreasonable to expect an employee to supervise the work of others unless both parties are clearly made aware of the managing relationship and that it is reinforced by the line of authority.

How am I doing?

No one likes to feel that he is working in a vacuum. In fact, management experts stress the need for recognition by employees. For this reason many organisations carry out regular 'appraisal interviews' which in a semi-formal atmosphere establish how an employee thinks he or she is doing, and how his or her work is assessed by superiors. In this situation many performance-inhibiting problems may be amicably thrashed out.

Where do I take my problems?

Most problems related to work are usually happily resolved in a private interview with an immediate superior. In large organisations personnel managers exist to help solve personal and work problems. Before taking a problem above an immediate superior it is essential to learn the organisation's complaints procedures, to avoid unnecessarily alienating the superior with whom one works closely, every day.

People in groups

'Any chance of joining your group?'

'Man is a social animal.' This self-evident truth has provided a basis of enquiry and analysis among anthropologists, sociologists and behavioural scientists alike. Wherever we look, from kindergarten to old people's nursing homes, we see individuals coalescing into groups and groups inter-acting with one another.

What makes a group? Certainly it is quite different from a random collection of individuals waiting for a bus or train. Firstly, a group has an identity which its members recognise. This identity may be formally acknowledged, as in a committee or working-party, or it may be totally informal, as in a children's gang or a set of commuters using the same train compartment daily. The establishment of a group identity leads anyone to being an 'insider' or an 'outsider' as far as the group is concerned.

The next aspect affecting the creation and composition of groups is that all human beings share the need to belong to one group or another. Very few people survive long periods of isolation. Indeed, long periods of solitary confinement have been proved to be positively injurious. Similarly, few actively seek the life of the hermit or recluse.

Belonging to a group involves an individual in accepting and being accepted. The whole purpose of some groups seems to lie in maintaining a jealously guarded exclusivity and in setting often very extensive formal or informal entry 'exams'. What the individual has to demonstrate is that he or she accepts and is willing to comply with the 'norms' of the group — that is to say the established outlooks, attitudes and behaviour patterns which the group displays. For example, it would be a reckless probationary golfer who never replaced divots, frequently picked up other golfers' balls, cheated on his scorecard and always wore his spiked shoes in the teak-floored club lounge! It is only by clearly demonstrating similar ideas and behaviour that an individual becomes accepted by a group.

In society groups exist in many forms. The basic, indeed fundamental group is, of course, the family. Extensions to this group are formed through relatives and close family friends.

Yet further, separate groups are readily identified in the local sports or social club, residents' association or parent-teacher association.

As well as possessing a discernible identity and norms of behaviour, groups also exist to achieve aims and objectives, whether commercial, cultural, sporting or community centred. Such groups will evolve, either formally or informally, procedures for choosing leaders and will also establish 'pecking-orders' which derive not only from official status, but also from length of membership, degree of assertiveness or demonstrated expertise. Most cricketers, for example, defer to the club's fast bowler or move aside to allow the 'Father of the House' to reach the bar.

It is interesting to note that within any group of reasonable size sub-groups will also exist or come together temporarily. Within a music society, for example, there may lurk a secret, hard-core nucleus wishing to oust Gilbert and Sullivan and to put Mozart on the throne! Such a group may only be identified when the future programme comes up for discussion and they form a solid caucus at a meeting. Once the purpose has been achieved, however, such a group may disperse as quickly as it was formed.

Groups at work

The characteristics of groups outlined so far are also to be found in company or public service organisations. Companies strive to establish a corporate identity among their employees and to build a corporate image through advertising and publicity to make themselves readily and pleasingly identifiable to the general public. Both private and public service organisations encourage staff to feel more involved and

The Attributes of a Group	
Identity	It is identifiable by its members and (usually) by those outside it
Norms of behaviour	It requires its members to conform to established norms or patterns of outlook, attitude and behaviour
Purpose	It has aims and objectives either clearly defined or intuitively understood which direct its activities
Hierarchy	It evolves either formally or informally a leadership and 'pecking-order' or hierarchy which its members accept
Exclusivity	It has the power to grant or deny admission and also to expel anyone from membership
Solidarity	It demands loyalty of its members and is capable of experiencing internal conflict while displaying an external front
Capacity for change	Its life may be either long or short. It may form, disintegrate and re-form depending upon external circumstances and stimuli.

committed by circulating house journals, newspapers and magazines and by staging social and sports events. Also, in very many organisations there is tremendous loyalty and a will to survive in members facing external competition and adverse circumstances.

If it is true that work-centred organisations embody characteristics shared by most groups, how are they to be identified? Firstly, it should be pointed out that, although an organisation as a whole may have a recognisable identity and character, the whole is, in fact, made up of many smaller groups, and, within them, sub-groups. As we have discovered, organisations are divided into specialist divisions, which themselves may take on the characteristics of a distinctly identifiable group – 'the marketing wallahs', 'those whizz-kids from R & D', 'the Scrooge brigade in accounts'. Indeed, groups are often formed as a kind of self-defence and means of survival in the face of other groups. In addition, within any specialist or departmental group there will form sub-groups of people who associate together for a variety of reasons – shared activities, outlooks, physical proximity, common goals and so on. The following represent some of the reasons why groups are formed within work organisations:

1 It is difficult as an individual to feel a part of a large organisation.
2 People need to have a sense of belonging and to feel that they make a meaningful and accepted contribution somewhere.
3 People are drawn together by striving to achieve common goals and objectives.
4 People often form groups by reason of daily proximity and shared work-places.
5 Common expertise may be the basis of a group as may also be common outlooks and interests.
6 Positions in similar grades may also form a group characteristic.
7 People may wish to join a group because its activities make it look desirable.

Some groups within organisations are created and then develop extremely tight-knit relationships as the result of a formal activity. For example, a committee may be set up to make an investigation or develop a product. Though its members may not, initially, know one another very well, being drawn from different departments and levels, nevertheless, if the work is protracted, and if the members become thoroughly committed to the group's defined goals – especially if the committee faces external criticism – then very often it will become distinctly recognisable as a group. Other groups, however, are formed quite informally, springing from likings which A and B and C may have for one another. Such groups are often to be found within departments, but may also span them.

Relationships at work

The employee, whether as part of a group or as an individual will create, maintain and develop a number of different relationships at work with those people with whom he has contact. The nature and extent of such relationships obviously depend a great deal upon the employee's job and position in the organisation's hierarchy. The diagram indicates the wide range of relationships which, in this case, a manager may have with people both inside and outside his company. (See page 20.)
What the employee communicates and how he communicates is very much influenced by the nature of the relationship between sender and receiver. Indeed, the success or failure of communication depends upon both sender and receiver perceiving that a relationship exists and that it places constraints upon the communication process. We regard the polite handling of a difficult customer by a sales assistant as 'professional'; we admire the way a resourceful secretary handles her boss, who may be under pressure; we applaud the manager who

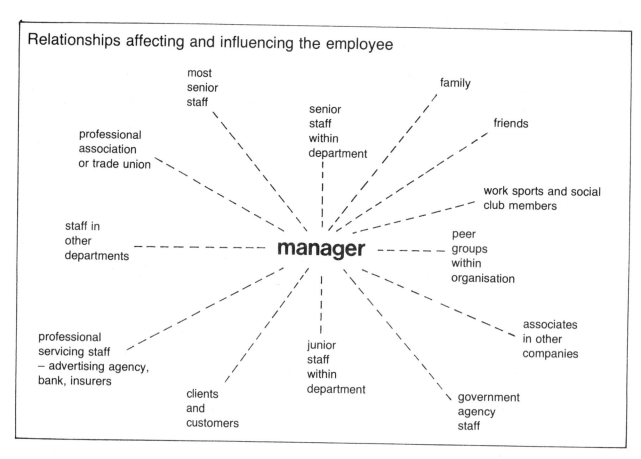

Relationships affecting and influencing the employee

executes an unpopular directive without alienating his subordinates. Each in his or her way has seen a relationship and has used communicating skills to overcome a problem without transgressing the protocols, etiquettes or conventions which undoubtedly characterise the relationship.

Conflicts

When communication goes wrong the fault may lie in any one of a number of different areas:

1 The communication process may break down in any one of the six main stages.
2 The wrong communications medium may have been chosen.
3 The route for communication may have been disrupted by 'interference' of one kind or another.
4 The context or background of a situation may have been misread.
5 Arising more particularly from 1 above, the relationship between sender and receiver may create a conflict in one or other or both.

This last area may cause deep-seated problems. One main reason for such conflict is that all members of an organisation embody within themselves a number of different obligations and responsibilities which come to the fore at different times, depending upon which particular duty they are discharging and with whom they are relating, whether to a group or an individual.

Jim Harper's problems

Take Jim Harper, for example. Jim works as senior clerk in the production department of a large manufacturing company. He is also the representative of an office staff trade union. For some years he has been actively involved in the works sports and social club and has recently been elected its chairman. He is also a husband and father. As the diagram illustrates, all these duties or 'roles' overlap and together go to 'make up' Jim both at work and at home:

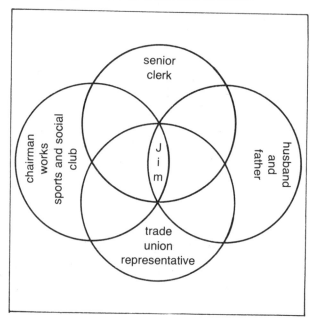

The various roles of Jim Harper

In some parts of each of his roles there is no problem – Jim is able to carry out his duties without feeling tension or conflict. But there are also areas which overlap, where aspects of one role and the relationships it creates with other people impinge upon another role with accompanying difficulties. Imagine, then, how Jim would feel in the following situations:

1 He has been asked to work late on the night he promised to take his family to the cinema – a treat they had all been looking forward to.

2 His trade union is in general dispute with employers over a pay settlement.

3 His departmental manager is appointed to the works sports and social committee saying, 'Don't worry about me, Jim, just treat me as another committee member'.

4 As trade union representative he is given confidential information to the effect that the company is likely to require the sports field for the expansion of the works.

The conflicts which are bound up in such situations are not easily resolved and membership of any organisation, in whatever capacity, is likely to involve the employee in similar, difficult circumstances. Resolving such problems requires much communication expertise and reserves of goodwill and mutual sympathy on both sides of a relationship.

Effective communication, then, is totally bound up with an understanding of how people behave in groups or as individuals and also with an appreciation of the ways in which relationships – managing director/senior clerk, foreman/operative, secretary/principal – affect the process of communication. For example, the managing director, because of his power and status may only get to hear what his staff think he wants to hear; the departmental group which represents the older, long-service staff may express resentment at the changes being energetically introduced by a newly-appointed young manager; the machine operator may have a disagreement with the foreman in fuller and franker terms than he would with the production manager.

Thus communication tends to be coloured by a number of factors based on group attitudes and person-to-person relationships:

1 Communication with a superior tends to be more formal or guarded than with an equal: 'I'd better be careful what I say here.'

2 Communication with a subordinate tends also to be formal and restrained: 'I don't wish to lose my authority by becoming too familiar.'

3 Communication with an equal tends to be fuller, franker and less restrained: 'What I tell Charlie will not affect my position.'

4 Informal groups may not always communicate directly, but 'let their feelings be known' in various ways.

5 People expect other people to communicate in ways associated with their position and mutual relationship: 'The boss don't stand for no nonsense,' or, 'Janet? Oh, yes, always polite. I'd be sorry to lose her.'

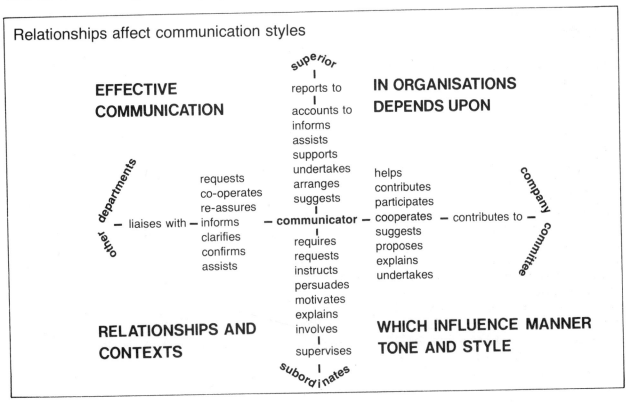

Relationships affect communication styles

EFFECTIVE COMMUNICATION — IN ORGANISATIONS DEPENDS UPON — RELATIONSHIPS AND CONTEXTS — WHICH INFLUENCE MANNER TONE AND STYLE

superior
reports to
accounts to
informs
assists
supports
undertakes
arranges
suggests
— communicator —
requires
requests
instructs
persuades
motivates
explains
involves
supervises
subordinates

other departments — liaises with —
requests
co-operates
re-assures
informs
clarifies
confirms
assists

helps
contributes
participates
cooperates
suggests
proposes
explains
undertakes
— contributes to —
company committee

Styles of communication

Directing
Instructing
Requiring

If the objectives of an organisation are to be achieved then orders and directives need to be sent down the authority line which are clearly expressed. The authority of the sender backs up the 'requiring' message which the subordinate is expected to accept.

Accepting
Undertaking
Executing
Effecting

Accepting and undertaking – doing – are central to the subordinate's role. In fact the directing/accepting relationship is the lynch-pin of organisational communication since it lies at the heart of the contract between the employee and the employer. Acceptance of employee status requires self-discipline and if the receiver cannot accept and undertake courteously phrased instructions he or she is probably in the wrong job!

Requesting
Suggesting
Proposing

Nevertheless, some directives are more tentatively phrased – especially when the receiver's active goodwill is central to the task. Requesting also characterises those liaising relationships between departments, while suggesting and proposing typify the manner of communicating up the authority line.

Informing
Clarifying
Confirming

A great deal of communication in organisations takes the form of passing information up, across and down. Since there is no attempt to secure action from the receiver the communicating style is much more neutral than in directing or requesting.

Persuading
Exhorting
Explaining
Reassuring

Despite the existence of lines of authority and the manager/subordinate relationship, people still need to be led rather than driven. Active cooperation is crucial to effective performance and very many communications need to be persuasive – employees may need encouragement to sell more, to accept changes or to be reassured over developments.

Motivating
Involving
Encouraging

Underlying *all* communication is the need for the sender to motivate the receiver to action or sympathetic understanding. If the receivers of messages are to want to carry them out, then the senders' communicating style must be motivating, involving and encouraging.

Helping
Assisting
Cooperating
Contributing

In many relationships where the communicator makes a contribution to a group activity – meeting, task-force or working party – then the communicating style needs to display a willingness to help, contribute and cooperate. In this way a team-spirit will be built up without which little will happen. Also, the communicator must be willing to accept criticisms and modifications to his or her contributions.

Questioning
Disagreeing
Criticising

Perhaps the most difficult task facing the communicator is coping with expressing disagreements or criticisms. Organisations with any commonsense accept the need for disagreement and criticism in the decision-making process, yet it is an area needing tact, discretion, restraint and above all timing – no one likes being dressed down in public before colleagues. Also, disagreeing while keeping on good terms is an art to be studied which pays handsome dividends!

Talking point: Before embarking upon a communicating process think carefully about your aims, the relationship, the context and prevailing attitudes. Then select thoughtfully the most appropriate manner and style in which to express the message.

Examples

'If production deadlines are to be met and the imposition of penalty-clauses avoided, it is essential that the above causes of delay are dealt with quickly.'

extract from managing director's memorandum to production manager

'Come on, Charlie, this ain't a sit-in!'

foreman to operator after tea-break

'I think your idea of introducing the mobile tea-trolley for tea-breaks by the machines would certainly secure increased productivity. The trouble is, mid-morning and afternoon tea-breaks have become traditional in the eyes of the men. . . .'

production manager to organisation and methods officer at a meeting

'It is therefore recommended that a working-party be set up to investigate the feasibility of introducing a voluntary retirement scheme.'

extract from an investigatory report from personnel manager to board of directors

'So I was wondering, Jack, if we could possibly borrow your slide-projector for the Bristol presentation.'

assistant sales manager to training officer over the 'phone

'This one's a tricky one, John, so I decided to ask you to handle it.'

extract from briefing of a personal assistant by the marketing manager

'I very much regret the trouble you have been caused and assure you that the defect is being given urgent attention at the company's Birmingham works. The machine will be delivered to you no later than . . .'

extract from regional sales manager's letter to a customer

'I appreciate that Mr Jenkins – it's just that no one appears to be controlling the flow of work and the girls are being pressured late in the afternoon and left with little to do in the mornings . . .'

extract from a secretarial supervisor's conversation with office manager about the recent introduction of a typing pool

'I know – and you know – that the company, and indeed the country, have been going through a difficult trading period. Equally, I know that the strength of Allied Products lies in its ability to meet a challenge. It hasn't been easy, and I can give you no guarantee that it will get better at all quickly. What I do know is that if anyone is going to lead the company into a better tomorrow, it is you, its sales representatives. And so my closing message to you all is: the company is proud of what you have done during a difficult year and will back you all to the hilt in the coming months; but it will only be your determination and continued enthusiasm which will turn the corner during the next year. I know I can rely on you!'

conclusion of managing director's address to the Annual Sales Conference of Allied Products

'If it will help, I don't mind staying on to type the letter – Monday's my stay-at-home night anyway.'

secretary to manager late Monday afternoon

Talking point: A major cause of communication failure occurs when the receiver considers the manner, tone or style of the sender's message inappropriate – '. . . he can't talk to me like that!' . . . 'Cheeky young puppy' . . . 'I can never take him seriously' . . . 'if only he'd come out and tell you what he really wants'. . . .

The communicating manager

The role of the manager in any organisation involves the acceptance of many responsibilities. It also places a number of constraints upon the person who manages, whatever his or her title or designation. Certainly the manager needs to be a good communicator, since communicating lies at the heart of what the manager is doing, achieving given objectives through other people. The following table indicates some of the principal managerial qualities; they all direct or influence what the manager says, writes or does and the manner in which it is done and add up to what is an asset in any organisation – the communicating manager:

'The trouble is, doctor, it takes so long – all this thinking about what I'm doing – I never seem to actually do very much. . . .'

As an executor of tasks

decision-making
problem-solving
accountability
authority
initiative
anticipation
effectiveness

That the manager often acts under pressure to achieve objectives imposed from above is not always fully appreciated by his subordinates. Such accountability imposes strains, tensions and conflicts reflected in daily inter-personal communication. Helping the manager – who usually is only too aware of his problems – is a duty of the subordinate. In such ways teams are built and climates established essential to enjoying life at work.

As a leader

delegating
motivating
developing
involving
counselling
reconciling
healing

It is, however, the manager's responsibility to provide the lead and impetus in building a team based on cooperation and goodwill. This involves trust on both sides. The communicating manager needs to make constant efforts to be aware of the expectations, needs and anxieties of his team. Indeed, as much time may be needed to develop and hold the team together as in achieving tasks, since the latter is wholly dependent upon the former.

As a subordinate

integrity
loyalty
discretion
tact
diplomacy
self-discipline

The manager is also, usually, a subordinate. Much of his effectiveness relies on the development of personal qualities, reflected in communication practices, which result in his being trusted. Access to confidential or privileged information assumes qualities of tact, discretion and integrity – and the total subordinate role requires a high degree of self-discipline.

As an information source

informing
disseminating
listening
relaying
interpreting

If his team is to perform effectively, then the manager needs to keep sources and routes of information as open as possible, allowing for obvious needs such as security and confidentiality. He will need to develop skills in ascertaining what his team needs to know in order to perform and then to supply that need.

As a contributor to the organisation's development

thinking
planning
proposing
suggesting
querying
disagreeing

The manager is also a contributor to his organisation's development. If he is to be of benefit, then he needs to put his experience and expertise to use by thinking about what he is doing, putting forward suggestions and proposals, criticising constructively and using instances of disagreement to re-appraise what he is doing as well as to cause others to think about what they are doing.

The communicating secretary

The secretary's role has been significantly enlarged in recent years, partly as a development of communications technology, partly as the result of the changing economic and social climates regarding women at work. Nowadays, the secretarial post is much more frequently a route to executive responsibility. In any case, secretaries have always been lynch-pins or sheet-anchors in many an organisation. Many discharge responsibilities out of all proportion to their designations as assistants to senior managers, and are, in effect, executives in their own right. Moreover, the scope of the secretary's role is enormous, embracing not only the routine duties of dictation, typewriting or filing, but also coping with unexpected potential disasters, using initiative and resourcefulness and often, extreme delicacy and discretion. Good secretaries are treasured by managers in all organisations, since their price is truly 'above rubies'! Perhaps the best definition of the secretary's role is as the hub of a communications wheel around which a manager, staff – in fact a whole department – may revolve.

As a subordinate

loyalty
integrity
discretion
tact
cooperation

The secretary is often, literally, 'at the right hand' of her principal, acting in co-ordination with and as an extension of the manager. In addition to qualities like those already outlined in the manager as subordinate, the secretary needs to be particularly aware of the need for personal loyalty.

As a supervisor

delegating
checking
maintaining standards
helping
developing

Very often the secretary acts as a supervisor to junior staff, and is, consequently, in a similar position in many ways to the manager. She will need to set high standards by personal example, yet be accessible to staff, many of whom may be young, diffident and inexperienced, and so also has a responsibility to enrich and develop the staff in her charge.

As an executor of tasks

accuracy
precision
editing
efficiency

Much of the secretary's work lies in written and oral communication, in producing as finished products the manager's messages. Such work entails painstaking care, and may include the discreet editing of rough drafts.

As an assistant

ability to cope
initiative
resourcefulness
perceptiveness
helpfulness

In addition to the routine range of secretarial duties, the secretary is very often given, or assumes the role of assistant or confidante to her principal. In fact very many management functions are, in reality, carried out by a team of two. Thus taking an interest and being committed may soon lead to a creative and fulfilling assistant's role.

As receptionist and 'filter'

charm
intelligence
poise
grooming
perception
alertness

Most secretaries have an involvement in reception work. In this role they may be understudies for an absent principal and may form a lasting first impression on a visitor or client. Also, alertness and perceptiveness may prove invaluable in relaying information or attitudes regarding customers or competitors who visit or telephone. Also, the secretary needs to be resourceful in deciding what she can deal with and what needs her principal's attention.

Conclusion

Nowadays people acknowledge much more readily the central part which good communication techniques can play in overcoming the problems which occur when objectives are to be achieved by people working in tiered structures or hierarchies.

This is not to say that all problems related to work are easily overcome – newspapers provide evidence to the contrary every day. Nevertheless, systems and processes are being improved. In many organisations employees are consulted and involved far more extensively than in the past. In the area of industrial relations, managements and unions have developed sophisticated 'negotiating machinery' and government agencies have been created to arbitrate where necessary.

The improvements in education during the last 100 years have resulted in individuals being more aware and articulate, with the result that, both as managers and as subordinates, they have more insight and perception of 'the other fellow's point of view'. More recently, the study of human behaviour and human relations has revealed much more of the psychology involved in human communication processes – of 'what makes people tick'.

In addition, organisations in recent years have been casting a much more critical eye over their systems and structures. Management specialists and consulting industrial psychologists are able to demonstrate the problems deriving from a line of authority which is too long or the problems arising from groups which are too big or from doing work which is unsatisfying. There is now a greater appreciation of the fact that people like, on the whole, to work in small, closely-knit groups; there is also more understanding of the need for people to be given the initiative to solve problems or to effect manufacturing processes in their own way. For this reason many organisations are now more loosely controlled from the centre and more independence is given to subordinate parts. The trends of the future, resulting from the findings of the communication and behavioural sciences, may well be away from the giant corporations and back to smaller, locally based manufacturing or servicing units.

One thing is certain, however. Whenever people, even in comparatively small numbers, are put together in a working environment, human nature will ensure that problems ensue! Overcoming the problems of human interaction in the world of work is, in effect, what business communication is all about.

This module aimed to set out some of the main theories and principles which underpin good communication techniques and to indicate some of the problems which only developed social skills and positive human relations attitudes will overcome.

All really worthwhile skills not only take time to learn, but also need daily practice to maintain. Communication is no exception.

The chances are that you already are, or shortly will be working in an organisation. Whether you love it or hate it, whether you become fulfilled or frustrated in your working life, will depend very much on how well you manage to put good communication skills into daily practice. Doing so requires self-discipline and dedication and the benefit of experience – plus the counsel of those who 'have been around' if you are wise enough to seek it.

But the effort is worth it – especially if you consider that you will probably spend some 80 000 hours of your life at work!

Assessment questions

Theory and process

1 Why do people generally imagine themselves to be good communicators?

2 What are the six main stages in the communication cycle?

3 Describe the main features of each stage in your own words. Draw any illustrative diagram which will help to explain the process.

4 How many communication 'languages' can you identify?

5 Draw up a list of the principal media for communicating. Outline the main advantages and disadvantages for each.

6 What is the importance of feedback in the communication cycle?

7 Outline the nature of the problems which may occur at each stage of the communication cycle.

8 List the main communicating activities of:
  a the manager
  b the secretary

Systems and structures

9 Describe how organisational structures are influenced by the activities of a company or public service institution.

10 What do you understand by the term 'hierarchy'? Illustrate your answer diagrammatically.

11 Why are organisations divided into specialist divisions?

12 What are the main advantages and disadvantages of hierarchy and division structures?

Routes

13 Explain what you understand by: vertical, lateral and diagonal communication routes.

14 What sort of communication problems develop as an organisation evolves from a one-man business?

15 What do you understand by formal, informal, bypassing and grapevine routes of communication?

People in groups

16 Explain the main characteristics of a group.

17 Why do people form groups in organisations?

18 How does the existence of groups in an organisation influence the routes and processes of communication?

Relationships at work

19 With what sort of other people does the manager tend to develop relationships at work?

20 Explain how conflicts may arise from personal relationships at work. Illustrate your answer with examples.

21 How does the relationship between sender and receiver affect the style in which a message may be communicated?

22 How many different communication styles can you identify?

The role of the manager and the secretary

23 Describe the various ways in which the component parts of a manager's role influence the manner and the content of what he communicates.

24 What do you consider to be the most important qualities in communicating which a secretary should possess?

Summarising

25 What do you think may be likely future trends in communication practices at work.

26 In what ways is a knowledge of communication principles and practices likely to help the employee commencing work?

Assignments, discussion topics

1 Draw an organisation chart of the organisation where you study or work. Indicate the communication routes.

2 Compose a written case-history (the description of a problem which actually occurred) stemming from your own experience of a communication break-down. Take care to keep places, people and events anonymous. Read your case-history to the group and explain why you think things went wrong.

For example, you could choose a shopping experience, a telephone-call or a conversation in which you were involved.

3 Devise a dialogue including a number of inappropriate communication practices or attitudes.

Your dialogue may either be in written form and duplicated or tape-recorded. Present your dialogue to your group for analysis and evaluation.

4 Draft a manual of helpful hints and tips on effective communication for the new junior staff joining your organisation, (which may be of whatever type you choose).

5 Devise a scene built around one of the following situations:
a a customer complains about a shoddy article recently purchased
b a sales representative neglects to send in his sales report two weeks running
c a member of staff is causing resentment because of arrogant behaviour and disciplining is called for.
After consultation and rehearsal, members of the group should simulate the scene for the group to analyse and evaluate.

6 Write an essay entitled:
The causes of communication break-downs in organisations and ways of solving them.

7 Write an article for your house-journal giving advice to newly-appointed sales assistants in your company's departmental stores on how to serve customers successfully.

8 Devise a case study (an open-ended presentation of a problem) based on your knowledge of communication problems and experience.

You may like to perform this task either as an individual or in a small group.

Suggestions for themes:
a a personality clash
b a blockage in a communication route
c a misunderstanding
d a wrong approach

Your case study may then be duplicated or tape-recorded for your group to analyse and discuss.

9 Interview a number of contacts – parents, relatives, friends or neighbours – privately and ask them what they consider to be the most important aspect of communication. Present your findings (anonymously compiled) to your group and compare notes. Draw up a comparative check-list. See if there is any connection between occupation and choice of important aspect.

10 Imagine the following situation:
The management and trade union officials of a manufacturing company are engaged in negotiating a pay-agreement for the next twelve months. The company's factory personnel comprises:
Grade I   30 specialist staff
Grade II   70 skilled staff
Grade III 100 unskilled staff

The specialists carry out highly skilled repair and maintenance work on the machines; the skilled work more complicated machines; the unskilled carry out more routine tasks and work more straightforward machines.

Negotiating background: management have put a ceiling of £41 000 on the total pay award for the whole of the year; the specialists and the skilled feel that their pay-differentials have been eroded; the unskilled resent that they were left behind in the last pay round.

Each grade of staff is represented by a different trade union.

Simulate the negotiations with three members forming the management team and three the trade union officials.

Discussion assignments – what went wrong?

Discuss the following extracts from conversations and establish what went wrong:

'I've never been so insulted in my life! All I wanted was to try the set on approval and I was informed over the phone that this was entirely possible. When I arrived your assistant asked me for a deposit against possible damage – anyone would think I was a stereo vandal!'

'Listen here, Smith, just because you won the Alfordale contract you think you're the bees-knees round here! Let me tell you, some of us in this office were winning contracts when you were still in nappies! So don't come so condescending with us – we won't wear it!'

'Well, you see, I'm new here. . . .'

'I don't know, it's all very frustrating. Sales are up in the air because of the extra paperwork. Accounts are complaining about the costs. Marketing are determined to push it through at all costs. And Personnel maintain we can't staff it. Still, I daresay it will sort itself out. . . .'

Don't ask me, I only work here!

'The trouble with Jonesy is, he ain't got the nerve to sort out the late-comers – too many of his golden boys among 'em. But I'm telling you, this place don't get started properly until half-past nine in the morning – and he calls isself a manager!'

'No, sorry. You're the sixth person to ask for the blue one this week. Trouble is, we don't get much call for the blue ones. . . .'

'I've had just about enough! This is the fifth week running that they've messed up my pay-slip. They ought to bury that wretched computer down the deepest coal-mine. They must know when the thing's gone wrong! Look, answer my phone for me will you? I'm going over to wages to sort this out right now!'

'Nothing to do with me, chum. Try Servicing . . .'

'I don't care who you are! There's nothing in my contract says I have to put up with your carry on!'

'You're wasting your time. Take it from me. Just keep your head down, wait for pay-day and keep your nose clean. I mean, if your idea was any good, they'd have thought it up years ago, now wouldn't they?'

'It's no good, Harry, you've just got to take the bull by the horns, or there'll be no factory. If you'd grasped the nettle six months ago it might have been easier. As it is, you'll have to handle it the best way you can. But it's got to be done!'

'Can't you read the notice? It says "No refunds on sales goods". I mean, if they didn't mean it, they wouldn't have put it there, now would they?'

'Look, Jenkins, when I want advice from you I'll ask for it. OK?'

'No, I didn't get it sorted out. He just waffled on about spirals and escalations or something. They always tie you up with words. Anyway, I'm going to be looking for something else now . . .'

'Yes Mr Theobald. Of course Mr Theobald. No, no, . . . it was nothing really. It was just that . . . ... No, I know. I realise you're busy. . . . Yes, I know I can see you any time. . . . No. Sorry to have troubled you.' (Puts down 'phone.)

Discussion topics

1 'If people concerned themselves less with communicating and more with doing some actual work, we might get something done round here!'

2 'You're either a born communicator – "gift of the gab" and all that – or you're not!'

3 'The trouble is, once you get everybody chipping in their two-penn'orth, you get further away from a decision, not nearer.'

4 'You either believe in all that communication mumbo-jumbo or you don't. Either way, I don't think it makes any difference.'

5 'As far as I can see, a lot of the communication thing goes on without people being aware of it. If that's the case, it doesn't seem to matter whether you develop these techniques or not.'

6 'I can't see how communication techniques affect me. You see, in my job I'm asked to do something and I do it. Simple as that.'

7 'It's all right, I suppose, if you're a manager, but if you're at people's beck and call like me, you don't get much chance to be a whatdoyoucallit, "communicator chappie".'

Case studies

A high price to pay!

Dick had worked in the Office Administration Department of the head office of Buy-rite Supermarkets Ltd for the past ten years. He'd started off as a junior clerk and was now responsible to the Senior Administrative Officer, who herself reported to the Assistant Office Manager.

Dick was fairly conscientious and tended to keep himself to himself. He prided himself on a faultless record in producing the weekly schedules of selling prices which were distributed to each branch manager, and displayed a certain touchiness if anyone strayed into what he considered his 'patch' or questioned his performance.

He liked to recall to his fellow-clerks in the pub the occasion when he'd 'put one over' Miss Jameson, the Senior Administrative Officer, when she had queried the price of butter on the schedules:

'Forgot clean about the government subsidy she had,' Dick would say, 'came over all hoighty-toighty When I told her she should do her homework first. Still, what d'you expect from a woman? Think they know it all. Still, I soon put her right!'

The other clerks would smile politely but kept their own counsel.

About six months ago, as the company's business had grown, it was decided that Dick should be given a junior assistant to help generally and to learn the job.

'I don't need any help Mr Richards,' Dick had said to the Office Administration Manager. 'That'll be the day when I'm not on top of my job!'

Nevertheless, John was appointed as Dick's assistant, and Dick was asked to bring the youngster along and show him the ropes. John was rather quiet and rather self-conscious about a stammer he would develop when nervous.

'Here you are,' Dick had said to John on his first day, giving him a bulky folder, 'when you've memorised these prices you can come and find me. Carry 'em all in my head I do. Never been caught out yet!'

Some weeks later, Dick was overheard shouting at John:

'Come on! Spit it out, you daft beggar! Why didn't you remember that two-pence off? I told you about that yesterday. – It's too late now, all the schedules have been duplicated. You m–m–m–might well be sorry! Here, give 'em me!'

Later that morning, Dick was called into Mr Richard's office and confronted with the fact that a complaint had been made about his treatment of John.

. . 'That's a lie!' said Dick. 'In any case, people have got to learn from their mistakes. Anyway, who's complained? Come on, you tell me! I don't see why I should have to justify myself for some anonymous Johnny. Was it the lad?'

The Office Administration Manager indicated that John had said nothing and that he wasn't prepared to divulge his sources:

'But I will say this; this is the second complaint I've received and called you in over, in the last two months. If there is another instance I shall further implement the provisions of the Employment Protection Act'.

To which Dick replied:

'Well, you know what you can do with your Act! Keep your job! I don't have to work in some kind of police-state outfit!'

And with that he stormed out.

What was the nature of Dick's shortcomings? Were they entirely his fault? Did Mr Richards handle the interview correctly? Could the outcome have been avoided? Make a written analysis of the case-study outlining problems and causes. Alternatively, analyse the case-study in syndicate groups and discuss your findings in your full group.

'As I see it. . . .'

Bettadecor is a large national company in the home decorating and furnishing retail and distribution markets. The company has over 150 branches throughout the country linked by divisional and regional offices. Its head office is in London and its national marketing headquarters are based in Bristol. The company has recently computerised its sales and accounts systems from a newly-established computer centre in St Albans. The growth of Bettadecor has been swift and is the talk of city financiers.

(Scene inside the Hightown retail store)
'Been waiting long?'
'About ten or fifteen minutes – everyone seems to be dashing about . . . but . . . three of 'em in there, engrossed in something or other . . . Well, I dunno. I think I'll call back . . .'

(The Divisional Office of the western district of the Southern Region)
'Could you put me through to the Regional Manager's Office, please. Hullo? Miss Davidson? Ah. Jack Griffin here . . . I was wondering whether you got my order for the new Peterson wallpaper range . . . Yes I know you sent out a questionnaire . . . Well I sent in an order about two weeks ago, asking for 300 extra rolls in about 30 patterns under the special arrangement . . . only I'm being badgered for them. Oh, there's a new special order form. How many copies? You're kidding! . . .'

(Bettadecor's Head Office. The Transport Manager meets the Assistant Accounts Manager in the corridor)
'How's tricks, Harry?'
'Don't ask! I've just done an exercise on town and country mileage. Could help to cut servicing costs. But you'd never believe the trouble I've been having getting the returns in from the branches. They must need cushions or something – sit on things so long!'
'Yeah, you don't need to tell me. Between ourselves, this computer's giving me grey hairs – we sent a processing manual to every branch, but the mistakes! It's not as if the new invoices are very different from the old ones. Dave Pritchard's tearing his hair out at St Albans. . . .'

(Sales Manager's Office The Quarterly Regional Managers' Sales Meeting. The Sales Manager is speaking.)
'Frankly, it's extremely disturbing. The company seems to have lost all impetus. The figures for the second quarter are simply not good enough. But before anyone starts blaming the computer, there are some questions I'd like answers to about the new order processing scheme to speed special orders. . . .'

(The Manager's Office of the Newtown retail branch)
'Fred, flip the closed sign on the door, will you. And come in here and give me a dig out with these sales analysis sheets. They've been on the phone from Divisional Office. Jack Griffin's been on the warpath. Wants 'em yesterday, or, preferably, the day before!'

What do you see as Bettadecor's fundamental problem? How is it manifested? What could be done to improve matters? Can you draw any conclusions about problems which beset large companies as opposed to small ones?

Write an analysis of the kind of problems which Bettadecor are experiencing and what could be done to improve matters. Alternatively, discuss the case-study in syndicate groups and discuss your findings in a full group analysis session.

Clean sweep at Visco

Jim Peters joined the head office of Visco Computers Ltd as Office Manager on 27th July 19—. His appointment was in no small way due to his record of achievement in a smaller company which had been in need of office reorganisation. At 28 Jim was ambitious and an extremely hard worker. He was given to making a total commitment to any work in hand and expected a similar commitment from those who worked for him. In his previous appointment he had a reputation for being hard but fair. His staff had been young and keen to benefit from the rapid progress the firm had been making. The Visco company, a much larger organisation, was one of the first in the computer industry after the war and after early successes had lost its lead in the market. Staff relationships were generally good and staff turnover low. The managing director had a favourite saying: 'What we lack in "whizz-kids" we make up for in continuity!'

Some six weeks after his appointment, Jim Peters sent the following memorandum to all office staff:

Subject: Office Reorganisation

You will doubtless recall my first staff meeting on 4th August 19— when I informed the department of the poor performance I had noted on arrival and that changes would need to be made.

Despite the introduction of an open-plan office to accommodate a centralised secretarial service, efficiency and productivity still leave much to be desired.

Staff are still wasting time in idle gossip and showing little consideration for others in the open-plan working area. Moreover, it is apparent that little effort is being made to promote the effectiveness of the reorganisation.

You are therefore reminded of the obligations implicit in your contract of employment in supplying a degree of commitment related to your remuneration. I shall expect to see an immediate improvement generally in the productivity of the work of the department.

Within three hours of the distribution of the above memorandum, Jim was called into the managing director's office. A stormy interview ensued. Jim was informed that Visco was not another HMS Bounty and that there was no room for any Captain Blighs. Jim's answer was that he expected support in remedying what he saw as an acute problem, 'a cosy and cushy complacency'. If his resignation was required, it was immediately available.

Assignment

Discuss or answer in written form the following questions:
1 Did Jim go wrong in his approach?
2 If so, where?
3 What would you, as Jim, have done to resolve the situation?
4 Consider Jim's memorandum. Re-write it if you consider it less than appropriate.

People and Communication

The Letter

Desmond W Evans

Contents

Acknowledgments

The author and publishers have made every effort to trace the
ownership of all copyright material and to obtain permission from
the owners of copyright.
Thanks are due to the following for permission to reprint the
material indicated:

EMI Records Ltd, Hoover Ltd, The Coca-Cola Company, Atlanta,
Georgia, and West Sussex County Council for the use of their
logos, p4.

Oxford University Press for the extract from *The King's English*,
H W and F G Fowler, p20.

BBC Radio Light Entertainment 'Frank Muir goes into . . . the
Office' for the Mongoose joke, p21.

PITMAN EDUCATION LIMITED
39 Parker Street, London WC2B 5PB

Associated Companies
Pitman Publishing Pty Ltd, Melbourne
Pitman Publishing New Zealand Ltd, Wellington

© Desmond W Evans 1978

First published in Great Britain 1978
Reprinted 1979, 1980

Text set in 10/12pt Sabon
printed and bound in Great Britain
at The Pitman Press, Bath

ISBN 0 273 01246 0 (bound book)
     0 273 01247 9 (module pack)

Introduction

'Ah, Miss Parker, could you make a few notes – there are a number of things I'd like you to tie up. . . . Firstly, we've had an enquiry through Jones down in Plymouth – Atkins Ltd are interested in the new range of fabrics. Better ring them up and describe the patterns and outline the price-structures. Now, these overdue accounts. Send Jenkins round to see the firms concerned to ask for the money. Forty-four of them. Well, tell Jenkins not to hang about! Oh, and Bentley's. What were the revised buying terms we agreed last month? Was it an extra 5% and $3\frac{3}{4}\%$ settlement, or an extra $3\frac{3}{4}$ and 5? Well, it was something like that. Anyway, Johnson wants to know. Tell him to make an intelligent guess and say they'll let us know if we're wrong. Now, about the Motor Show. Ring round all our customers. What do you mean you won't have time? We always ask them! Ring round all our customers and say we'll be exhibiting on Stand 146. Invite them for the usual hospitality. It's on the 13th . . . or is it the 31st? Well, ask Jenkins to check on his way through London. . . .'

Imagine the crazy chaos which could overwhelm today's hard-pressed executives if they suddenly had to do without that most essential of written documents – the business letter!

Telephone networks would soon be jammed as hundreds of thousands of organisations tried to pass messages to customers and creditors, accountants and suppliers. Communications would have to be passed by word of mouth without the written record to act as a subsequent memory-jogger. Costs would soar and efficiency would go by the board as organisations in the private and public sectors endeavoured to find alternative means of routing the thousands of millions of business and official letters which the Post Office handles in Great Britain each year.

Developments in paper-making technology, supported by electronic printing and copying processes have resulted in making the letter one of the major means of written communication between companies and public sector departments and their host of daily contacts.

The modern business letter is used as a means of making enquiries, confirming information, collecting outstanding debts, selling, advertising, tendering, giving quotations, complaining and answering com-

'It's no good, Robosec. No offence. It just doesn't seem the same . . .'

plaints. It is also used as a means of relaying the thousand and one 'one-off' messages which arise from the specialisations and situations which make up the day-to-day business of the commercial and public service worlds.

In many instances, the letter forms the only contact between organisations and acts as ambassador or salesman or both. Managers set great store by the appearance of the letters they send, since they know that the reputation of their organisation may depend entirely upon the appearance of such letters – whether upon the image evoked by the printed letterhead or upon the typescript. They also realise how important is the composition of the message in eliciting a positive response from the letter's recipient.

In the future, paper technology will be replaced by a computer-based, electronic method of relaying and storing messages using visual display units and computer data banks. But, until all organisations and individuals are linked on a 'super-computer', the letter, typed or hand-written on paper, will continue to form the basis of most external written communication between organisations and individuals.

A mastery of the skills of letter writing, and an appreciation of the displayed letterhead and letter layout are therefore essential to the efficient communicator.

Format

The letterhead

The letterhead is basically the printed part of the letter sheet. Its design is extremely important, and skilled graphics designers take great pains to produce a format of letters and colours displaying the trading-name, logo, address and other legally required components of a company or institution, which will create an appropriate image of that concern for the letter's recipient.

In recent years the development of a 'corporate image', by which the company's activities are publicised in designs for uniforms, stationery, company vehicles, shop-fronts, packaging and so on has played an important part in transforming companies' services or products into household words. The total effect of the design of the letterhead (as a result of the type, coloured inks, paper colour and quality of paper employed) is to create a sense of, say, reliability, modernity, efficiency or flair.

The letterhead indicates the nature of an organisation's activities, where it is located and how it may be reached by letter, telephone, telegram or telex. In addition to this, the letterhead also includes certain other information required in law as a result of The

Companies Act 1948, Sec 201, and The European Communities Act 1972, Chap 68 Sec 9, para 7:

The company's trading name
Its status as a limited company, if appropriate
A list of company directors, if founded after 23rd November 1916
The address of its registered office
The company's registered number
The location of registration e.g. England, Scotland.

All this information must be displayed legibly and there are also stipulations covering any changes in directors' names and the indication of nationality in certain instances. The legal requirements are to protect the letter's recipient from difficulties of identification or communication resulting from unscrupulous dealings.

The logo

One particularly fascinating element of letterhead graphics design is the logo. Simply explained, the logo is a visual symbol or device which communicates memorably what a company or institution does, or with what it would like to be associated.

Local authorities, for example, often use the heraldic coat of arms of the county or city with which they are associated.

Many companies utilise the same symbol both as a letterhead logo and as a registered trade-mark on their range of products. The electrical giant E.M.I., for example, still uses on some of its products the old 'His Master's Voice' symbol of a dog listening to an early gramophone. H.M.V. is now part of the E.M.I. group. And the 'Hoover' symbol, which has perched on millions of vacuum cleaners has been a household word for many years.

Letterhead example

In arriving at an effective design, a university bookshop might well wish to associate its wares with the consumers on whom it relies for much of its business, bringing both together in a visual statement of its activities:

Student Bookshops Ltd

21-25 High Street
Oxford OK19 4QZ

Telephone: Oxford 46912 Telex: 8694173
Telegrams: Stubooks Oxford

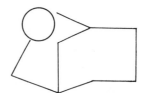

Directors: K. Harris (Managing) H. Klein (U.S.A.) J. Jermyn P. Weston

Registered Office: 12-20 Richmond Street London WC2B 4TZ

Registered No: 694892 Registered in England

Letterhead components

Trading name	must be registered and displayed
Logo	see page 4
Postal address	see annual Post Office Guide
Post code	Now incorporated in postal address
Telephone number	Either preceded by name of town or city or STD code if universally used e.g. 01-632-1000
Telegraphic, cablegram address	usually an abbreviation of trading name with city location
Telex number	see GPO Directory of Telex Numbers
Reference entries	some companies include in letterhead 'Your ref: Our ref:'
Names of directors **Address of registered office** **Registered number** **Registered location**	see reference previous page for details of legal display requirements

Letter layout

Just as much care is devoted to the letterhead design, so also is particular attention given to the overall appearance of the typescript when it is set out beneath the letterhead. One business communication researcher ascribed as much as 25% of the business letter's total impact to its visual appearance. Thus both graphics designer and secretary or typist have an extremely important combined role to play in the production of an elegant, crisp letter.

Many organisations have developed personalised ways of displaying their letters, and display conventions vary from one company to another – especially since, ultimately, there are no absolute rules governing letter layout, but rather sets of generally accepted conventions which are consistently applied, and which most letter-writers agree to accept. Thus the elements of letter layout are constantly subject to change, as one practice is superseded by another in order to achieve greater simplicity, speed of production or pleasing appearance.

The following models indicate in outline the principal shapes of currently popular typescript letter-layouts, which are used in conjunction with whatever letterhead design a company or institution has chosen to adopt.

Blocked

The date is displayed near the right-hand margin and the complimentary close to the right of a central position.
Otherwise as for 'fully-blocked'.

Fully-blocked

All the typed entries commence from the left-hand margin, forming a 'vertical line' down the page.

Semi-blocked

The date and complimentary close are situated to the right of centre and each paragraph is indented.

Open and closed punctuation

An integral part of the appearance of the typescript section of the letter is the use of either an 'open' or 'closed' punctuation system at the end of the lines of type outside the main body of the letter – the letter references, date, recipient's name and address, complimentary close, writer's name and official designation etc. (See The Typescript Component – The Recipient's Address.)

When the open punctuation system is employed, particularly in the Fully Blocked layout, *all* punctuation outside the body of the letter is omitted. The absence of apostrophes, commas and full-stops enables the letter to be typed more quickly, thereby increasing the typist's productivity. Closed punctuation is the name given to the practice by which the type outside the body of the letter is normally punctuated.

Paper and envelope sizes

The most frequently used sizes of letter stationery are A4, (approximately the size of this page), and A5, half the size of A4:

A4 = 11.7″ × 8.3″ or 297mm × 210mm
A5 = 8.3″ × 5.8″ or 210mm × 148mm

Paper sizes used for stationery and some printed matter range from A0 (841mm × 1189mm) to A10 (26mm × 37mm).

In the Post Office Guide, the range of envelope sizes which the Post Office prefers (P.O.P.) is listed. The maximum envelope size allowable is 2′ × 1′ 6″, and the minimum is 4″ × 2¾″, 610mm × 460mm and 100mm × 70mm respectively.

The envelopes most frequently in use are coded:
DL = 110mm × 220mm and
C6 = 114mm × 162mm

Envelope size reproduced below: quarter DL size, normally 110mm by 220mm.

The envelope address

In the 'Method of Address' section of the Post Office Guide, full details are given of the preferred method of addressing envelopes. A frequently used example is shown below.

The typescript component

The typist's role

The importance of the typist's role in the production of a letter cannot be over-emphasised. As the last link in the letter-producing chain, after the graphics designer and dictator, whether as personal assistant, secretary or typist, he or she has an extremely important job to perform. Sometimes poorly dictated or structured ideas have to be transcribed from the shorthand pad or audio-cassette into a legible, correctly displayed letter, free from unsightly typing errors or erasures, and expressed in accepted, grammatical English, without spelling or punctuation mistakes.

During their busy days, managers and executives are inclined to take for granted the many hundreds of hours of hard work needed to acquire the range of shorthand, typing, transcription and communication skills which go to produce the typescript component of a letter. Yet the finest graphics letterhead design in the world, and the most carefully constructed letter message will all count for nothing in the face of a sloppily typed and error-ridden typescript. And so the typist's contribution, though sometimes undervalued, must never be under-estimated.

```
Mr. R. J. Thompson,
Better Business Equipment Ltd.,
14 Broad Street,
MAIDENHEAD, Berks,
SL6  1FH
```

Letter references	commonly author, typist, filing ref.
Date	day, month, year
Recipient of letter	company, institution or individual
Recipient's address	name, street, town, county, post-code
Attention reference	identifying specified recipient
Salutation	greeting prefacing letter message
Subject-heading	brief summary of letter's theme
Letter message (main body)	letter message, or content
Complimentary close (or subscription)	closing assurance e.g. Yours faithfully
Signature space	location of author's signature
Author's identity	typescript of author's name
Author's official designation	author's title or job designation
Enclosure reference	indication of accompanying material
Letter copy(ies) reference	indication of recipients of copy(ies)
Continuation sheet details	recipient's name, page number and date

The Letter Reference

The need to file correspondence, whether originals or copies, for future reference requires that each letter carries two reference entries. 'Our ref' prefaces the

Our ref

Your ref

reference given to the letter being dictated, the out-going letter, while 'Your ref' indicates the reference given to an incoming letter which is being acknow-ledged. Commonly both references have the follow-ing components:
1   the letter-writer's initials
2   the letter-typist's initials
3   a coded file reference.
The first and second parts of the reference are separated by a solidus:

Our ref   HT/JN

Sometimes the typist's initials are typed in lower-case:

Your ref   LMK/pb

and the following filing reference perhaps indicates an account file:

Our ref   HT/JN   WA 151

Sometimes the reference entry is simply indicated by, 'Ref'. Often, the typist types the letter reference prefixes, although some companies include them in the letterhead.
The model letters on pages 11, 25 and 27 show where the letter references may be located.

The Date

The date on business or public service letters is displayed in the order:

day   month   year

For example,

16th July, 1978

Sometimes a comma separates the month from the year, but increasingly, the date is being displayed without the 'th', 'st', or 'nd' and 'rd' after the day, and also without the comma:

16 July 1978

Neither the month nor the year should be abbrevi-ated as 'Jan' or '78' and the abbreviation 16/7/78 should be reserved for sales slips, or invoices etc.
In the United States the date is usually set out as:

July 16th 1978

but the European practice as set out above should be adhered to.
The locations of the date on the letter-sheet are shown in the model letters on pages 11, 25 and 27.

The Letter's Recipient

Letters may be addressed to entire organisations or departments, as well as to an official function within a department or lastly to a personally named indi-vidual:

Gourmet Restaurants Ltd

The Department of Employment

Wessex County Council

The Accounts Department,
Gourmet Restaurants Ltd.

The Education Department,
Wessex County Council.

The Sales Manager,
Gourmet Restaurants Ltd.

The County Architect,
Architect's Department,
Wessex County Council.

Mr P J Harrison,
Managing Director,
Gourmet Restaurants Ltd.

J P Knight, Esq, MA, Dip Ed,
Assistant Director of Education,
Education Department,
Wessex County Council.

The recipient's postal address follows on directly beneath the various forms of identifying the letter's recipient, whether, as shown above, it is a company, local authority, department or individual, either addressed by his or her name, or by official designation only.

Styles of address

The following are the principal styles of address currently in use:
male recipient   Mr, Esq, Dr, Rev, Sir, Lord
female recipient   Miss, Mrs, Ms, Lady, Dame
male partnership   Messrs
Note that 'Messrs' is sometimes used as a courtesy style to address companies where a personal name forms the basis of the trading name:

Messrs H G Cartwright & Co, Ltd,

In the case of Messrs prefixing a partnership, it is followed by the names of the partners:

Messrs Trueman and Wellstead.

Note also the following styles of address:

Sir *Richard* Hargreaves
Lord Chilgrove

Increasingly women in business are tending to use 'Ms' as their style, since it indicates neither single nor married status, thus preserving a personal matter for a private life.

Frequently the recipient of a letter has letters or qualifications after his or her name. Some people spend years of hard study to acquire the degrees, diplomas or awards which appear after their names, and it is important to take care in setting them out correctly, even if this means making a preliminary call to an executive's secretary to check.

In broad terms, orders and decorations precede degrees and diplomas, which are themselves followed by memberships of professional bodies:

James Gray Esq, OM, DFC, MSc, MBIM

Note that men with letters after their name are usually addressed as 'Esq' (as above). Mr is rarely used in this case. Ladies with letters to their names are styled thus:

Miss P Singleton, MA,
Mrs H Grantham, BMus, DipEd,
Or the style 'Ms' may be used in either case.

The recipient's address

The recipient's postal address follows immediately beneath the name of the recipient or his department. It is set out in the sequence: street or road, town or city, county and, lastly, post-code. In the case of larger conurbations (listed in the Post Office Guide) the county may be omitted.

In order to avoid commencing the letter's message too far down the page, it is a common convention to restrict the postal address to no more than four lines whenever possible.

The combination of personally identified recipient, designation, organisation and postal address will look like this:

Open punctuation version:

```
Mr R O Jefferson
Marketing Director
Fleetway Transport Ltd
14 Queen's Road
MANCHESTER     M60  2DA
```

Closed punctuation version:

```
Mr. R. O. Jefferson,
Marketing Director,
Fleetway Transport Ltd.,
14 Queen's Road,
MANCHESTER.     M60  2DA
```

For further examples of layouts of the recipient's address consult the model letters on pages 11, 25, 26 and 27.

Note that when a letter is written to an organisation or department, the official nominated to deal with it may be indicated by typing the following 'leader' above the salutation:

For the attention of:

with the specified person's style and name following on the same line.

Components of the letter

Salutations and complimentary closes

Bracketing the letter's message, which comprises the body of the letter, are the Salutation and Complimentary Close.

Conventions exist to follow certain salutations with particular complimentary closes (see table). Some pairings are regarded as more formal and some less so. In addition, there exists a protocol or etiquette which determines their use. 'Dear Sir, ... Yours faithfully,' is reserved, broadly, for situations in which the letter is formal, where dictator and recipient have not met, and where their respective positions in their hierarchies differ in vertical terms. 'Dear Mr, ... Yours sincerely,' is considered more friendly (hence its use in sales or advertising letters) and can show a closer, established relationship. While pairings such as, 'Dear Jim, ... Kind regards, Jack' or 'My Dear Susan, ... Sincerely, Janet' display a close relationship within the working environment.

Table of linked salutations and complimentary closes in use

Salutation	Complimentary close
Dear Sir, Dear Madam, Dear Sirs, Dear Mesdames,	Yours faithfully,
Dear Mr Green, Dear Miss Sharp, Dear Mrs Howes, Dear Dr Ivors, Dear Reverend Wilson, Dear Lord Chilgrove, Dear Sir Richard, Dear Lady Hatton,	Yours sincerely,
Dear Jim, Dear Jenny,	Sincerely, Kind regards,
My Dear Susan, My Dear Harry,	Affectionately, Best wishes,

Note that: 'Yours truly' as an alternative to 'Yours faithfully' is declining in use.

The salutations and complimentary closes other than, 'Dear Sir, ... Yours faithfully,' or 'Dear Mr Green, ... Yours sincerely,' are becoming less bound by conventions as contemporary letter-writers give their letters a more personal stamp.

Location check-list

1 Letterhead

Trading name
Postal address
Telephone number
Telegraphic address
Logo

2 Typescript component

References
Date
Recipient
Recipient's address
Salutation
Subject-heading

Body of Letter with
Indented paragraphs for
semi-blocked layout

Complimentary close
Signature
Writer's identity
Job designation

Enclosure reference
Copy reference

3 Letterhead – legal requirements

List of directors,
includes a United States citizen
Address of registered office
Registered number of company
Location of registration

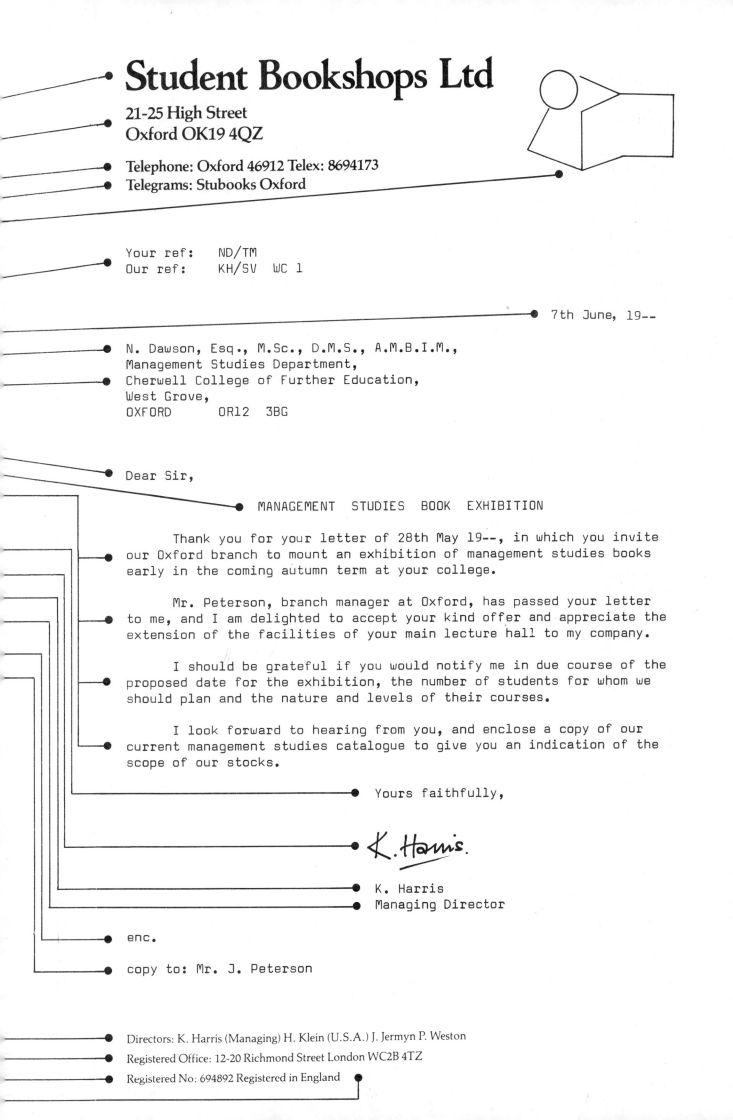

Student Bookshops Ltd

21-25 High Street
Oxford OK19 4QZ

Telephone: Oxford 46912 Telex: 8694173
Telegrams: Stubooks Oxford

```
Your ref:    ND/TM
Our ref:     KH/SV    WC 1
```

7th June, 19--

```
N. Dawson, Esq., M.Sc., D.M.S., A.M.B.I.M.,
Management Studies Department,
Cherwell College of Further Education,
West Grove,
OXFORD        OR12   3BG
```

Dear Sir,

                MANAGEMENT STUDIES BOOK EXHIBITION

        Thank you for your letter of 28th May 19--, in which you invite
our Oxford branch to mount an exhibition of management studies books
early in the coming autumn term at your college.

        Mr. Peterson, branch manager at Oxford, has passed your letter
to me, and I am delighted to accept your kind offer and appreciate the
extension of the facilities of your main lecture hall to my company.

        I should be grateful if you would notify me in due course of the
proposed date for the exhibition, the number of students for whom we
should plan and the nature and levels of their courses.

        I look forward to hearing from you, and enclose a copy of our
current management studies catalogue to give you an indication of the
scope of our stocks.

                                        Yours faithfully,

                                        K. Harris.

                                        K. Harris
                                        Managing Director

enc.

copy to: Mr. J. Peterson

Directors: K. Harris (Managing) H. Klein (U.S.A.) J. Jermyn P. Weston
Registered Office: 12-20 Richmond Street London WC2B 4TZ
Registered No: 694892 Registered in England

The subject-heading

Dear Sir,

SEMPERFLO DISPENSERS

The subject-heading summarises the theme of the letter and not only focusses the reader's interest, but also aids mail sorting and filing. Examples are shown in model letters on pages 11, 25, 26 and 27.

Signature, identity and designation

The complimentary close is followed by a space for the letter-writer's signature, which in turn is followed by a typescript entry of his or her identity and job title or designation to assist the letter's recipient in replying:

Yours faithfully,

R. J. Enwright

R J Enwright
Production Manager

Note that when letters are signed by, say, a secretary for his or her principal, 'for' is commonly inserted before the typescript name. Although derived from a legal context p.p. is also used in this case.

The letter's paragraphs

The fully-blocked paragraph:

————————————————————
———————————————— (See fully-blocked
———————————————— and blocked layout)

The indented paragraph:

————————————
———————————————— (See semi-blocked
———————————————— & indented)

The letter's message is divided in the body of the letter by one of the paragraph layout conventions. Each paragraph is commonly separated by 2 spaces.

Enclosure(s) and copy(ies)

It is essential that material accompanying the letter is 'signalled' to the reader:

enc. encs. Enc. Encs.
enclosure enclosures

The above methods are currently in use. See model letters on pages 11 and 27 for location points.

When letters are copied in order to inform a third party, usually within the writer's organisation an acknowledgment prefaced by:

copy to
copies to
c.c.

is given at a suitable place on the page.

The continuation sheet

At the head of page 2 and subsequent pages of a letter the following information is typed:

recipient's name, page number, date

Status of the letter

When the letter's contents are confidential the following 'warning headings' may be prominently displayed on both the letter-sheet and envelope:

CONFIDENTIAL or
PRIVATE AND CONFIDENTIAL

Note: if the heading PERSONAL is used the letter will only be opened by the person to whom it is addressed.

Common categories of letter

Although it would be impossible to categorise the myriad of different uses to which business and public service letters are put, nevertheless, it is helpful to be acquainted with the more common categories which recur frequently.

Area	Letter classification	Explanation of use
General	Enquiry	to seek information, confirmation
	Acknowledgement, Information	to provide information, confirmation
	Complaint	to seek redress of a deficiency
	Adjustment	to rectify a complaint
Financial	Collection 1, 2, 3	to obtain settlement of a debt
	Letter of credit	to authorise an advance of credit
	Financial standing	to check credit-worthiness
	Solicitor's letter	to procure debt settlement etc.
Sales, Advertising	Sales letter	to sell goods or services
	Follow-up sales letter	to remind of sales offers
	Unsolicited sales letter	to advertise goods or services
Orders, Estimates	Order	to place an order for goods etc.
	Confirmation of order	to confirm a submitted order
	Estimate	to submit a projected price
	Tender	to submit a contractual price
Appointments	Application	to apply for a post
	Resignation	to confirm resignation from a post
	Reference enquiry	to seek confidential particulars
	Reference reply	to provide confidential particulars
Circulars	Circular to personnel	to reach a group, organisation
	Circular to customers	or company customer in one despatch
Special category	Letter requiring especial tact	to convey delicate information etc. tactfully

As the brackets indicate, some letters are 'paired' in a sequence of broaching a matter and of responding to its implications – the enquiry is answered, the sales letter wins an order, the complaint is adjusted or the order is confirmed. Sometimes letters are produced in a related series, like the three-part collection letter series making a request for payment in progressively more stringent terms.

In some circumstances the frequency with which certain categories of letter are despatched makes it worthwhile having a pre-printed supply of letters in which only certain items need to be entered – recipient's name, an amount in pounds sterling, or a signature. Such letters are called **form letters.** Their advantage lies in the time that may be saved in producing virtually identical letters individually, although such economies remove the benefits which come from the 'personal touch' of individual letters. Letter writers must therefore decide in which situations a form letter may be appropriate.

Content

Structuring the message

1   The opening paragraph – puts the message into a context

The function of the opening paragraph is to put the detailed message into a clearly defined context, either by initiating an action, by responding to a received stimulus or by introducing the next stage in a sequence or exchange.

This may be achieved by:

1 Acknowledging the date, receipt and subject of any received correspondence

2 Supplying the reason for the letter being written

3 Providing essential names, dates, locations or other data to put the message into context.

2   The middle paragraph(s) – develops detailed message

In the middle paragraph(s) the detailed data which comprises the letter's message is logically, briefly and clearly set down. For example, the precise nature of a complaint may be described, the benefits of goods for sale enumerated, the chronology of payment requests reiterated or the essence of bad news gently imparted.

In complex letters, several middle paragraphs may in turn, deal with one principal aspect of an involved message. This will make it easier for the reader to assimilate.

To aid impact, some data may be displayed in tabular form, perhaps as a table of discounts, schedule of supplementary benefits, list of selling points or specification of building materials.

3   The closing paragraph – states action needed

In addition to providing a résumé of the main points of a complex letter's message, the essential function of the closing paragraph is to state simply and unequivocally what action the writer needs from the recipient.

The time and effort needed to send a letter (estimated currently at several pounds) require that it promotes an active desire in its recipient to act upon its message, whether by paying a bill, ordering some perfume or meeting a rates demand.

Since the action statement is the entire reason for writing letters other than informational ones, the requirement or request for action appears virtually at the letter's end, thus remaining uppermost in the recipient's mind, followed only by a courteous closing statement.

Analyses of structures

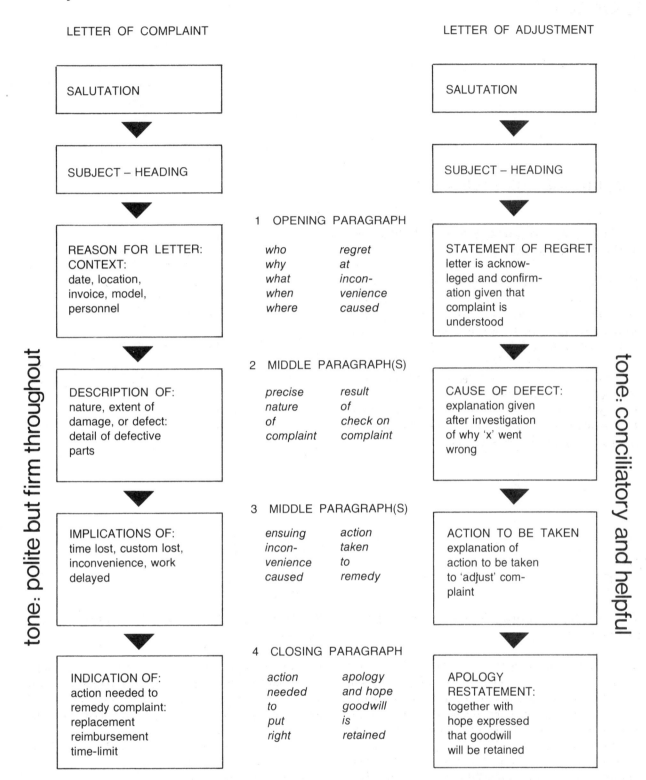

LETTER OF COMPLAINT

tone: polite but firm throughout

SALUTATION

▼

SUBJECT – HEADING

▼

REASON FOR LETTER:
CONTEXT:
date, location,
invoice, model,
personnel

▼

DESCRIPTION OF:
nature, extent of
damage, or defect:
detail of defective
parts

▼

IMPLICATIONS OF:
time lost, custom lost,
inconvenience, work
delayed

▼

INDICATION OF:
action needed to
remedy complaint:
replacement
reimbursement
time-limit

1 OPENING PARAGRAPH

who	regret
why	at
what	incon-
when	venience
where	caused

2 MIDDLE PARAGRAPH(S)

precise	result
nature	of
of	check on
complaint	complaint

3 MIDDLE PARAGRAPH(S)

ensuing	action
incon-	taken
venience	to
caused	remedy

4 CLOSING PARAGRAPH

action	apology
needed	and hope
to	goodwill
put	is
right	retained

LETTER OF ADJUSTMENT

tone: conciliatory and helpful

SALUTATION

▼

SUBJECT – HEADING

▼

STATEMENT OF REGRET
letter is acknow-
leged and confirm-
ation given that
complaint is
understood

▼

CAUSE OF DEFECT:
explanation given
after investigation
of why 'x' went
wrong

▼

ACTION TO BE TAKEN
explanation of
action to be taken
to 'adjust' com-
plaint

▼

APOLOGY
RESTATEMENT:
together with
hope expressed
that goodwill
will be retained

Remember!

When writing a letter of complaint, remember that the recipient must receive clear details of the transaction and a careful explanation of the faults complained of. He must also be informed of what action is expected to put the matter right and any deadline required. Correspondingly, the adjustment letter must, while expressing regret at the inconvenience caused, take pains to explain *why* things went wrong and what is *speedily* being done to put them right, especially since the customer's goodwill is the lynch-pin of commerce.

Model letters

Complaint

Letter to the Wessex County Treasury Department, for the attention of Mr. Johnson.

12th May 19--

Dear Sir,

L. R. Ross. Ref: 42PG 14

I am writing to express my concern at not yet having received a refund of £28.18, in respect of a surcharge deducted from my March 19-- salary to cover sickness benefit cheques paid to me during a period of illness between 21st January and 15th February 19--.

Between 30th January and 24th February, I received three cheques from the Department of Health and Social Security totalling £42.06.

In my March pay-slip, however, I was deducted £70.24 in respect of sickness benefit under code AG. On 4th April I telephoned your department and spoke to Miss Martin, who promised to adjust the surcharge on my next paycheque. I notice that, apparently, I have received a normal month's salary for April.

I had reckoned on receiving the repayment by the end of April, in order to budget for a Spring Bank Holiday excursion.

I should be grateful, therefore, if you would now kindly arrange for me to receive the repayment of £28.18, less tax payable, before the Spring Bank Holiday.

Yours faithfully,

L. R. Ross
Wessex High School

Adjustment

Letter to Mr. L. R. Ross, teacher at Wessex High School from Mr. Johnson, County Treasury Department.

18th May 19--

Dear Mr. Ross,

Salary Ref: 42PG 14

I was sorry to learn of the inconvenience you have been caused regarding the repayment of £28.18 to adjust a surcharge relating to sickness benefit payments outlined in your letter of 12th May 19--.

On looking into the matter, I discovered that your refund was, in fact, being processed for the April computer salary run, but was delayed as a result of departmental reorganisation which, I hope will shortly improve the service which the Treasury Department provides to the authority's personnel.

I have now made arrangements, however, to send you by separate cheque, a refund for £28.18, less tax, which will reach you in good time for the Spring Bank Holiday.

I regret the delay in resolving the adjustment to your salary, and trust that the action I have taken will enable you to enjoy your break as planned.

Yours sincerely,

J. Johnson
Treasury Department
Wessex County Council

Perhaps the most difficult of all letters to write are those whose messages must either affect the reader adversely, or which require great tact or delicacy, so as not to offend the recipient – particularly when the writer hopes to elicit action in spite of difficult or unwelcome circumstances. Many managers or officials find themselves all too frequently having to impart bad news, having to say 'no' gracefully, or to communicate an unpopular directive.

The diagram illustrates how a four-paragraph structure could be employed to break bad news to a recipient – perhaps of failure in a promotion application, or a transfer to a different position with less authority, or the closing-down of a branch-manager's store because of falling turnover. The permutations are numerous.

Although the letter-writer's aim is basically to convey the bad news clearly and unambiguously, he or she has an equal obligation not to wound the recipient's feelings by insensitivity, indifference or terseness. As the diagram illustrates, the letter must be carefully structured to cushion the impact of the bad news, which can neither be baldly stated in the first paragraph, nor 'tacked on' to the closing paragraph almost as an after-thought.

The context and circumstances surrounding the bad news are used carefully to prepare the reader for what is to come. Similarly, once the bad news has been imparted (towards the end of the second paragraph in the diagram), the writer must take pains to ensure that some positive factors are found, with which the reader may identify and so not be left feeling entirely overlooked, discarded, incompetent or passed over.

The most difficult task is to avoid any sentiments which may be interpreted as being insincere. And, as may be readily imagined such letters require careful drafting and scrutiny before despatch.

Now turn to page 25 and study the model letter which aims to convey disappointing news tactfully.

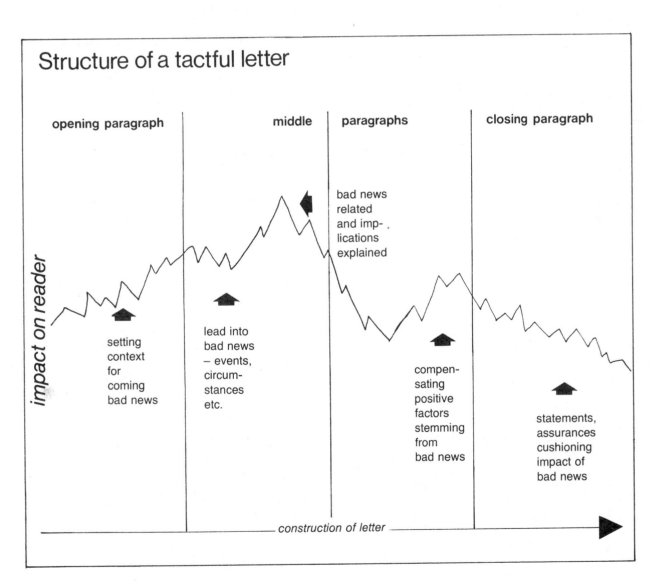

Structure of a tactful letter

opening paragraph   middle   paragraphs   closing paragraph

impact on reader

bad news related and implications explained

setting context for coming bad news

lead into bad news – events, circumstances etc.

compensating positive factors stemming from bad news

statements, assurances cushioning impact of bad news

construction of letter

FINOSA FABRICS LTD require a PRIVATE SECRETARY to the EXPORT SALES MANAGER (EUROPE)

A knowledge of two EEC foreign languages is required and experience of export sales procedures is an advantage. The successful candidate will work on her own initiative and be able to handle incoming telephone calls and documentation from French or German agents. He or she must also be prepared to travel abroad.

The company provides excellent conditions of service, including four weeks' paid holiday per annum subsidised insurance and restaurant facilities. Salary negotiable according to age and experience.
Apply in writing to: The Personnel Manager, Finosa Fabrics Ltd,

4 York Way, London WC2B 6AK

Applications to be received by 30 May 19—

Model letter of application

Dear Sir,

I should like to apply for the post of private secretary to your Export Sales Manager recently advertised in 'The Daily Sentinel', and have pleasure in enclosing my completed application form and a copy of my curriculum vitae.

The advertised post particularly appeals to me, since my own career aspirations and education have been specifically directed for the last two years towards a secretarial appointment in the field of export sales.

In the sixth form at Redbrook High School I specialised in Advanced-level German, French and English and proceeded in September 19 to Redbrook College of Technology, where I embarked upon a bilingual secretarial course leading to the Commercial Secretary's Diploma in Export Studies.

The course includes intensive commercial language studies (I am specialising in German), communication, office administration and export studies with particular emphasis on E.E.C. procedures and documentation. In addition, the Diploma course provides shorthand and typewriting components, including work in the special foreign language.

I anticipate achieving a good pass in the June Diploma examination and attaining shorthand and typewriting speeds of 100/50 w.p.m., having already secured passes at 80/40 w.p.m.

During my full-time education, I have travelled extensively in the Federal Republic of Germany and in France, and have become familiar with the customs and outlooks of both countries. In August 19 I gained a valuable insight into German business methods during a month's exchange visit to a Handelsschule in Frankfurt-am-Main.

Assisting my father for the past two years in his own company has afforded me an opportunity to use my own initiative and to obtain helpful work experience in areas such as sales documentation and customer relations.

If called, I should be pleased to attend for an interview at any time convenient to you.

My course at Redbrook College of Technology finishes on 30th June 19 and I should be available to commence a full-time appointment from the beginning of July onwards.

Yours faithfully,

Jane Simmonds. (Miss)

(Note: It is usual for letters of application such as the one above to be handwritten.)

Commentary

Jane Simmond's letter of application begins by acknowledging the source of the advertisement, makes a formal application statement and refers to relevant enclosures.

In her second paragraph, Jane endeavours to establish a close link between her own career aspirations and vocational education and the essential nature of the advertised post.

Jane goes on to draw particular attention to those aspects of her more recent education which she considers have equipped her with a sound preparation for the post.

In case her prospective employers may be unfamiliar with them, Jane outlines the relevant course components of the Diploma, emphasising those parts which would be most likely to interest her potential principal.

Jane endeavours to display self-confidence without immodesty, and evidence of existing achievement.

Since she lacks full-time work-experience, Jane makes the best of her travels and knowledge of the countries relating to the advertisement. She also includes mention of a course of study which has provided relevant insights.

Realising that her lack of work-experience could prove a stumbling-block, Jane emphasises the practical work-experience she has had, and highlights aspects of it which she hopes will be relevant to her application.

Availability for interview made as easy as possible.

Since she needs the job, Jane displays a willingness to start just as soon as possible after the end of her course, thus demonstrating her 'earnestness of intent'.

Assignments

1 In syndicate groups, study Jane Simmonds' letter from the point of view of Finosa's Personnel Manager and consider the following questions:

Has Jane's letter succeeded in arousing your interest? If so, why? If not, why not? Does Jane's letter succeed in meeting the aims suggested in the commentary? Do you have any criticisms to make of Jane's letter in terms of the information supplied, its structure, its tone and style? Could it be improved upon? Does it adequately match the requirements implied in the advertisement?

2 Draft letters from Finosa to:
  a call Jane Simmonds to attend an interview
  b inform Jane Simmonds of her failure to obtain the post after interview
  c offering Jane Simmonds the post after interview

3 As Jane Simmonds, assume that, while awaiting news from Finosa after interview, you have been offered, and accepted a post with another company as a result of an earlier application. Write a letter to Finosa appropriate to the situation. Invent a suitable home address.

Style

Language

Essential to conveying the letter's message effectively is the form of language used – the style in which the letter is written.

Immediately any written form of communication is employed problems occur which are much more easily overcome in, say, face-to-face oral communication. The transmission, assimilation and feedback cycle of the oral conversation are supported and reinforced by a range of non-verbal communication signals such as the smile, nod, gesture or posture. In oral communication offence caused by misunderstandings over inappropriate tone or ambiguity is much less likely to occur and much easier to put right. Correspondingly the permanence of the letter as a written record and the absence of the supportive effect of non-verbal communication mean that special care must be given to the way in which the letter's message is expressed. The construction of the message, the 'what', should be carefully organised in the letter's structure, and in the same way, the 'how', the choice of words expressing the message, should be just as carefully chosen so that the letter's basic aim is reinforced and the desired action from the recipient thereby generated.

Some letters are written principally to convey information, while others are active selling 'weapons' in the armoury of the advertising manager, and seek to persuade. Yet others may seek to inform and persuade simultaneously.

Simply put, style may be defined as 'the most effective words in the most appropriate order', and the letter-writer must be continually checking to ensure that the words he or she is using are creating the right effect, whether it be to inform objectively, or to sell subjectively:

The emulsion paint embodies a vinyl additive which improves both its covering capacity and durability.

Wondacover! Its warm and satiny vinyl finish makes it go on great! And then go on and on and on!

The Latin, Saxon, Norse and French roots of English have rendered it extremely rich when it comes to finding alternatives or synonyms to express an idea or sentiment, and, in *The King's English*, H W and F G Fowler have synthesised three proverbial guide-lines which the letter-writer would do well to follow:

1   Prefer the short word to the long
2   Prefer the Saxon word to the Romance
3   Prefer the single word to the circumlocution.

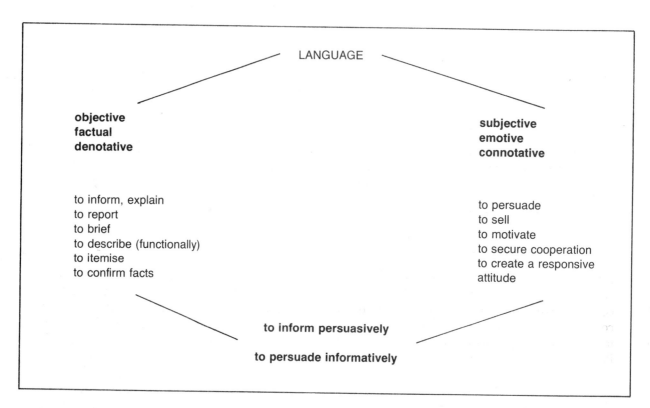

LANGUAGE

**objective
factual
denotative**

**subjective
emotive
connotative**

to inform, explain
to report
to brief
to describe (functionally)
to itemise
to confirm facts

to persuade
to sell
to motivate
to secure cooperation
to create a responsive
attitude

to inform persuasively

to persuade informatively

When the letter-writer poses the question, 'What action do I wish to generate?' he is thinking of the effect of his words on his recipient. His style will also be affected, however, by the 'strength dimension' of the letter's context and the relationship between writer and recipient, where the writer may be:

directing
requiring
requesting
asking a favour
seeking help
in dire need of
'baling out'.

The recipient

As well as developing a style in a letter appropriate to its aim, the letter-writer must also keep firmly in mind the kind of person for whom the letter is intended:

how old is the recipient?

what sort of education?

what kind of business background?

what professional interests?

what tastes, preferences, leisure interests?

what prejudices, *bête-noires*?

The response of the recipient is bound to be affected by a wide range of factors which have moulded his or her life and experiences – either a wealth of practical experience, or a lengthy higher education, a specialism in a narrow field, or a succession of varied appointments, either a metropolitan, sophisticated life-style or a traditional, rural background.

To remain indifferent to the recipient's personality is to run the risk of communication breakdown, perhaps by using terminology and syntax which the reader does not understand, or to cause unpremeditated offence or tactlessness by an insensitive reference. Whatever the cause, failure to write specifically for the letter's recipient may well cause him or her to ignore the letter's message and to refuse to act upon it.

Use this plan and your letters will always 'IMPRESS'!

I DEA	– Decide upon the principal aim(s) of the letter
METHOD	– Structure the letter's main points in a plan
P ARAGRAPHS	– Follow the opening, middle and closing scheme
R ECIPIENT	– Remember who will receive the letter
E MPHASIS	– Guide the letter's progress to its action statement
S TYLE	– Employ a style appropriate to the letter's aim(s)
S AFETY	– Check the letter for errors or omissions before despatch

---

Above all, keep thinking!

... 'Ah, take a letter, please, Miss Smith. ... Bombay Animal Supplies Ltd, etc. ... Dear Mr Singh comma subject-heading Order No. 8692. ... Letter begins ... Further to my order of 21st August 19— comma please supply comma in addition comma three elephants open bracket Indian close bracket comma two tigers open bracket striped close bracket comma three cobras with hoods if possible and two mongooses ... er no, mongeese. ... No, start again ... and one mongoose. Letter ends Yours etc. ... P.S. Please send another mongoose.' ...

Examples

Don't   **. . . but do**

Keep it brief but polite

In view of the recent increase in postal rates and because of rising labour costs, a surcharge of 10% will be levied to cover the cost of postage and packing.

A 10% surcharge is, regrettably, payable on orders under £1.00 to cover postage and packing.

Keep it clear and simple

Although the holiday which you request is now fully booked, the latter holiday to which you refer is still on offer, together with Holidays 164 and 169 in our Sunny Days brochure, although the former is more expensive than the latter.

    I trust this information will help you to make your choice.

I regret to inform you that Holiday 161 is fully booked. You referred, however, to Holiday 179, which is still on offer, and I also strongly recommend Holidays 164 and 169 in our Sunny Days brochure. Of the three holidays, number 164 is more expensive, but features additional attractions. . . .

Be helpful

The aerial to which you refer is no longer available from stock, since the radio was withdrawn six years ago. I suggest you try local stockists.

The radio, model XL49, was withdrawn from our product range six years ago. I have located a spare aerial at our Oxford service depot, however, and have made arrangements for it to be posted to you c.o.d.

Be positive

We are unable to deliver the goods you ordered before mid-July.

The goods you ordered will be delivered by 16th July 19— at the latest.

Be persuasive

Our new range of wall-coverings are advantageously priced. We also supply on request our merchandiser free-of-charge.

Not only will our new range of wall-coverings give you a much better deal, the free-of-charge merchandiser ensures they sell themselves!

Avoid officialese

The extent of rate-relief for which rate-payers are eligible is dependent upon the level of earnings in gainful employment.

The amount of rate-relief to which you are entitled depends on how much you earn.

Be tactful

I regret that I shall be unable to keep our appointment on 21st March 19—, as I have to see one of our larger account customers.

I am sorry to have to ask you if we may postpone our appointment for 21st March 19—, as a matter has arisen requiring my personal attention.

Remember the recipient

Dear Sir,

    Your application for a reduced-fare omnibus pass is awaiting process pending receipt of a photostat birth-certificate in compliance with public transport departmental regulation 46, our letter 16th June, 19— ref. AT/TG refers.

Dear Sir,

    I should be grateful if you would kindly send a photostat copy of your birth-certificate as soon as possible to enable us to send your reduced-fare pass by return of post.

Don't	... but do

Avoid clichés

We acknowledge receipt of yours of 15th January 19— re our new upholstery fabrics catalogue.

Thank you for your letter of 15th January 19—, in which you request our new upholstery fabrics catalogue.

Be courteous

I am obliged to inform you that your claim against warranty in respect of your hair-dryer cannot be met, since accidental damage lies outside the terms of the conditions laid down.

On receipt of £1.40 the company is prepared, without prejudice, to undertake the repair of your hair-dryer, although it accepts no responsibility to ensure that such repairs are efficacious.

I am sorry to inform you that your claim against warranty for a replacement hair-dryer cannot be met, since upon inspection, it was discovered that the appliance had, apparently, suffered from accidental damage.

The company would, however, be most happy to undertake the repair of your hair-dryer at a nominal charge of £1.40. As I feel sure you will appreciate, however, such repairs do not carry our guarantee.

Avoid over-familiarity

Dear Sir,

Sorry we haven't been round yet to fix your t.v. The van has been on the blink since Monday, and the service engineer is off with 'flu.

As you can imagine, things have been a bit tricky lately, but we hope to send someone round before Saturday.

Sorry about the waiting.

Yours truly,

Dear Sir,

Please accept my apologies for the delay in repairing your television set.

Our service engineer is ill with influenza, and the service van has suffered repeated breakdowns, now traced to an electrical fault.

Nevertheless I am very hopeful that a service engineer will be able to call before Saturday.

I hope the delay will not prove too inconvenient.

Your faithfully,

Avoid irrelevance

Dear Sir,

I am writing to complain about the way I was treated by your counter-clerk last Thursday, when I came in to enquire about a tax rebate, to which I feel I am entitled, since I have been off work for the past three weeks, as a result of an industrial accident, which was occasioned by the negligence of a colleague, although I do not hold him personally responsible. . . .

Dear Sir,

I wish to complain about the way I was treated by your counter-clerk when I came in on Thursday 14th April 19— to enquire about a tax rebate.

After a long, but admittedly unavoidable wait, I was curtly informed that . . .

Approach checklist

Don't

Allow a letter to become formless

Lapse into long-windedness

Allow the letter to become obscure or ambiguous

Let the message become irrelevant or trivial

Opt for jargon, officialese or deliberate complexity

Ramble or 'butterfly' around the message

Adopt a tone which is aloof, hostile, over-familiar, condescending or mixed with slang expressions.

Talk down to the letter's recipient or baffle him or her with inappropriate language

Be vague or ineffectual, or overlook the action to be generated by the letter

Ever allow a letter to degenerate into rudeness, sarcasm, offensiveness or tactlessness

Allow the language to become stale, cliché-ridden or hypocritical

Settle for a half-hearted or indifferent approach

Allow a letter to be despatched which contains careless errors either in its composition or typescript

Forget that a letter provides a written record – don't commit to paper what you may later regret having written

Do

Keep the basic aims firmly in mind

Plan the letter's points before starting to write or dictate

Aim for brevity

Ensure that ideas are clearly expressed

Keep to the relevant points

Prefer the simple to the complex

Check that the message is logically structured

Adopt a tone appropriate to the letter's aim

Remember who will be receiving the letter and adopt the appropriate vocabulary, syntax etc.

Be positive

Write a clear action statement or request

Take care at all times to ensure that the letter is courteous and tactful

Take trouble to keep the language fresh and sincere

Use your powers of persuasion when it matters

Check carefully for careless mechanical errors –
spelling
punctuation
usage

Remember that every letter is an ambassador

Wessex County Council

**County Hall High Street
Avalon Wessex DO14 6QZ**

Telephone: Avalon 86000

Education Department Ext: 247

Your ref:

Our ref: JPK/AT HCS 41

12 February 19--

P K Harrison Esq BSc Cert Ed
Headmaster
Highgrove Comprehensive School
AVALON
Wessex   AV12 4KA

Dear Sir

PROPOSED EXTENSION TO THE SCHOOL LIBRARY

As a result of recent discussions between the Wessex Education Committee
and the Education Department arising from the reduction made in the
rate-support grant for the coming financial year, I am now able to tell
you the decision on the proposed extension to the Highgrove Comprehensive
School Library.

After having given careful thought to what money will be available to
the secondary education sector, and bearing in mind other essential
renovation and maintenance obligations, it is with regret that I inform
you of the Committee's decision to postpone the building of the proposed
library extension.

I realise that this decision must come as a disappointment to you,
especially after the work which both you and your library staff have
put into the design of the proposed provision.

Nevertheless, I feel sure that you will appreciate the difficulties facing
the Education Department at this time, and I should welcome an opportunity
of discussing with you ways and means by which additional library facilities might be provided within the existing accommodation.

I shall look forward to hearing from you when you have had an opportunity
of re-appraising the distribution of your accommodation resources.

Yours faithfully

H P Knight MA Dip Ed   This letter is typed in
Assistant Director of Education   FULLY-BLOCKED LAYOUT
Wessex County Council
                                                      with

copy to: Director of Education   OPEN PUNCTUATION

Home Insulation Service Ltd

Kingsway House Ealing Broadway London W7 5AQ
Telephone: 01-401 3986/9

Directors: J. Kent (Managing) P. Brown A. Wilson
Registered Office: Kingsway House Ealing Broadway London W7 5AQ
Registered Number: 846971 Registered in England

Date as post-mark

Dear Householder

                A SURE WAY YOU CAN SAVE MONEY THIS WINTER !

        Will your bank balance get blown away by an 'over-draught' of
cold air again this winter?

        Our research has proved that up to 30% of all money spent on
home heating virtually goes up in smoke!

        The culprits are ill-fitting, single-glazed windows and
doors, poor insulation in lofts and attics and exposed cavity walls.

        Can you afford to let yet another year go by with your heating
bills far larger than they need be?

        Or will you be sitting pretty when winter winds rage, secure in
the knowledge that your family, home and income are being protected by
Home Insulation Service's unrivalled products?

        Our FREE expert advice and NO-OBLIGATION quotations are tailor-
made to suit the insulation needs of YOUR home.

        Our policy specifically excludes high-pressure salesmanship and
gives you a 7-day 'make-your-mind-up' period.

        Special low-interest credit facilities are also available to
suit your pocket.

        ACT NOW! Ring 01-100-9000 free-of-charge and our specialist
insulation consultant will arrange to visit your home when it suits
you to give you an on the spot FREE QUOTATION!

        REMEMBER: a FREE phone-call now to 01-100-9000 could prove the
wisest investment you ever made - and your family will love you for
it all winter long!

                                    Sincerely
                                    John Grant
                                    JOHN GRANT
                                    SALES MANAGER

This UNSOLICITED SALES LETTER is typed in SEMI-BLOCKED LAYOUT

Registered Office:
42 Warrington Road
Liverpool LW4 9RT
Registered No. 468973
Registered in England

Telex: 349764
Telegrams: Lancstyre L'pool

Directors
A. Rowe (Managing)
F. Piercey
T. Rowlands
S. Wainwright

LANCASHIRE TYRE DISTRIBUTORS LTD

42 Warrington Road, Liverpool LW4 9RT
Telephone: 051-423 6934/5/6

Ref: SGS/JB/ATC 16   7th June, 19--

H. R. Baxter,
Proprietor,
Ajax Tyre Centre,
Stretford,
MANCHESTER. MS14 3RF

Dear Sir

OVERDUE ACCOUNT: £649.43

        In spite of the copy statement and reminders sent to you on
3rd April, 15th May and 29th May, 19--, your account for February
19-- totalling £649.43 remains outstanding. A final statement is
enclosed.

        As previously stated, the period of credit extended to your
company was agreed as one calendar month from the receipt of a
statement.

        Unless the overdue account is settled in full within seven
days, I shall be compelled to instruct my company's solicitors
to take legal action to recover the debt.

                          Yours faithfully,

                          S. G. Simmonds
enc.   Accounts Manager

This COLLECTION LETTER, the last of a series of three, was typed in
SEMI-BLOCKED LAYOUT with CLOSED PUNCTUATION.

Assessment questions

Letter format

1 What contribution do the letterhead and logo make to the impact of the business or public service letter?

2 What parts of the business letter are required by law for some companies? Can you remember the names of the Acts concerned?

3 Describe two principal methods of setting out the typescript component of the business or public service letter.

4 What are the two acceptable methods for setting out the letter's date?

5 How are letters usually referenced under 'Your ref.', 'Our ref.'? How does the letter referencing system contribute to the filing and retrieval of letters?

6 Describe the difference between the 'open' and 'closed' methods of letter punctuation. What advantages does open punctuation provide in letter production?

7 List the various ways in which the letter's recipient may be styled in the recipient's address.

8 Specify the technical terms for the letter's 'greeting' and 'signing-off'.

9 Complete the following: a Dear Sir, . . . b Dear Mr Smith, . . . Describe the circumstances in which you would use the former and the latter.

10 List the appropriate methods for styling a man, a married woman, and a single woman with letters after their names.

11 What is the order by which letters after a person's name are set out?

12 What is the function of the subject-heading?

13 Why are the letter's paragraphs separated, most frequently, by double-spacing?

14 Why are the letter-writer's name and job-designation typed beneath his or her signature?

15 How should a secretary sign a letter on behalf of an absent principal?

16 How does the typist indicate that a letter is accompanied by additional material?

17 How does the typist indicate that a copy of a letter has been sent to a third person?

18 What are the components of the recipient's address on the envelope?

19 How should an envelope indicate that its contents are only to be read by the recipient specified?

20 Make a check-list of as many of the letter's components as you can remember.

Letter classification

21 What is a letter of adjustment?

22 Why are collection letters produced in a series?

23 What is an unsolicited sales letter?

24 Under what circumstances might a circular letter be used?

25 What is a form letter? What are the advantages and disadvantages of its use?

26 List and describe the use of as many different classifications of the letter as you can remember.

Structure

27 What is the usual function of the opening paragraph of the letter?

28 Outline the type of information most generally provided in an opening paragraph.

29 What is the function of the middle paragraph(s)?

30 What considerations should be borne in mind when planning the content of the middle paragraph(s)?

31 What is the function of the closing paragraph?

32 What do you understand by the term 'action statement/request'?

33 Outline the typical paragraph structure of:
   a a letter of complaint
   b a letter of adjustment

34 Describe the way in which a tactful letter might be structured which conveys bad news to its recipient.

35 Describe the considerations to be borne in mind when planning the structure of the letter's message.

Style

36 What sort of difficulties in communication face the letter-writer which are more easily resolved in oral communication?

37 What do you understand by 'objective, denotative language'?

38 What do you understand by 'subjective, connotative language'?

39 Outline the sort of message which might be expressed in the language referred to in:
   a Question 37
   b Question 38

40 Why is the English language so rich in alternatives and synonyms by which an idea might be expressed?

41 Can you remember the three style guide-lines advocated by H W and F G Fowler? Set them down.

42 What factors of the letter's context might affect the tone which the letter-writer adopts in influencing the recipient?

43 Why is it important to keep the recipient's personality and background firmly in mind when choosing the language in which a letter is expressed?

44 Specify the aspects of the recipient's make-up which should be borne in mind.

45 In planning and composing a letter, why is it of paramount importance to have arrived at a clear idea of the letter's over-riding aim(s) before commencing to write or dictate?

46 Can you remember the key words in the planning and expression of a letter signified by the mnemonic, 'IMPRESS'? Set them down.

Written assignments, discussion topics

1   Imagine that your principal has recently heard about a new typewriter marketed by 'Electric Business Equipment Ltd', Queensway House, Great Russell Street, London WC1 3AQ, which embodies an erasure strip in its ribbon, and has a means of employing interchangeable type-faces.

Write a letter to enquire about the availability, performance and cost of this machine. Provide a suitable letter-heading. Note that your company prefers to use the semi-blocked letter format.

2   Assume that you are Mr Peter Jones, Sales Manager of 'Electric Business Equipment Ltd.' Write a letter which embodies an appropriate letterhead replying to the letter outlined in Question 1 above, providing a suitable recipient's address. Bear in mind that you have published a brochure advertising the 'E.B.E. Moderna' typewriter referred to above. Also, demand has greatly exceeded supply, and at present, there is a six weeks waiting period for delivery. Your company has a nation-wide sales force, and demonstration machines are available. Use the fully-blocked open punctuation format.

3   Your company recently purchased a beverage dispensing machine from Semperflo Beverages Ltd of Highdown Industrial Estate, Birmingham BS3 4RA. Since its installation it has repeatedly broken down, and your company has no alternative means of providing for coffee-breaks etc.

Write a letter of complaint with a suitable letterhead employing the closed punctuation semi-blocked format.

4   As Sales Manager of Semperflo, you learned upon investigating the complaint outlined in Question 3 that the defect was caused by faulty installation by subcontractors whose services you no longer employ.

Write an appropriate letter of adjustment, with letterheading, to redress the complaint, providing recipient details as necessary, using the blocked format.

5   Write a final letter of collection to R J Hill Esq, BSc, Econ, ACMA, Accounts Manager of Maxi-Markets Ltd, whose head-office is at 14–18 Richmond Way, Edinburgh ED14 6ST.

Maxi-Markets are a chain of retail supermarkets. Your company has been supplying their Newcastle branch with a range of delicatessen sausages. Your company is owed £98.34 in respect of purchases invoiced for the month of September 19—. Your letters are neither being acknowledged nor replied to.

Provide your letter with a suitable letterheading and adopt an appropriate format.

6   Your company sells a range of household cleaning products which are sold on a cash basis by door-to-door salesmen and women.

Recently your company decided to adopt a change in policy by offering householders an opportunity to inspect your products by appointment at times suitable to them.

Draft an unsolicited sales letter, embodying an appropriate letterhead, which actively promotes these points:

Your company manufactures and retails a wide range of brushes, polishes, detergents and shampoos.

Your policy is to keep prices down by 'cutting out the middle man'.

Sales representatives are well-trained and able to demonstrate your products.

By returning in the envelope provided a detachable slip, customers can specify a date and time for representatives to call.

You are making a special offer of a free tin of furniture polish to all customers who reply with an appointed time.

You may add any additional supportive material. It may be helpful to collect and discuss a range of unsolicited sales letters before attempting this question.

7   Your company has employed Mr Fred Jenkins for the past 17 years. During that period, Mr Jenkins, who is well-liked in the company, has had a variety of jobs mostly of a handyman, storeman nature. Currently he is in charge of your mail-room, but recently, his disability occasioned by injuries sustained during military service has worsened. His doctors have advised him that he should give up his job or run the risk of a severe deterioration in his health. He has a small disability pension, but is 58 years old, and personnel in your company are not entitled to a pension until aged (males) 65.

Mr Jenkins could be kept on in a part-time capacity if his health improved. Ex-gratia payments are at the managing director's discretion.

As personal assistant to the managing director, you have been asked by him to draft a suitable letter to Mr Jenkins, who is at home following a set-back. You have been told to use your discretion and submit the draft when the managing director returns from a visit.

8   Assume you are personal assistant to Mr Richard Brown, Sales Manager of Sceptre Garages Ltd, a company with a chain of garages specialising in car sales and servicing, motor-accessory retailing, petrol trade and retail sales, and general parts and body-repair sales to the trade.

In six weeks' time your branch at Midchester is to be relocated at: 8–16 Bedford Road, Midchester, Bucks. ME12 2BG. Telephone: Midchester 4631/2.

The new premises afford the following advantages:
Showrooms for 15 new cars
Sales area for 50 used cars
Ample customer parking
A diagnostic centre
Large body repair shop
10 self-service petrol pumps
8 while-you-wait tyre, battery and exhaust fitting bays
A motor-accessory supermarket.

Write a circular letter:

a to trade customers
b to account customers

to advise them of the forthcoming relocation. You may add any additional material you consider justifiable.

Choose a format you think appropriate, supplying a letterhead and logo.

9 Write a letter in support of your application for the post which you hope to obtain either at the end of your studies, or as your next appointment. Assume that your letter is accompanied by a completed form of application and a copy of your *curriculum vitae*.

Such letters are customarily handwritten.

Discussion topics

1 Is the business or public service letter ever likely to become obsolete? If so, why?

2 Are the pains taken in letterhead and logo design worthwhile?

3 Are the conventions governing letter format unnecessarily complex, or do they contribute positively to the letter's impact?

4 In what ways does Mr Harris in his letter on page 11 try to initiate a good relationship with Mr Dawson?

5 How does Mr Ross in his letter of complaint on page 16 manage to maintain a polite but firm tone in his letter?

6 In what ways are the extracts in the left-hand columns on pages 22 and 23 inferior to those preferred in the right-hand columns? Do you agree in every case?

7 How does Mr Knight endeavour to break his bad news tactfully in his letter on page 25?

8 What advertising techniques do you detect in the unsolicited sales letter on page 26?

9 What aspects of the collection letter on page 27 reveal a formal, reserved tone?

10 What advice would you give to someone about to begin a job involving much letter-writing?

11 Why is it so important that the letter is pitched at a level appropriate to its recipient?

12 In what situations would you consider the letter to be the only suitable medium in which to transmit a message?

Case studies

Gayglo burns fingers

In order to promote a new range of eye make-up, Gayglo Cosmetics Ltd recently placed a series of advertisements in women's magazines to offer a free mascara kit (brush, mascara disc and mirror in a plastic wallet) to all women ordering the new pack of Gayglo eye-liners, cost £2.50. The total cost value of the mascara kit was 32p on the basis of an order for 12 000 kits. Gayglo had anticipated a demand for some 12 000 kits and had budgeted some £5000 for the whole promotional venture. To Gayglo's consternation, however, more than 30 000 replies were projected on the basis of the initial level of demand. As the advertisements had already been published, there was no way of reducing the demand. To meet the demand for an additional 18 000 kits would mean that a loss would be incurred on the first production run of the eye-liners, since in making the original offer, Gayglo had banked on establishing repeat-purchases of the eye-liners. The company's directors reached a conclusion that their only solution was to refund the postage to the disappointed customers for their mascara kit orders, and to send out a form letter explaining the situation as tactfully as possible as orders came in.

In such circumstances should Gayglo have absorbed the cost of the additional kits to maintain its favourable public image?

Given the directors' decision, what should the form letter aim to do?

Could any mitigating factors be introduced? Draft an appropriate letter, either singly or in syndicate groups, which you think most suitable. Then discuss and justify your draft.

Goodfellow says 'No'

In order to help out a friend, Robin Goodfellow recently stood in as a stage-manager for a local amateur production of *West Side Story*. Although he had no previous experience, Robin was an undoubted success with both the back-stage crew and cast. So much so, that shortly afterwards he received a letter from the honorary secretary of the Newtown Players offering him the permanent position of stage-manager. Robin was flattered, but had too many business and social commitments, and did not wish to commit himself to the many nights of rehearsal and production involved. Neither did he have any wish to offend the Newtown Players' committee, partly because his friend was a member, and also because some of his business associates were patrons of the Players.

What sort of letter-plan should Robin devise before drafting a letter replying to the invitation?

How could he best excuse himself tactfully? What tone should he adopt?

As Robin Goodfellow, draft a suitable letter to Miss Penny Haslemere, Honorary Secretary, Newtown Players, 'Cawley House', Cawley, Near Newtown, Herts. CW12 8MG.

Trouble bubbles at the Cauldron

Recently production at the Cauldron Engineering Ltd's factory has been declining dramatically. The root of the trouble is a long history of industrial disputes. Both management and factory-workers have been to blame for the deteriorating relations which have left both sectors mutually antipathetic. Yesterday the board of directors held a meeting after productive consultations with the unions involved to try to find a peace formula. It was decided to send out a circular letter to all company personnel outlining the gravity of the situation. Unless a solution is made to work, large-scale redundancies seem inevitable, as the factory is losing money. The basis of the management offer is that, provided production is increased by 15% within four weeks and at least maintained at that level, the company would re-introduce overtime working, re-negotiate productivity bonus payments and make substantial investments in re-tooling, which is much needed.

What would be the letter's main aims? What tone should it adopt?

Draft an appropriate letter, either singly or in syndicate groups and then evaluate each version.

Multi-letter – writing assignment

Leisure Press Limited

Situation

The sales of *Home Hobbies*, a monthly magazine aimed at 'do-it-yourself' home improvers have slumped badly in recent months.

The magazine is written, printed and marketed by Leisure Press Ltd, 42 Regency Crescent, London, SW1 4TD.

Home Hobbies is produced monthly and marketed by direct subscription to householders responding to unsolicited sales letters followed up by calls from the company's representatives.

At present the 64 page magazine costs £6.00 per year and is supported by a wide range of advertising. The peak circulation nine months ago was 84 000 copies per issue.

The managing director is of the opinion that what is needed is some 'young blood and fresh ideas'.

Assignments

1 For the past two years Leisure Press Limited has used the services of the Grafix Advertising Agency. The Home Hobbies account is being managed by Mr Peter Cos, senior accounts manager. His address is:

Grafix Advertising Ltd,
Grafix House,
22 Hampstead Park Road,
London
SW1 4TD

As assistant sales manager, you have been requested to draft a letter for the sales manager, Mr John Lloyd's signature, expressing your dissatisfaction with the current unsolicited sales letter used to promote the sales of *Home Hobbies* to householders.

You would like Grafix to submit for your approval two specimen unsolicited sales letters, one for young, married house-owners, and another for established householders. You will need to outline your ideas clearly.

2 The management of Grafix takes the letter from Leisure Press (Home Hobbies Dept) very seriously, and the managing director calls a meeting to see if a 'brain-storming' session will come up with some new ideas for the unsolicited sales letters. Your group should simulate the meeting (syndicate groups may be used), produce two suitable drafts, and set them out with a suitable covering letter to Mr Lloyd.

3 For the past two years, you have been a regular subscriber to *Home Hobbies*. Unfortunately, for the past six months delivery of your copies has been late and two copies never arrived. On another occasion, an 'enclosed' free gift of a tape-measure was not included.

Write a letter of complaint to the sales manager of the Home Hobbies Department at the London address, outlining your complaint and what you would like done to remedy it.

4 As sales manager of Home Hobbies Department of the Leisure Press Ltd compose an answer to a letter you have received from the customer making the above complaint. The problem has arisen because of staff turnover in your despatch section. Conditions of service have now been improved.

5 Compose an appropriate letter of application in response to the following:

ASSISTANT SALES MANAGER required by LEISURE PRESS LIMITED for *Home Hobbies* Magazine Dept.

Energetic, well-educated young person with business administration ability needed to assist sales manager of successful magazine. Top conditions and excellent salary for right applicant. Drive and ideas more important than experience.

Apply in writing to:
The Personnel Manager
Leisure Press Limited
42 Regency Crescent
LONDON
SW1 4TD

The above letters should include letterheads and may be composed either by individuals or by syndicate groups. The assignment should conclude with a group evaluation and analysis session.

People and Communication

Memoranda and Reports

Desmond W Evans

Contents

Acknowledgments

The author and publishers have made every effort to trace the ownership of all copyright material and to obtain permission from the owners of copyright.

Thanks are due to the following for permission to reprint the material indicated:

Michael Joseph Ltd for the extract from *Up the Organisation*, Robert Townsend, p8.

John Offord (Publications) Ltd for the article 'Employ a vending machine' by Ralph Braybrook in *Municipal Entertainment* vol 4 no 11 on p 32.

PITMAN EDUCATION LIMITED
39 Parker Street, London WC2B 5PB

Associated Companies
Pitman Publishing Pty Ltd, Melbourne
Pitman Publishing New Zealand Ltd, Wellington

© Desmond W Evans 1978

First published in Great Britain 1978
Reprinted 1979, 1980

Text set in 10/12pt Sabon
printed and bound in Great Britain
at The Pitman Press, Bath

ISBN 0 273 01246 0 (bound book)
      0 273 01247 9 (module pack)

Introduction

This module will examine those types of written communication which are most frequently used by companies and institutions as *internal* channels of communication: memoranda, reports, abstracts and summaries.

Some of the means of communication listed above are used externally as well as internally in the same way as the letter, while one, the memorandum, is *only* used within an organisation.

Fig. 1 illustrates how internal communications within a commercial company are organised.

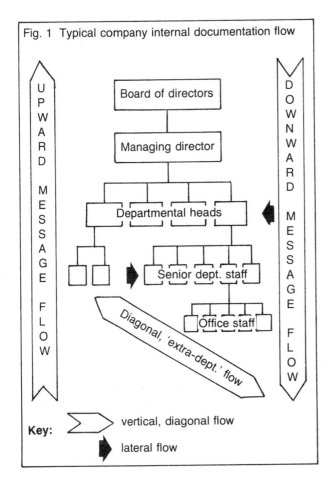

Fig. 1 Typical company internal documentation flow

Key: vertical, diagonal flow

lateral flow

The structure of institutions such as a county council is similar to that of industry or commerce — policy decisions initiated by county councillors (board of directors) are implemented by the various departments which report to a chief executive (managing director). See Fig. 2.

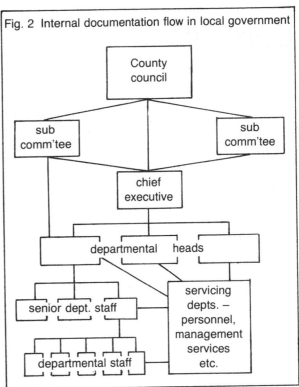

Fig. 2 Internal documentation flow in local government

The recording and storage of the details of a host of policies, decisions and routine daily business is essential to the efficient running of hierarchic organisations — though it is equally essential that the flow does not become a torrent! The internal flow of documents, vertical, lateral and diagonal can keep widely dispersed offices, branches or outlets constantly in touch with one another, as Fig. 3 indicates.

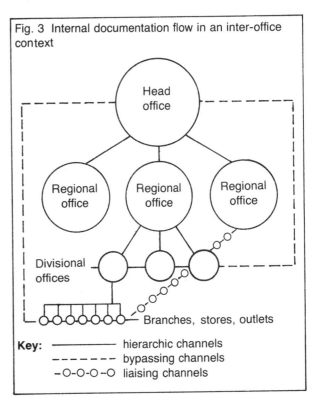

Fig. 3 Internal documentation flow in an inter-office context

Key: —————— hierarchic channels
- - - - - - - bypassing channels
-O-O-O-O liaising channels

The memorandum

Home Insulation Services Ltd
MEMORANDUM

To: **Date:**

From: **Ref:**

Subject:

---

copies to: **signed:** J Grant

Format

The format of many memoranda begins with the name of the company or institution, although this is probably unnecessary since the document is intended for internal use only. The title 'Memorandum' is usually centred at the head of the page. The names, and sometimes job designations, of author and recipient are displayed after 'To' and 'From', omitting courtesy titles. The date is set out as for the letter – day, month, year, and often a space is allocated for entering a reference for administrative purposes. The essence of the message of the memorandum is briefly stated after 'Subject', and space must be given for the inclusion of 'cop(y)-ies to', 'enclosure' and, if company practice, for a signature.

Memorandum component check-list

Organisation's name	Some organisations' names appear above 'Memorandum'.
'Memorandum' heading	'Memorandum' is usually employed as a central heading.
'To'	'To' precedes the space for the recipient's name.
'From'	'From' identifies the writer of the memorandum.
'Date'	The date is entered as for the letter: day, month, year.
'Reference'	Some memoranda carry a reference for filing purposes.
'Subject'	The memorandum's theme is briefly stated after 'Subject'.
'Signed'	Some memoranda include a space for the writer's signature.
'Cop(y)-ies to'	Memoranda should indicate the recipient(s) of copies.
'Enclosure'	Memoranda should also indicate accompanying material.
Memorandum's message	The memorandum's message is set out in spaced paragraphs in the same way as the letter's, but salutations and complimentary closes are dispensed with.

Although typists learn a helpful format for setting out a memorandum on blank paper, there is no single, universally accepted memorandum format. Many organisations adapt the basic format indicated above, or add to it location points for the inclusion of information which they require as part of their individual administration. The inclusion, for example, of a space for the writer's signature or initials is optional, although there are sound reasons for ensuring that no memorandum is despatched before its author has seen it in print and authorised its despatch by the initialling or signing of the memorandum.

Page size

Memoranda are usually produced in two standard sizes: A5 – 8.3″ by 5.8″ or 210 mm by 148 mm (about the same width as this page, but half its depth) and, A4 – 8.3″ by 11.7″ or 210 mm by 297 mm (approximately the same size as this page). A5 memoranda are used when the message is brief, conveying a single major point, and A4 memoranda are employed, sometimes with continuation sheets, when messages are involved and complex, perhaps including schematically set out components.

Colour-coded filing systems

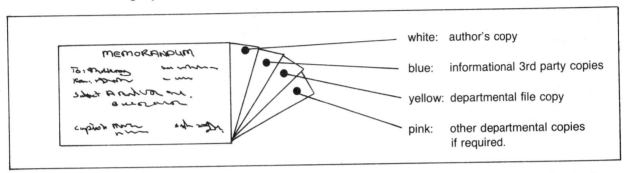

Instead of using a number of white sheets for the carbon-copies of a given memorandum, some organisations have adopted a colour-code for memoranda copies similar to that illustrated. The advantages of this system include prompt identification for filing, and speedy interpretation for possible action on the part of a recipient. For example, the recipient of a blue-coded copy would know immediately that it was for him to read, but not act upon, whereas, the recipient of the top copy of the same memorandum might need to act instantly upon its contents.

Application check-list

The memorandum provides an extremely useful channel of communication for transmitting unsolicited ideas or suggestions upwards in an organisation, as well as enabling policy decisions, routine instructions to flow down the hierarchic structure of a company or institution. Additionally, the memorandum is employed laterally or 'diagonally' between departments to seek advice, assistance or cooperation. By means of the copies despatched, memoranda also help to keep interested personnel 'in the picture' regarding a situation or development, in which they are not required to act directly.

Some of the principal uses of the memorandum are to:

send unsolicited suggestions or ideas upwards
instruct, require, advise downwards
request, seek help or cooperation
confirm, especially following a telephone conversation or discussion
seek information, confirmation or advice
clarify, explain, introduce
amend or modify existing policies or practices
brief, or inform via copies

Production process

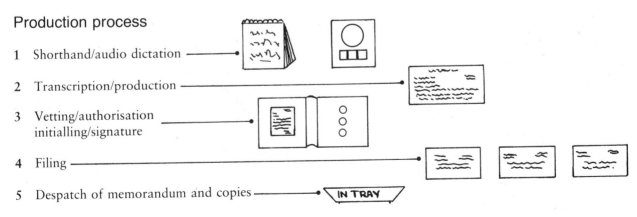

1 Shorthand/audio dictation

2 Transcription/production

3 Vetting/authorisation
   initialling/signature

4 Filing

5 Despatch of memorandum and copies

Content

The *Concise Oxford Dictionary*'s definition of the memorandum is, a 'note to help the memory'. Such a definition emphasises the brevity of many memoranda messages and focusses attention on their *supportive* function in helping personnel to recall, plan or act upon the flow of business activity.

In view of the space-restrictions deliberately imposed on authors by the A5 paper size, it is essential that the content of any message is condensed, so that only its essentials and any arising action requirement are transmitted to the recipient. Some memoranda, however, are produced on A4 paper and may run to a number of continuation sheets. Therefore, it is wrong to think of the memorandum solely as a means of transmitting short, 'one-point' messages.

The heading of the message after the entry, 'Subject' serves to pin-point the reason for the memorandum's production:

Regional Sales Meeting: 3rd June 19—
Reduction Of Days Of Credit
Revised Personnel Induction Procedure
Reorganisation Of Reprographic Service

and such headings, as well as summarising the subsequent message, also assist in allocation, ranking for action and filing.

Memoranda convey many different types of message: procedures to be followed, policies to be implemented, changes in established practices, clarifications or confirmations, motivation or exhortation of staff, disciplinary action, requests for assistance or liaison with other staff or departments.

Some memoranda are written by one individual to another, others by one department to another, yet others by an individual (perhaps a senior executive) to a large body of staff at different levels in the organisational hierarchy.

The structure of the memorandum's message will vary according to its context but the following diagram illustrates the three principal content components which form the basis of many memoranda.

Memorandum	
Subject:	SYNTHESIS OF THEME
Para 1: or **(sentence)**	1 Puts message in **context** past – present – future 2 Identifies the related components – people, places, events, time: **who, why, what, when, where?**
Para 2: or **(sentence)**	Details the **essence** of the memorandum's message.
Para 3: or **(sentence)**	1 Identifies clearly the **action** either required or requested of the recipient. 2 Puts a **time-scale** or **deadline** on the completion of the action – '...*by*...'.

Written confirmation

Perhaps the most important single aspect of the memorandum's application lies in its provision of a *written* record (for retention, future reference, circulation etc.) of previously conducted oral communications – conversation, telephone calls, meetings, informal corridor encounters and so on.

It is therefore essential that the content of the memorandum in such circumstances is factually accurate, unambiguous, devoid of inference or 'sideswipes' and fair to quoted third parties.

Copy to: The Reader – for future action.
'Memos and all other documents should always bear dates and initials. One of my colleagues once spent a twelve-hour night working on an undated document which turned out not to be the current draft. Why he was not convicted of mayhem remains a mystery.'

Robert Townsend, *Up the Organisation*

Style

The dictates of context

The style of memoranda varies enormously. Directives, for example, from a managing director or chief executive may be couched in formal, depersonalised terms and delivered with all the crisp authority of an electric typewriter. On the other hand, hasty, handwritten messages produced on a 'memo-pad' and passed to a colleague's desk may be written in a much more personalised and familiar language.

Factors affecting style

The style of the language in which the memorandum is couched depends very much upon the following:

1 *The context of the message:*
– a crisis, congratulation, reprimand, routine order etc.

2 *The status, personality or background of the recipient:*
– high/low position in organisation, higher education, practical background etc.

3 *The nature of the message:*
– factual, informational, congratulatory, persuasive, soliciting, requiring etc.

4 *The urgency or priority of any action needed:*
– crisis, routine re-stocking order, need for liaison or cooperation, instructions for all staff etc.

Appropriateness

In such varying situations the mechanics of the style will be different:

1 **Syntax** – sentence length may be longer or shorter, may include or exclude subordinate clauses or phrases.

2 **Vocabulary** – the choice of words will vary enormously: some may be complex technical or specialist words or phrases, others may be deliberately factual, devoid of emotive overtones (in an explosive situation), still others may be engaging and familiar in a persuasive role.

3 **Tone and nuance** – the shades of meaning, or connotations given to the message's component parts will differ, depending on whether the message is factual or persuasive the situation is 'fraught' or routine, the recipient responsive or obstructive.

Reaching the recipient

The style of the memorandum is also very much dependent upon the kind of recipient:

1 *Fellow specialist* 'in the know' – understands specialist, 'jargon' terminology.

2 *Peer group* – colleague(s) among whom is an unconstrained familiarity and directness.

3 *Junior personnel* – where the difference in authority, experience and 'reports-to' situation affects the way in which a communication is made.

4 *Range of staff within hierarchy* extending from senior to junior levels, where age, experience, background require a 'consensus' style approach avoiding obscurity, condescension or a patronising tone.

Message situations

The choice of either subjective or objective language or a mixture of both will also be decided by the nature of the memorandum:

1 **Informing:** where the message may confirm a revised discount, call a meeting or raise an order.

2 **Directing:** where action requirements are 'passed down the line' (persuasion may also be needed here to secure active cooperation).

3 **Requesting:** where there is no 'line-control' and colleagues may need 'wooing' for their help.

4 **Motivating:** where senior management needs, perhaps, to boost morale, exhort or persuade in engaging, motivating terms.

5 **Suggesting:** where junior executives attempt to 'sell' an idea to busy, sceptical seniors.

6 **Confiding:** where closely-working executives exchange highly personalised information informally and directly.

Models for analysis

Jim Grainger is a good salesman – he could sell ice to eskimos – but when it comes to routine paperwork, Jim is a laggard! Despite exhortations at a recent Area Sales meeting, he still isn't submitting his weekly reports on time.
   Which of the following alternatives do you think his Area Sales Manager should send to Jim to motivate him to meet his Monday deadline? What criticisms can you make of the memoranda you reject? Or are they all inappropriate?

A Further to the Area Sales Meeting of 13th May 19--, you are reminded of my reference to punctuality in despatching weekly sales reports. This reference was occasioned by the need for the efficient compilation of Area Sales figures, Head Office statistics and Company Bonus Scheme returns.

I note, however, that I am still not receiving your returns by first post on Mondays. Unless your performance improves, I shall be compelled to take the matter further.

B At our last Area Sales Meeting on 13th May 19--, I stressed the need for all sales representatives' weekly sales reports to reach me by the first post Monday mornings.

You will recall that I emphasised the importance of sending in weekly reports on time, not only to allow me to appraise the area sales situation, but also for our Head Office to produce national sales turnover statistics and monthly bonuses.

I should, therefore, be grateful if you would ensure that your weekly sales report reaches my office in time for me to deal with the Area Sales Report without delay.

C At our last Area Sales Meeting on 13th May 19--, I mentioned how important it was for your weekly sales report to reach me early on Mondays. My own sales picture, Company sales figures and the monthly bonuses all rely on my receiving sales representatives' reports in good time.

Your own territory is playing an important part at the moment in our area sales recovery programme, and for this reason I am relying on you to send me those figures for Mondays' first post, so that I can finalise my own report to Head Office.

I know you won't want to hold up my report unnecessarily, and I set too much store by your ability and enthusiasm to feel that I need to remind you again.

D I'm concerned about not receiving your weekly sales report on time. You remember I raised the problem at our last Area Sales Meeting on 13th May 19--, and told everyone how important it was to send in their reports to me by first post Mondays.

Well, I don't seem to be receiving yours until Tuesday or Wednesday, and so I'm held up in sending my own report to Head Office, giving our own situation and supplying information for our overall sales and bonus scheme.

It would certainly help me on a Monday, if I had your figures along with everyone else's. I know I can rely on you to rally round.

Keep up the good work!

NEWSHIRE COUNTY COUNCIL
Memorandum

Ref: HT/JR CS 46

Date: 24 February 19--

To: B. Martin, County Surveyor.

From: H. Taylor, County Information Officer

Subject: ACCEPTANCE OF PRESS RELEASE: RE-ROUTING TRAFFIC

I write to confirm our telephone conversation of 22 February 19--
regarding the submission of a press-release to the 'Newtown Evening
Post' concerning the re-routing of traffic in the centre of Newtown.

I received confirmation today from the editor that the press-release
and map would be given space on the front page of the edition for
Friday 4 March 19--. As I assured you during our telephone conversation, the explanatory statement accompanying the map will be published
in full.

As you requested, I have now arranged for copies of the press-release
and map to be available for distribution in Newtown public libraries
and the information kiosk in the pedestrian precinct.

I enclose a final draft of the press-release for your files.

HT

enc.
copy to: K. Mills, Chief Executive.
          P. Allsop, Printing Dept.

memorandum

to   All Sales Representatives.

from M. Franks, Sales Manager.

ref MF/kg SGC 116

date 8 August 19--

subject Achievement of Sales Targets: July 19--

I want to thank you all for the superb sales performance you achieved
in surpassing the company's national sales turnover target for July
19-- by £110 000.

The difficult trading situation experienced throughout the building
trades sector during the past three months of national recession has
made your successful efforts especially praiseworthy and particularly
satisfying for me.

I am confident that, with your continuing determination and enthusiasm,
not only shall we achieve our national sales target for 19--, but also
that I shall need to review the sales bonus targets next year!

Well done, one and all!

M.F.

A-4 memorandum

MEMORANDUM

TO   All Company Personnel   **REF** SK/RD

FROM S. Kilbride, Managing Director   **DATE** 7th September 19--

SUBJECT A PROPOSAL TO INTRODUCE A FLEXIBLE WORKING HOURS SYSTEM

For some time past, the board of directors, in consultation with senior members of staff, has been considering the introduction of a system of working known as 'Flexible Working Hours', or 'Flexitime'.

Under this system, personnel work an agreed total of hours each week or month (in the case of Kaybond Ltd. 37½ hours each week), within a framework of agreed starting and finishing times which allow for commencing work before the current 9.00 a.m., and continuing after the present finishing time of 5.30 p.m. to a maximum of 7½ hours each day.

In addition, <u>all</u> personnel are required to work during a 'core-time', say, between 10.00 a.m. and 3.50 p.m. excluding a lunch-break.

At the request of the board of directors, I have been asked to give you a schedule of possible flexible working hours (enclosed), together with a detailed explanation of the scheme which the board would like you to consider, with a view to its implementation after a period of discussion and trial if the consensus views received prove favourable.

Broadly, staff would be required to work 7½ hours each day, between 8.00 a.m. and 6.15 p.m., with a core-time from 10.00 a.m. to 3.50 p.m., and a minimum lunch-break of 45 minutes to be taken between 12.00 p.m. and 2.15 p.m. Thus the time available within which personnel may choose to work a period of 7½ hours totals 9¼ hours each day, after a 45 minute lunch-break has been subtracted.

In this way, a 'late-starter' may elect to commence work at 10.00 a.m. and to finish at 6.15 p.m. Alternatively, an 'early bird' may begin work at 8.00 a.m. and end at 4.15 p.m., both having worked the required 7½ hour period, both having taken a 45 minute lunch-break during the period 12 noon to 2.15 p.m.

There are distinct advantages, it is felt, to be gained from embarking upon a flexible working hours scheme; from the company's point of view, both punctuality and productivity would improve since peak rush-hour times could be avoided and staff could elect to work at times best suited to their 'internal clocks': similarly, the office would be manned for longer periods to take incoming sales enquiries, and the pressure on the staff restaurant would be relieved. From the viewpoint of company personnel, greater opportunities would be afforded to <u>plan</u> work and leisure times; shopping journeys and the collection of children from school would be made easier and there would be quieter periods during the working day for uninterrupted, concentrated work.

A detachable form has been included with the schedule referred to; you are requested to give serious consideration to the proposed introduction of the 'Flexitime' scheme and then to deliver your conclusions on the form provided to your departmental head no later than Friday 20th September 19--. Additional information may be obtained from your head of department or the Personnel Manager. I anticipate that I shall be in a position to provide you with a decision by 8th October 19--.

encs.

The report

The commission and production of reports plays a crucial part in achieving the goals which organisations set themselves. The more important decisions become, whether about people, finance or production, the more it is likely that specialist reports will be required by decision-makers to ensure that the process of decision-making is informed, impartial and considered.

The popular conception of a report is of a long, schematically set-down document, full of 'paras' and 'sub-paras', punctuated by references such as 'B 4 (iii) d', and it is true that some complex reports do require a logical referencing system. The format and methods of reporting are, however, many and varied, both spoken and written, and produced in a number of different contexts.

Classification and context

1 Regular and routine reports
equipment maintenance report
sales report
progress report
safety inspection report
production report etc.

2 Occasional reports
accident report
disciplinary report
status report etc.

3 Especially commissioned reports
investigatory report
market-research report
staff report (personnel)
market forecasting report
product diversification report
policy-changing report etc.

The range of reporting may be illustrated by the following two examples:

Situation one:

Jim Pearson, personal assistant to the Sales Manager, has just emerged from a meeting on administering a new bonus scheme. By chance, he encounters his principal, the Sales Manager.

'How did the meeting go, Jim?' he is asked. What follows will be an orally communicated report which synthesises the main features of the meeting as Jim saw them.

Situation two:

Later the same day, Jim is called into the Sales Manager's office:

'I'm worried about the steady fall in sales turnover at our Bournemouth branch, Jim. You'd better have a thorough look at the situation, get down there and let me have a report on what's gone wrong and how we put it right. Oh, and I'll need it by next Wednesday. I'll write to put the Regional Sales Manager in the picture.'

Such orally communicated instructions, or 'terms of reference' define the limits within which Jim may act, and are usually confirmed in a memorandum. Having collected and classified his information, Jim will present it to the Sales Manager as a written report to assist his principal in making a decision – whether to close the branch, redeploy staff or institute a hard-hitting advertising campaign.

In addition to the orally-delivered or detailed, investigatory reports, there are numerous routine reports the formats of which are designed to allow information to be inserted into boxes following questions or to permit a tick or cross to show a 'satisfactory/unsatisfactory' message. Such 'check-list' reporting systems save time and simplify routine reporting procedures.

Format

The format of reports varies considerably. Some may run to hundreds of pages, such as those produced by Royal Commissions, others may be quite short and set-out on an A4 memorandum sheet. Some may be produced as a succession of paragraphs of continuous prose, while others may be displayed under a series of headings and sub-headings with lists, tables and diagrams.

The following table indicates some of the principal contexts and forms in which reporting takes place.

Applications

Messages in letters or memoranda

Oral briefings or reporting back

Minutes of meetings

Routine 'check-list' reports

Progress reports – architects' site meetings

Annual reports to shareholders

Profiles of candidates for interview

Sales reports

Newspaper reports/ news releases

Technical reports

Balance sheets for annual audit

Statistics in various visual formats

The choice of format for a report is most important. Therefore, before producing his report the report-writer should decide carefully which layout will best relay his message.

In some circumstances the powers of persuasion and emphasis of a direct oral report may outweigh the advantages of producing a written document – particularly when a time-factor is an over-riding consideration. Similarly, when more than one recipient is concerned, a report may best be delivered orally at a meeting, where the information may easily be verified, confirmed, questioned and examined.

In many situations, however, the sheer wealth and complexity of report data require that it be transmitted in a written form, so that recipients keep a record for reference, and have repeated access to it and so assimilate it more easily. Moreover, in the context of the meeting, it is common practice to circulate reports in advance to allow participants to arrive at the meeting prepared to discuss a report's contents on an informal basis.

The following check-list provides a guide to the components which, in various combinations, form the parts which go to make up the whole of a range of different report formats:

Component check-list

1   Title
2   Author
3   Identity of report's commissioner
4   Date
5   Reference
6   Contents, pagination
7   Status e.g. Confidential
8   Background/history/introduction/terms of reference
9   Method/procedure/*modus operandi*
10 Information/findings/data input
11 Conclusions/synopsis/synthesis
12 Recommendations/suggestions for action

13 Footnotes
14 Appendices
15 Index

16 Circulation list

The extended formal report

This format is used for high-level, extensive reports by central or local government and large companies.

Layout

Sectionalised with schematic organisation and referencing.

Format key: extended report

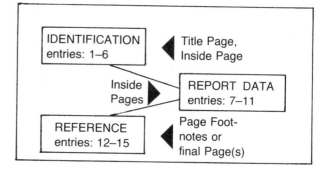

Principal components

1 Title page
2 Contents, pagination
3 Synopsis of findings
4 Terms of reference
5 Procedure
6 Sectionalised findings
7 Conclusions
8 Recommendations
9 Appendices
10 Bibliography

Note: Where a reporting committee cannot agree, some members may submit a 'Minority Report'.

The short formal report

This format is used in formal reporting situations (mostly internally directed) where middle or senior management reports to senior or top management.

Layout

Sectionalised with schematic organisation and referencing.

Principal components

1 Title page or heading
2 Terms of reference
3 Procedure or identification of task
4 Findings
5 Conclusions
6 Recommendations (where required)
7 Appendices (if appropriate)

Note: This format should be reserved for situations where the context, nature and complexity of the data warrant a formalised report.

The short informal report

The short, informal format is used when the information is of a lower status and less complex than that of the 'short formal report'. It is frequently used in 'subordinate reporting to departmental head' situations.

Layout

Usually three-part and less elaborately schematic in its organisation.

Principal components

1 (variously styled) background
               introduction
               situation etc
2 (variously styled) information
               findings etc
3 (variously styled) conclusions
               action required etc

Note: Any recommendations required are usually included in the final, 'conclusions' section.

The memorandum report

The memorandum format is used for internal reporting, especially within and between departments. Its format is extremely flexible, since the 'title' information is contained in the memorandum heading and the space of the sheet below 'Subject' may be employed in a variety of ways to display the content of the report.

Layout

Heading as for memorandum. May be sectionalised with headings and include tabulated information.

Principal components

No pre-determined components – the format of the memorandum report may be structured to suit the nature of the data.

```
D O U B L E   S P A C I N G   O F   C A P I T A L S     used for titles, title
                                                        pages etc.
USE  OF  CAPITALS                                       used without underscoring
                                                        for main section headings.
Initial Capitals Underscored                            used to introduce sub-
                                                        headings within a main
                                                        section.
Initial Capitals Without Underscore                     with use of space around
                                                        it, this form of heading
                                                        may be used for minor
                                                        headings.

Use of numbers and letters for referencing
schematically:

Roman Numerals: I,II,III,IV,V, etc.)                    best employed to intro-
Capital Letters: A,B,C,D,E, etc.   )                    duce main section head-
                                                        ings.
Arabic Numerals: 1,2,3,4,5, etc.                        used to introduce sub-
                                                        sections after Roman
                                                        numerals or capital
                                                        letters are used for main
                                                        sections.
Lower Case Letters: a,b,c,d,e, etc.             )       used to introduce minor
Lower Case Roman Numerals: i,ii,iii,iv,v, etc.)         points; used in conjunc-
                                                        tion with indentation.

(Note that such letters or numbers are sometimes
 displayed within brackets thus; (i), (a).)
```

Alternative referencing system

In the Civil Service and Local Government an alternative system is frequently employed, which utilises a system of numbered sections:

1. 2. 3. 4. etc.

to introduce major sections of the report. Successive sub-sections within a major section are referenced:

1.1, 1.2, 1.3. etc.

and subordinate points or paragraphs within such sub-sections are referenced by the addition of a further full-stop and number:

1.2.1, 1.2.2, 1.2.3, 1.2.4, etc.

In the references illustrated immediately above, the points being referred to would be the first, second, third and fourth points of the second sub-section of the first major section. This system has the advantages of using only one 'code', the Arabic numeral system and full-stops, and is economic to display.

Use of space and indentation

Apart from considerations of logically discriminating between major and minor sections or points, the use of space – either by centering titles, or leaving lines blank above and below a section heading is extremely important in enabling the reader's eye to travel more easily down the page and to take in the impact of the report more readily. Long paragraphs of continuous prose are extremely difficult to digest, particularly when the information they contain is specialised or technical. The use of progressive indentation, similarly helps to convey the report's information quickly.

Content

Title page headings

All reports are prefaced with certain information which is displayed either on a title page (in the extended, formal report) or as a series of headings (in the memorandum or short, informal reports):

1 The subject of the report, displayed as its title
2 The identity of the report's recipients
3 The identity of the report's author
4 The date at completion
5 A reference (optional)
6 A circulation list
7 An indication of priority or confidentiality as required.

Structure of the short formal report

The structure of this report is divided into four or five sections (depending on whether recommendations have been asked for in the 'Terms of Reference'). The report is set down schematically as the following diagram broadly illustrates:

```
I    TERMS OF REFERENCE

II   PROCEDURE

III  FINDINGS
     1 Main Section Heading
     2 Main Section Heading
     3 Main Section Heading
        a Section 3 Sub-Heading
          i  Sub-point of a
          ii Sub-point of a

IV   CONCLUSIONS

V    RECOMMENDATIONS
     1 First main recommendation
     2 Second main recommendation etc.
```

The principal features of the schematically organised report to remember are that each section or point has a code for reference:

I or II or V or, III 3 a ii.

Also, headings are either in upper case, initial capitals underscored or initial capitals only, depending on whether they introduce a major section or a subheading. Lastly, as points become more detailed, they are progressively indented.

I TERMS OF REFERENCE
In this first section of the report, the author details the scope of the report, or its 'parameters', within which he may investigate. Sometimes the report's commissioner asks for recommendations; at other times they are made by the recipient(s) of the report.

II PROCEDURE
Having outlined the report's scope, the writer identifies the means he or she adopted to collect its data:
        by scrutinising documents
        by interviewing personnel
        by visiting branches
        by observation
        by examination, analysis etc.

III FINDINGS
Here the detailed information which has been collected is sifted for relative importance and relevance and classified under appropriate headings, usually in descending order of importance, where the most important comes first.

IV CONCLUSIONS
In this section a résumé or synopsis of the principal findings is written, and is particularly helpful to those who may not wish to read the entire report.

V RECOMMENDATIONS
Having classified the detailed information of the report and summarised its main conclusions, the writer's last duty, if required, is to identify the means by which a problem may be solved or a deficiency remedied, so that decisions may be made or advice acted upon.

Structure of the short informal report

The content of this report falls into three principal sections, equating to a 'beginning, middle and end', and may be used in a variety of situations where the subject of the report is neither too long nor complex. Its sections may be variously titled but the three sections may be considered as follows:

```
1  Background outlined
2  Problem/situation analysed
3  Problem/situation resolved
```

The content of each section is detailed in the three boxes below.

---

1 First Section – headed:

Background or

Introduction or

Situation etc.

This opening section puts the report into a context and briefly outlines the essential background information needed to make the detailed information which follows in the middle section intelligible to the reader.

For example, if the report were entitled, 'Economic Use of Stationery Supplies', the first section might well indicate a situation in which waste of stationery had been detected and a dramatic increase in stationery costs discovered. This section would also indicate who had commissioned the report, its author and any further details corresponding to the 'Terms Of Reference' section of the Short Formal Report.

---

2 Middle Section – headed:

Information or

Findings or

Analysis of problem etc.

This section displays systematically the detailed information which has been collected by similar methods to those identified in the 'Procedure' section of the Short Formal Report.

The detailed information of this middle section may be organised as a series of continuous prose paragraphs beneath sub-headings, which may also contain numbered lists or tabulated information. Generally the input of this section is not sufficiently complex to justify a highly schematised, indented layout.

---

3 Final Section – headed:

Conclusions or

Action required or

Resolution etc.

In this last section the main points of the report are summarised as conclusions and any actions required, recommendations or means of resolving a problem outlined. Thus the 'Conclusions' and 'Recommendations' sections of the Short Formal Report are combined.

The final section may be set out as a single continuous prose paragraph (or as a series of paragraphs), or may itemise its main points in a numbered list of sentences or phrases.

Structure of the memorandum report

If the subject may be treated analytically, the structure of the Memorandum Report will correspond to that of the Short Informal Report. Indeed, the A4 memorandum sheet, and continuation sheet(s) if needed, may be used for the Short Informal Report.

Additionally, the structure of the Memorandum Report is extremely flexible, and by employing the various display techniques available in typescript, it may be used for a range of internal reporting situations.

Detailed information in the form of charts, graphs and tables is often placed at the end of a report as an appendix.

Illustrated below are the section headings for a candidate profile in a job application situation:

1   Personal details
2   Education
3   Qualifications
4   Experience
5   Personality/disposition
6   Interests
7   Circumstances

Each section will be displayed in whatever manner is easiest for the reader to absorb.

Style

The style of report-writing should be factual and objective. In the case of investigatory and analytical reports, the decisions to be made and actions to be taken should be based on information and recommendations devoid of self-interest or bias.

The author of the report should not allow prejudices or emotional responses to intrude into the presentation of the Findings, Information or Recommendations sections of the report. Even when opinions are presented, these should be supplied in an *informed* and balanced way.

In practice, however, it is difficult for the report-writer to avoid influencing his or her report by subjective value-judgments, whether made consciously or subconsciously. Indeed, it is often the case that the member of personnel assigned to investigate and to report upon a situation is chosen on the basis of possessing a sound reputation in matters which require judgment. Subjectivity or bias may be exercised, not only in the style in which the report is written, but also in the *selection* of points or topics to be included and in the omission of other material which may be deemed irrelevant or too trivial to warrant attention.

Some reports may be couched in entirely denotative language, devoid of rhetoric or persuasion. Frequently, however, the report writer is seeking not only to inform but also to persuade. Therefore, the report writer must always be on his guard to avoid subjectivity creeping in.

Most experienced senior executives, usually the recipients of reports, have a developed sense for detecting unfairness, biased selection or partiality in a report, the effect of which is usually to detract from the reputation of the writer. It is therefore extremely important when choosing the style of writing for a report to check continually, both in the organisation of the data and the use of language, for signs of inappropriate subjectivity or partiality.

Impersonal constructions

One important convention employed particularly in the writing of formal reports is the use of impersonal constructions to convey information. The use of 'I' or 'we' and their respective cases is avoided. Instead, ideas are expressed, not with a first, but with a *third* person subject. Instead of writing:

I found that . . .

constructions are preferred such as:

It was evident that . . .

or,

The statistics revealed that . . .

The underlying reason for preferring such impersonal constructions lies in the exclusion of any subjectivity associated with 'I', 'me', 'my', 'mine' and 'we', 'us', 'our', 'ours'.

Both before drafting a report and during composition, it is helpful to keep in mind a check-list of guide-lines or yard-sticks to ensure that the end product accords with the intentions or aims which are to be met:

Style check-list

1 What is the principal aim of the report – to inform by presenting a body of facts, to persuade by supplying a distillation of opinions, or both?

2 What sort of people are the report's recipients? Are they specialists who will understand specialised or technical language, or laymen for whom facts must be presented simply?

3 What is the context of the report? Does it require the use of formal language, or may points be made informally and familiarly?

4 What sort of language will be appropriate? Should the report be couched in objective terms, using impersonal constructions and the passive voice? Should its vocabulary deliberately seek to avoid connotative, emotive meanings? Should technical and jargon words be avoided, or may they be employed? Should sentences be kept short and simple, or may they contain provisos and modifying ideas?

5 How should the data be organised? Are the themes of the major sections all relevant and important? Is the material of each section connected and related to its heading? Does the complexity of the report's data require the use of a detailed schematic format?

6 Do the recommendations or suggestions given derive from the Findings rather than from personal bias?

REPORT ON THE SERVICE PROVIDED BY THE STAFF RESTAURANT

For the attention of: 18th November 19--

A.J. Murchison, Esq., O.B.E., M.Sc.
Managing Director

A   TERMS OF REFERENCE

In response to increasing complaints and following the formation of a
Staff Restaurant Working Party, the Managing Director requested the
Working Party to investigate the nature and quality of the service
currently provided by the Staff Restaurant and to make recommendations
for improvements. The report was to be submitted by Friday 21st November
19--.

B   PROCEDURE

In order to ascertain the precise nature of the service provided and to
identify the specific areas of complaint the following investigatory
procedures were adopted:

    1 a cross-section of 30 members of staff selected from all grades
       and departments were interviewed
    2 questionnaires were sent to all departments to obtain information
       on staff attitudes and expectations (Appendix I refers)
    3 the Staff Restaurant Manageress, Mrs. Ivy Patterson, was interviewed
    4 the Staff Restaurant personnel were interviewed
    5 observations of the Staff Restaurant in action took place on four
       occasions between 25th October and 8th November 19--
    6 a range of modern kitchen equipment was evaluated (Appendix II refers)

C   FINDINGS

    1 The Current Provision

       (a) staff are currently served at a single sitting between
            12.30 p.m. and 1.45 p.m.
       (b) currently some 220 three-course meals are served at a
            cost to staff of 40p
       (c) the Staff Restaurant personnel currently comprises:
                 the Manageress
                 4 Cooks
                 3 Serving/Cleaning Staff
                 1 Cash Register Operator
       (d) the Staff Restaurant is being subsidised at present by
            approximately £735 per week

    2 Staff Attitudes and Expectations

       As a result of interviewing 30 members of staff and analysing 72
       complete questionnaires, the following main responses were
       collated:

       (a) some staff spent up to half their lunch-break queueing to be
            served
       (b) the current provision of tables and chairs used in a single
            sitting was inadequate
       (c) both the choice of dishes and the general quality of food was
            considered by a majority of those interviewed to be inadequate
       (d) accusations were levelled (particularly by junior staff) that
            senior staff members were enjoying favouritism, both in terms
            of queue-jumping and receiving prepared lunch-trays

3   Staff Restaurant Personnel Problems

Interviews with Mrs. Patterson and her staff revealed that:

(a)   the rush to prepare some 220 meals between 12.30 p.m. and
      1.45 p.m. placed impossible pressures on the staff and had
      resulted in a decline in the quality of food served as well
      as a lack of choice in dishes offered
(b)   job satisfaction was being sharply eroded, particularly as
      a result of abuse from members of staff
(c)   much of the kitchen equipment was obsolescent and was
      responsible for the increasing deterioration in quality
      of food prepared

4   Use of Equipment and Serving Procedures

Observation of cooking and serving procedures and an evaluation
of modern equipment indicated that:

  1 Kitchen Equipment

    (a)   the equipment in use was no longer satisfactory - food
          took too long to cook and was not being kept hot
          satisfactorily
    (b)   the constant renewal of food being kept hot contributed
          to delays in being served
  2 Serving Procedures

    (a)   the system of users forming a single queue was the
          principal factor in causing delays
    (b)   the use of a single cash register was quite inadequate
          and caused severe bottlenecks

D   CONCLUSIONS

The principal conclusions drawn by the Working Party were that user
criticisms were largely justified, that the current single sitting
placed impossible demands upon the Staff Restaurant personnel, that
the kitchen equipment currently in use was in urgent need of replacement and that the current single user flow-system was a main cause of
delay. Failure to introduce corrective measures would almost certainly
result in staff finding alternative lunch provisions.

E   RECOMMENDATIONS

In order to rectify the unsatisfactory situation summarised in Section
D, the Working Party recommends that urgent consideration be given to
implementing the following measures:

  1   two lunch sittings should be introduced
  2   the quality of food and choice of dishes must be improved
  3   the kitchen should be re-equipped with cost-reducing equipment
  4   a second user queue to a second cash register should be introduced

                          signed:

                          Chairman   Staff Restaurant Working Party

MIDSHIRE COUNCIL

Memorandum

<u>CONFIDENTIAL</u>

To: Director of Education   **Ref:** HJK/RT   DE 156

From: Personnel Services Manager   **Date:** 12th August 19--

Subject: Appointment of Personal Assistant to Director of Education
Candidate Profile: Miss Jean Harris

PERSONAL DETAILS

Full Name: Jean Olivia Harris   Date of Birth: 22nd April 19--
Age: 24   Status: Single   Nationality: British
Address: 14 Highmoor Drive, Midtown, Midshire. ME12 4TG

ATTAINMENTS
Secondary School: September 19-- to July 19-- Waverely College.
'A'-levels: English Lit A, History B, Sociology B.
University: October 19-- to June 19-- Cumbria University.
Graduated B.A. Hons in English Literature,
Second Class.
Post-graduate: September 19-- to June 19-- Midtown College of F.E.
R.S.A. Diploma for Personal Assistants: Distinction

GENERAL INTELLIGENCE
Miss Harris's academic record evidences a lively intelligence and her
success in higher education courses suggests an ability to deal with
problems conceptually and analytically. Reports from Cumbria University
and Midtown College of F.E. confirm initiative and resourcefulness in
problem-solving situations.

SPECIAL APTITUDES
During her post-graduate course, Miss Harris did particularly well in
shorthand and typewriting, achieving 110w.p.m. and 50w.p.m. respectively,
and gained distinctions in Communications and Administration.

While studying at Cumbria University, Miss Harris served on the Students'
Union Education Committee and published a paper entitled, 'The Future
of Higher Education - Freedom Now!'

INTERESTS
An accomplished violinist, Miss Harris is Honorary Secretary of the
Midtown Orchestral Society. She also enjoys sailing and is interested
in industrial archeology.

DISPOSITION
Reports indicate a tendency towards impatience with viewpoints commonly
identified with the 'establishment' but also reveal a willingness to
modify a point of view when faced with a superior argument. Miss
Harris's personality has been variously described as 'forceful' and
'dynamic' and she is generally held to possess a cheerful, outgoing
personality and a good sense of humour. She has been universally
described as a young woman of integrity and loyalty.

CIRCUMSTANCES
Since completing her course at Midtown College of F.E., Miss Harris
has been staying with her parents and would be immediately available
for employment if successful in her application.

signed...... H J K ....

Summaries

One of the most essential needs of business is for the succinct presentation of ideas, information or opinion. The communications revolution of the past one hundred years has resulted in incredible mechanical and electronic advances. The wide-spread use of telephones, telex, typewriters, computers, and so on speaks for itself.

Such universal adoption of communications equipment has meant that managers and secretaries are deluged by a flood of documentation and oral communication. The pressure on people's time and the increase in data production and relay costs have impelled organisations to develop sophisticated summarising techniques which, by reducing communication to bare essentials, achieve an essential saving in reading, processing and assimilation time as well as a reduction in expenditure.

The plight of the senior executive amply illustrates the need for summarising practices. If an organisation is to benefit from the years of experience and developed expertise present in such people, it must appreciate that their time is a precious asset. Such executives need not only to keep abreast of activities and developments, but must also regulate their contact with the large numbers of colleagues, associates or subordinates who make pressing demands upon their time.

In order to cope, senior managers need to avoid time-wasting minutiae and to encourage those in contact with them to discipline themselves, both orally and in writing. Ideas, factual reporting, feedback or suggestions should all be condensed to a main core which represents the main points of a complex problem, a synthesis of a discussion or meeting, or a brief analysis of an involved situation.

All those who produce information in such circumstances need to acquire summarising skills broadly identified as:

comprehension
classification
analysis
evaluation
selection

Essentially, they will exercise their powers of discrimination in deciding which parts of a given piece of material need to be extracted and relayed in a particular format to meet the needs of a third party.

'Can you shorten this, Miss Kirby? I've a meeting at 10.30. Schematic layout, you know the sort of thing . . .'

Indeed, one of the most valuable assets of the executive, personal assistant or secretary is the ability to relay the essence of a 'message' which will involve meeting the following objectives in whole or part:

1 Ability to comprehend a range of information, data or opinion
2 Ability to identify salient points for a particular purpose
3 Skill in analysing and evaluating material to distinguish the essential from the trivial
4 Practice in working objectively so that personal attitudes do not influence selection processes
5 Skill in using language to convey the tone or attitudes of the original
6 Familiarity with business practice to ensure that appropriate formats are used when reproducing data

Whether we realise it or not, the techniques of summarising pervade the whole range of communication activities. For many of us that schoolboys' scourge, the précis, was the first 'baptism of fire' in acquiring the skills of summarising, yet it is not used to any extent in business, though the skills it develops are valuable in a host of situations. The following table indicates just some of the communication contexts which involve the application of summarising techniques:

Relaying to a principal the outcome of a meeting
As chairman, summing up a discussion at a meeting
Passing a message, either orally or on a message pad
Designing an advertisement for a job
Delivering the chairman's report at a company's annual general meeting
Producing a sales report
Writing a letter or memorandum conveying information or a point of view
Relaying instructions from above to subordinates
Editing a press-release for inclusion in a newspaper
Writing an article for inclusion in a house magazine
Drafting a notice or circular
Using the telephone – particularly over a long distance!
Interviewing a candidate for an appointment
Giving a briefing to a group, working party or task-force
Getting across a point of view or suggestion
Despatching a telegram or telex message

many oral and writing situations arise daily requiring summarising techniques

Though the summarising process is present in so many communications channels, nevertheless there are a number of documents produced frequently in an organisation which require a specific summarising technique:

Documents needing specific summarising techniques

Précis	a faithful, selective miniature reproduction
Summary	selective reproduction of *required* data
Abstract	selective data from long article, paper
Abridgement	shortened version of a book, thesis etc.
Précis of documents, correspondence	summary of a series of related documents
Minutes	summary of decisions (background) of a meeting
Conclusions, synopsis sections of the formal, extended reports	summary of main points of 'Findings' section (or Synopsis) introductory essence of report
Telegram, Telex message	abbreviated message reduced to essentials
Press release	submission to newspaper of newsworthy item

(For a more detailed examination of minutes see the 'Meetings' module.)

Note the difference: The **précis** seeks to reduce a passage to about a third, and aims to retain both its major features and attitudes in a faithful. miniature reproduction. The **summary** selects points to meet a specific brief or requirement and is therefore selective of the passage's material, extracting only those points relevant to a desired purpose. The **abstract** is also selective, reducing a much longer article or passage far more extensively, but again, its length is determined by the *specifically directed* requirements of its recipient.

'Here's that summary of your after-dinner speech to the Rotary Club, Mr Hardacre. The trouble was, by the time I'd cut out your jokes and eight references to a fact-finding mission to the Folies Bergère, all that was left was your thanks to the catering staff. . . .'

Principles of summarising

Stage one

Check that you understand clearly the requirement or brief – which may only involve *part* of the item for summarising.

Stage two

Read the item *thoroughly*, since you cannot summarise what you do not fully grasp. Read for:
a The general drift or meaning
b For the meaning of individual words or phrases
c For the structure of the item and the development of its ideas or arguments.

Stage three

Give the item a title conveying the essence of the summary. This will act as a yard-stick against which to measure points for importance and relevance.

Stage four

Select the principal points, keeping the 'terms of reference' of Stage One in mind. A useful technique is to identify the 'key topics' of paragraphs as a starting point.

Stage five

Check your list of points against the original in case something has been overlooked. Check your points against your title for relevance.

Stage six

Establish which format is appropriate for the summarising version – schematic layout or paragraphed continuous prose.

Stage seven

Compose a rough draft leaving room for subsequent refinements and using your own words to convey the sense rather than copying phrases or sentences; remember, that you need not find alternatives for specialist terms like 'inflation' or 'wage-freeze' etc.

Stage eight

If you are limited to a specific number of words, it is wise to aim to exceed this limit in a rough draft by some 10–15 words in the context of a passage of 300 words to be reduced to some 110, since it is easier to prune further than to insert extra points into a rough draft.

Stage nine

Check the rough draft to ensure that the points are linked in connected sentences that read smoothly and where the progression is logical and intelligible. Then polish into a final version by improving vocabulary, syntax, tone etc. Ensure that the final version has been checked for transcription errors of spelling, punctuation etc.

Stage ten

Add the details of the item's sources, the author's name and status, as well as your own. The summary may be passed to its recipient by means of a covering memorandum. All such work should bear a completion date, to indicate that it is current work.

The acid test

The acid test of all summarising work is that its recipient can clearly understand it without ever having seen the original!

Example

Let us assume that the material of page 21 is required to be summarised to form a guide for would-be summarisers. It comprises some 470 words, which we shall try to reduce to 160.

The requirements of our brief require that we keep our summary simple and present only the main points in a way which will help the reader to follow them easily.

A first reading indicates that the passage deals with the need for executives and their assistants to develop expertise in summarising in order to cope with the flood of communications and to make best use of the time available.

The second reading will, perhaps, produce a number of words and phrases which require careful scrutiny:

succinct	time-wasting minutiae
deluge	synthesis
data production	exercising their powers of
saving in reading,	discrimination etc.
processing and	
assimilation time	

Some dictionary work may be needed, or in an examination situation intelligent guesses may be required by looking at the *context* of difficult words or phrases.

Structurally, the passage embodies five stages:

1 Introduction – communications revolution
2 The communication flood
3 The plight of senior executives and how assistants may help
4 An identification of the main areas of summarising techniques
5 A check-list of the basic skills needed by the summariser.

The title required in Step Three might be:

'Summarising Techniques: Why They Are Needed And How They Are Applied In Organisations.'

Following the structural plan, the main points are then listed, using the title as a yard-stick of relevance.

Main points list

The Main Points Check List will appear, broadly as follows:

First para:
1 Summarising – essential need in organisation – need for *brief* statement of info, ideas
2 Communications revolution – reliance on wide range of business equipment

Second para:
3 Communications revolution – flood of documentation, inc. oral comms.
4 Consequence – pressure on person's time and increase in production and distribution costs
5 Essential reduce flow to be able to cope

Third para:
6 Senior executives – their time and expertise wasted if spent on trivialities
7 Calls on their time must be rationed to 'core material' and brief analyses

Fourth para:
8 Those who summarise – need to acquire skills in: comprehension, evaluation, selection
9 Must have ability to discriminate to meet a *specific* requirement

Fifth para:
10 The summariser needs to develop these specific skills:
a Comprehension
b Recognition of main points
c Analytical skill
d Objective working
e Facility with language
f Sound knowledge of business practices
g Familiarity with document formats
Note: In terms of the target 160 words, the notes are rather generously written, but since they are not for personal use, they need to be intelligible to the reader.

The rough draft

The next stage, having established a format, would be to compose a rough draft:

The ability to summarise effectively is essential in organisations ~~if personnel are to cope~~ [to enable personnel to cope] with the flood [of information]

brought about [caused] by the communications revolution and the [consequent] wide-spread use of business equipment.

Organisational personnel are being 'flooded' by oral and written communications, causing staff to waste time and ~~resulting in~~ increasing [the] costs [of] ~~in the~~ produc~~tion~~[-ing] and distribut~~ion~~[-ing] of information.

Senior executives cannot use their time and expertise [effectively] if forced to waste time on trivialities. Calls on their time must be rationed and communications reduced [by those servicing them] to 'core material' or brief analyses.

To help senior ~~executives,~~ [staff] those who summarise need to acquire skills in comprehending, evaluating and selectively reproducing data ~~:~~ [– They] they must learn to discriminate.

Specifically, ~~they should develop their expertise in the following areas~~ [expertise is needed in:]:

comprehension
~~recognition of main points~~ [selection]
~~analytical skills~~ [analysis]
objective ~~working~~ [writing]
~~facility with language~~ [fluent expression]
sound knowledge of:business practice
~~familiarity with~~ document formats   (143 words)

The next step is to include the title and any other helpful headings and to polish the rough draft, taking care not to exceed any prescribed word limit.

The final version

The final version will then appear like this:

SUMMARISING TECHNIQUES: WHY THEY ARE NEEDED AND HOW TO APPLY THEM IN ORGANISATIONS

Background
The ability to summarise effectively is essential in organisations to enable personnel to cope with the flood of information caused by the communications revolution and the consequent wide-spread use of business equipment.

The current situation
Organisation personnel are being 'flooded' by oral and written communications causing staff to waste time and increasing the costs of producing and distributing information.

The senior executive's problem
Senior executives cannot use their time and expertise effectively if forced to waste it on trivialities. Calls on their time must be rationed and communication reduced by those servicing them to 'core material' or brief analyses.

Skills needed by the summariser
To help senior staff, those who summarise need to acquire skills in comprehending, evaluating and selecting data. They must learn to discriminate.
    Specifically, expertise is needed in:

comprehension
selection
analysis
objective writing
fluent expression
sound knowledge of:
    business practice
    document formats
(160 words)

Last word
More communication fails from being too long, than from being too short!

When summarising . . .

Don't ... but do

Don't	... but do
Skimp the reading stages – the original *must* be clearly understood	Check your brief carefully before starting
	Check unfamiliar words
Include items in your points list which are trivial, repetitious, and, broadly, illustrations or examples	Convey fairly the author's own attitudes and outlooks
Abbreviate your points list too dramatically or allow yourself to be verbose	Measure your points list against relevance and importance to theme
Allow your own personal views to obtrude into the summary	Cross-check against passage and chosen title
Forget that it takes at least twice as many words on average to expand a points list into continuous prose	Convey the sense rather than the wording of the original
Try to 'borrow' phrases or sentences from the original – they won't fit into your smaller version comfortably – and you may use them wrongly	Think of reducing the original to its basic 'skeletal' form
Allow your rough or final version to suffer from 'over-compression', where the meaning is lost in a kind of shorthand language	Keep essential illustrations short – use collective nouns when possible
Allow your summary to look like a list of unconnected and hence meaningless statements	Bear in mind that authors tend to repeat main points several times and 'say it only once'
	Make a draft before attempting a final version
Overlook the fact that the recipient may never see the original. Your version must stand on its own two feet and not rely on a reading of the original to render it intelligible	Ensure that your tone and style are appropriate either to the author's approach or the recipient's needs – e.g. factual or persuasive
Forget that the context dictates the format of the final version – a schematic layout may be essential for quick reference in a meeting	Ensure that the rough draft to final version stage is free from mechanical errors – spelling, punctuation, syntax
	Choose an appropriate format

Précis of documentation or correspondence

Sometimes it is necessary to produce a summary of an exchange of letters or of a number of related documents. Such techniques involve selecting only the most essential points and connecting them as follows:
1 Specifying the context, authors' names and designations and organisations in a title section.
2 Proceeding chronologically showing dates and authors and the essential point of each document or letter.

The abstract

In compiling an abstract, it is extremely important to act only upon the requirement of your briefing – do not produce a précis when the recipient has asked for a particular aspect to be synthesised from points dispersed in the original. Follow the method shown on page 23. Remember that you will need to be far more stringent in excluding non-essential material, and that a schematic presentation may be needed for the abstract to be used in a discussion or meeting. Lastly, always cite the source, authorship and date of the original, together with your name, status and the completion date.

Assessment questions

The memorandum

1 How does the use of the memorandum differ from that of the letter?

2 What are the main components of the memorandum format?

3 What are the limitations of a memorandum set out on A5 paper?

4 What sort of message does the memorandum tend to convey?

5 List the various stages of producing an inter-departmental memorandum.

6 What considerations govern the construction of a memorandum subject-heading?

7 Outline the composition of each of the three parts of the suggested structure of a memorandum.

8 What aspects of the recipient's make-up should the memorandum-writer keep in mind?

9 What communication factors would affect the style in which a memorandum is written?

10 What dangers do you think might stem from an executive sending too many memoranda throughout his organisation?

11 In what circumstances might it be necessary to send a memorandum?

The report

12 What principal functions does the report perform in organisational communication?

13 What are the differences in use and format between a routine report and an especially commissioned, investigatory report?

14 In what situations might it be appropriate to deliver an oral as opposed to a written report?

15 What are the main components common to the majority of reports?

16 What are the principal differences of format of:
 a The short informal report?
 b The short formal report?
 c The memorandum report?

17 What are the advantages of using a schematic layout in report-writing? Identify two methods for schematic referencing.

18 When would you opt for the short formal report format?

19 What do you understand by the headings:
 a 'Terms of reference'?
 b 'Procedure'?

20 What considerations would you bear in mind when classifying the data collected for the Information or Findings section of a report?

21 What principal features of style should the report-writer adopt when writing a report?

Summarising communication

22 In what ways are summarising communications employed in organisations?

23 How can summaries help senior executives?

24 List some of the communication activities which require summarising techniques.

25 Identify some communication documents which specifically require summarising techniques.

26 List the ten stages of summarising.

27 What advice would you give to someone about to commence a summary?

28 What do you understand by:
'Précis of Documentation or Correspondence'?

29 When is a précis of correspondence likely to be required?

30 What is an abstract?

31 What is the 'acid test' by which the success of a summary may be gauged?

Written assignments, discussion topics

The memorandum

1 Recently there have been several instances in your company when confidential information about your products and activities has been secured by rival firms. As a result, your office administration manager has asked you to draft a memorandum to all office staff reminding them of the need for maintaining security and confidentiality at all times, and outlining the procedures they should follow.

2 A fire-drill in your offices last week revealed a number of alarming inadequacies. Many members of staff behaved quite indifferently; others seemed to have no idea of what they should do, while one or two simply did nothing at all, saying that they were 'far too busy'. As a consequence, you have been detailed to draft a memorandum to all staff aimed at emphasising the possible dangers in remaining indifferent to company regulations in case of fire and at securing an improved response.

3 As assistant sales manager you recently clashed with the deputy works manager at a marketing meeting over the need to have a batch of refrigerator motors produced by what he thought was an impossible deadline. Now you need to secure his cooperation, following complaints feedback from your sales representatives, to reduce the time taken by the Works to repair defective refrigerators sent back under warranty.

Draft a memorandum which you think will result in the repair time being reduced.

4 After deliberating on ways to overcome persistent late-coming on the part of the factory and office staff, your managing director decided three weeks ago, in the spirit of industrial democracy, to introduce clocking-in and off for *all* company staff, himself included! Your departmental office staff did not particularly welcome such an innovation, and feelings since have been running high. You have therefore been requested to draft a memorandum to departmental staff aimed at improving the situation and securing cooperation while reiterating the need for punctuality in all staff.

5 Write a critical evaluation of the four alternative memoranda on page 8 and justify which version you consider as being likely to secure the punctual submission of Jim Grainger's sales reports.

6 Analyse the three memoranda on pages 9 and 10 from the point of view of the style in which they have been composed and comment on the ways in which the choice of words and syntax is likely to contribute to the effectiveness of the memoranda.

7 Assume that you are a departmental head at Kaybond Ltd, and that your staff have indicated that they are not keen to work under the proposed flexible working hours system. (See model memorandum, page 10.)

Write a memorandum to S Kilbride, managing director, outlining the staff's response to and misgivings about the proposal and stating clearly what you consider to be the best next step.

The report

8 You work as a trainee manager in the Gifts Department of a large departmental store. Three days ago, one of the sales assistants was involved in a difficult situation with a customer who wished to make an account purchase but who did not have her account credit card with her. Following company regulations, the assistant declined to give credit, whereupon the customer became abusive. You witnessed the scene and have been called in by the departmental manager to report on what you saw.

Deliver your oral report. (Note this assignment may be carried out in a role-playing situation).

9 Gourmet Enterprises Ltd is a company manufacturing a wide range of kitchen utensils. After initial rapid expansion, the company did badly last year. Profits slumped and its share of the market fell by a third. The company's factory is in need of investment and there has been some industrial unrest. Fortunately, the company's small but resourceful research unit has just developed and patented a revolutionary new inner coating for saucepans, frying-pans etc. which enables them to be cleaned by a wipe with a cloth – thus doing away entirely with the need to wash them up. As chairman of the Board, draft that part of your annual report releasing news of this development, bearing in mind that you and your co-directors are anxious to keep your seats on the board and need to win back the confidence of the shareholders.

Before attempting this assignment collect a number of company annual reports, extracts of which often appear in newspapers. Discuss their style and tone.

10 Recently your superior, the office administration manager, expressed his dissatisfaction with the number of different ways in which your department's secretaries and typists are unilaterally producing letters and memoranda in widely differing formats.

He thinks it should be possible to standardise such formats in a way which would make a more economic use of time and human resources. At the same time he thinks that guide-lines could be established to assist new staff on an induction and familiarisation programme. The active cooperation of departmental executives would, however, be needed.

As his personal assistant, he has asked you to look into the matter and to submit a written report to him indicating the nature and extent of the problem he has perceived, together with your recommendations for implementing an acceptable and workable system for producing letters and memoranda.

Research current commercial practices and then compose an appropriate report.

11 Last week a row broke out among the office personnel in your department over the drawing up of the annual summer holiday staff rota.

In past years it has been the practice to approach senior and long-service staff first and to follow an informal and delicate 'pecking order'.

Two weeks ago, however, the senior clerical officer, over-worked and under pressure at the time, delegated the job to a relatively new and inexperienced subordinate. Unaware of the customary procedure, he compiled a list on a 'first come, first served' basis, and then circulated the list without any consultation.

Several members of staff took exception to the way in which the rota had been drawn up and a row occurred which had the effect of polarising attitudes between senior and junior, older and younger departmental personnel.

In order to retrieve the situation and to improve departmental staff relations, your office manager has informed staff that he is currently 'looking into the matter', and has asked you, his deputy, to investigate the situation and to produce a written report for him, establishing what went wrong and why, and suggesting how the current problem may best be resolved and how an equitable procedure may best be established for the future.

Write a suitable report, adding any additional authenticating material you consider appropriate.

Discussion topics

1 What do you think some executives mean when they refer to 'memo warfare'?

2 How can the proper use of the memorandum improve internal communication in organisations?

3 What advice would you give to someone new to a job involving the regular writing of memoranda?

4 What problems do you think could result from sending 'blind copies' of memoranda to an organisation's personnel?

5 Some organisations distribute memoranda which are neither signed nor initialled by their authors. Can you see any dangers arising from this practice?

6 Some senior executives consider the production of a detailed investigatory report to be one of the most demanding tasks which an executive can be given. Why do you think this might be?

7 What contribution do a precise referencing system and an indented schematic layout make to the communication of report data?

8 Why is so much store set by 'objectivity' in report-writing? Can a report ever be truly objective? Does it matter?

9 What problems do you envisage in the collection of data for an investigatory report of a controversial or delicate nature? What could the report-writer do to avoid embarrassments, confrontations or indelicacies?

10 Assignments involving summarising techniques are sometimes viewed with distaste by those deputed to undertake them. Why should this be so?

11 What do you think is the best way to acquire summarising skills?

Case studies

The Bournemouth problem

'I'm getting seriously concerned about the slide in sales at Bournemouth, and from what I hear, there's also a staff problem there. I think the time has come to get to the heart of the matter. I want you to have a good look at the picture as we have it here at Head Office, and then get down there and find out what's gone wrong. Let me have a report by Wednesday week, in time for my meeting with Mr Green (the regional manager for the Southern Region). Oh, and you'd better let me have your own views on how the matter can best be put right. Now, about this draft advertisement. . . .'

It was with these words that Harold Grafton, managing director of Countrywide Food Stores Ltd briefed his personal assistant on the need for an investigatory report into the slump in sales at the Bournemouth branch.

After having carefully researched the relevant documentation at head office – sales statistics, personnel files, marketing reports and the like, and having visited the Bournemouth branch, Harold Grafton's P.A. uncovered the following information:

After a steady increase during the last five years, sales have dropped by 31% during the past nine months.

Company advertising and sales promotion has recently been criticised by a number of branch managers and divisional managers.

Customer relations at Bournemouth suffered for two months as a result of a faulty cash-register which has now been repaired.

Branch stocks are replaced by a system of drawing from a regional warehouse to ensure fresh stocks, quick turnover and avoidance of shortages.

A rival company opened six months ago a branch some three-quarters of a mile away, which has been engaging in price-cutting and extensive sales-promotion.

Mr Harris, the branch manager, was appointed 12 months ago. His background was sales assistant, assistant branch manager and temporary branch manager at three of your company's branches in Lincoln, Harrogate and Warrington.

A memorandum from the Central Southern Divisional Manager drew attention four months ago to the increasing demands of head office regarding the completion of a host of returns issued by various head office departments to all branches.

Telephone and customer serving techniques leave much to be desired at the Bournemouth branch.

The fixtures and fittings of the branch are old and were put in as a 'temporary' measure some three years ago.

Basically, office administration, merchandising and branch appearance are satisfactory if unremarkable.

An urban redevelopment plan is at present reponsible for the demolition of 500 houses about half a mile from the branch as part of an urban renewal and rehousing scheme.

Marketing Department wrote a eulogistic report about the business potential of the area when a decision to purchase was being made three years ago.

Company branches at Poole and Christchurch are eclipsing the Bournemouth branch's turnover.

Assignment

As Harold Grafton's personal assistant, draft a suitable report according to his brief above, incorporating whatever aspects of the above information you consider relevant, and adding any appropriate, additional material you wish.

The Sherbury Leisure Centre

For several months public unrest has been growing in the town of Sherbury, county town of Wealdshire, about the lack of leisure amenities and facilities in the town, particularly for young people. A recent police report revealed that cases of vandalism had risen by 32% in the last 12 months, and teenage arrests for drunk and disorderly behaviour by 24%. Social workers have also expressed their concern about the mounting incidence of teenage alcoholism, and teenage gangs roaming the town centre and housing estates, bred as they see it, from boredom deriving from little or nothing to do in the evenings. The town's two youth clubs are over-subscribed, and there have been incidents when older teenagers have attempted to disrupt youth club activities when denied entrance.

During the past six weeks the local weekly news-paper, *The Sherbury Chronicle* has been campaigning for improvements in leisure facilities, with hard-hitting editorials under headlines such as, 'Council Fuddy-duddies Forget Their Youth'. The paper has also carried a lively correspondence on the subject. Readers' views have ranged from the sympathetic to the condemnatory – 'Sherbury's years of indifference towards the needs of the young are now bearing a bitter fruit,' and, 'In my youth people were too tired from a hard day's work to worry about whether they could play ping-pong or not. As a ratepayer I fail to see why I should subsidise the indolent by forking out for some white elephant Leisure Palace!'

Some town councillors have been actively canvassing for a Leisure Centre to be built to provide what they consider as sorely lacking amenities. At a recent council meeting, Councillor James Hillingdon referred to 'the shocking state of affairs that exists when a town of this size should have nothing to offer its young people in the evening but violent films from its one cinema and and alcoholic beverages from its ten central public houses.'

Local sports clubs and associations have been making representations to councillors and to County Hall officials. Some sports enthusiasts are travelling thirty miles or more to find the amenities they seek. The existing facilities are predominantly those for outdoor sports on recreation park pitches or for a few indoor sports such as judo in the small and over-crowded Community Hall at the western end of the town. The activities which have been suggested for inclusion in any future Leisure Centre include table-tennis, badminton, basketball, tennis, swimming, judo, karate, volleyball, ten-pin bowling, snooker and billiards, gymnastics and for older members, yoga, relaxation classes and keep-fit courses, together with a club-room for darts, dominoes and other 'less strenuous pursuits'.

A rough projection has put the cost of building a Leisure Centre at £1.3m, for a centre suitable for existing needs. Two sites have been identified as suitable. The first is at the end of the Charles Bowley Memorial Recreation Park, in the town's southern suburb, and the second is a central site which would require the centre to be built as a multi-storey building. Obviously, to meet the costs the rates would have to be increased, although it might be possible to secure a grant from central government, and local sports clubs have intimated that they would group together in a cash-raising drive.

As a result of the mounting pressure to provide a Leisure Centre, Sherbury's Chief Executive has decided to form a working-party made up of representatives of the Planning, Architect's and Education departments, including the Youth and Community Officer, the Sports Advisory Office and co-opted representatives from local sports clubs and associations. He has asked this working-party to investigate the need for a Leisure Centre, to make projections as to its likely building and maintenance costs, suggestions as to its location having regard to parking and transport considerations, proposals as to the kind of activities it should house and the kind of rooms or halls it should contain. Lastly he wishes the working party to make recommendations which could be submitted to the Council. As secretary to the working party you have been asked to draft the report.

Employ a vending machine...

Ralph Braybrook talks to Douglas Lee

We started something when we told you, in the May issue, how Lyons Maid's Russell Boorer felt about wasted potential catering sites. Douglas Lee, catering advisor to the big GKN Sankey vending machine concern, shares his views to a great extent and has entered the arena.

"What," he asks, "about those coach parks where 8000 or so people disgorge in a day and head straight for the toilets. Just the place for some impulse buying by people who have sat long hours in a coach.

"Look at it this way," he says to civic caterers. "We can help you compete on more equal terms with your commercial competitors. After all, you can employ a machine on a coach park or some similar site at no extra cost throughout the 24 hours. There is no argument with a machine about unsocial hours.

But, he hastens to say, it is no good putting in vending and leaving it at that. "People must be more sensitive to service through a machine than through a service counter. The machine is dead, thus presentation must, if anything, attain a higher standard than normal kitchen standards.

Particularly where there is a captive audience, and where people will be using the machines day after day, a good image has to be established, he says. "Yet people do not pay sufficient attention to customer requirements. They feel that a machine comes in and takes over and their responsibilities are at an end."

Constant attention to the needs of the people you are feeding is essential," he says. "Too long vending of food has been looked upon as a second-class catering operation."

This view was confirmed by his predecessor, Ron Lawrence, who though now in retirement, is still associated with the company. He said, "If you give a second-class service of food through vending equipment you might just as well not bother to put the food in at all. It does not take any longer to do the job properly; in fact, it takes less because no time is wasted in catching up on mistakes. Yet it is terribly difficult to get this over to some wooden-headed caterers."

At one time, he said, it was possible for a company like theirs to insist on certain standards.

Another essential, said Douglas Lee, is for caterers to get away from the habit of merely banging machines against a wall. A great deal depended upon environment. For example, in a sports centre, vending units should be close to the area of activity, furnishings should be good - a few well-placed seats made a lot of difference - and decor was all-important. "If you are going to give people decent food in vending machines, you must let them eat it under decent conditions."

There was a tendency, when aiming to save labour, to try and save everything else as well; to take automated selling to its ultimate. Saving labour did not necessarily mean becoming spartan. "One must not become too grasping, and interchange of menu is all important.

"Given that, there was very little feeding that could not be carried out through vending machines, and much of his company's success in the past had been in basing food vending on the "home" kitchen. On the caterer preparing the food in-house, that is. This, he said, vested direct control in the catering manager, from the point of view of portioning, price structure and quality. Though, of course, in smaller establishments, vending was based entirely on hand-snacks and beverages.

He could see a trend away from the main meal to the snack type of item, but, whether one was selling meals or hand-snacks and wrapped confectionery, it was vital to go through the same merchandising techniques.

He pointed out that, in most staff canteens, most items were provided at an overall loss. But beverages and snack items were profit makers and could ease their subsidy. "In addition," he asked, "does everyone feel hungry and thirsty at the same time? That is why we like the system of open vending, where people can feel like a snack and go and get it at will."

He foresees a great increase in leisure activity and, through vending, it was possible to feed people round the clock. Moreover, it was essential to encourage impulse buying by having, say, a snack machine next to a beverages machine. "If they go to one it is likely they will also use the other."

He could see instances where, at a seaside resort, for example, it would be viable to install vending for weekend trade only. After all, the machine would last longer and was costing no more. However, he added that it was of paramount importance that sites should come under frequent inspection.

He foresaw vending moving into such establishments as schools, where costs were such a problem, especially where they were multi-purpose buildings that were in use in the evenings, or in instances where senior pupils studied on their own and did not keep normal school hours.

"Give vending the first-class image it should have and there is no feeding requirement it cannot meet," he says. And he is not averse to talking to people like yourselves about the possibilities.

Assignment

People and Communication

Meetings

Desmond W Evans

Contents

Acknowledgments

The author and publishers have made every effort to trace the ownership of all copyright material and to obtain permission from the owners of copyright.
Thanks are due to the following for permission to reprint the material indicated:

Chichester and District Angling Society for the extract from their Constitution, p9.

West Sussex County Council for the extract from their Standing Orders, p9.

PITMAN EDUCATION LIMITED
39 Parker Street, London WC2B 5PB

Associated Companies
Pitman Publishing Pty Ltd, Melbourne
Pitman Publishing New Zealand Ltd, Wellington

© Desmond W Evans 1978

First published in Great Britain 1978
Reprinted 1979, 1980

Text set in 10/12pt Sabon
printed and bound in Great Britain
at The Pitman Press, Bath

ISBN 0 273 01246 0 (bound book)
      0 273 01247 9 (module pack)

Introduction

The term, 'meeting' is used so widely nowadays, and given so many different interpretations that it has come to mean almost all things to all people. At one end of the meetings' spectrum are those which are formally conducted and governed by rules of procedure as laid down by a company's Memorandum and Articles of Association or the Standing Orders of a county council. At the other end are the easy, informal types of meetings such as the managerial brain-storming meeting at which executives keep making suggestions about, say, product development, in the hope of crystallising a totally new idea or approach.

Some types of limited company and various local government councils are required to hold certain meetings by statute, as a result of government legislation. A company's Articles or a council's Standing Orders will prescribe rules about giving adequate notice of a meeting, what constitutes a quorum (the minimum number of members needed to be present for a meeting to be held), what sort of business a meeting should conduct, and when and where certain types of meeting, such as board meetings or Annual Meetings of a council should be held. In addition, such rules will indicate what rights the shareholder or member of the public possesses in areas such as voting or admission.

Meetings are held by people from all walks of life and in countless company, public service or sports and leisure contexts. At the top of an organisational pyramid company directors may meet to evolve company policy and decide future strategies. Members of trade unions may meet to hammer out an approach to imminent pay negotiations. Alternatively, members of an angling club committee may meet to discuss the dates and locations of the following season's fishing matches.

Indeed, whether as a tool of management, instrument of local or central government, or forum of the voluntary club, the meeting has, for many years, been employed as a means of making decisions – usually binding, upon those participating in the meeting, of spreading information or as a means of resolving a particular problem. Through the medium of the meeting, people are able to make suggestions, voice criticisms and express opinions. Moreover, the physical proximity of people seated round a table to 'thrash things out' creates a special type of relationship among those present which no form of written exchange or electronic substitutes is able to produce.

Like most communications channels, however, the meeting is also a potential source of communication failure or break-down. It may become sterile and unproductive, costly to call and a source of time-wasting. Much depends upon the qualities of the members attending and their respective skills in communicating effectively through the constraints imposed by rules, procedures or conventions. Certainly all types of meetings share certain common factors which serve to unite those attending and to direct their thoughts and actions.

Meetings:	common factors
Goals:	Goals or aims have been identified which the meeting elects to achieve
Outcome:	The members of the meeting have an interest in the outcome of its business
Interests:	Participants represent sectional or official points of view
Action or Information:	A problem, situation, plans or attitudes need to be resolved or crystallised; information needs to be imparted and disseminated
Deadlines:	The business of the meeting takes place within a limited time-scale which affects the potential effectiveness of decisions or the relevance of information
Leadership:	Someone has assumed or been assigned the leadership of the meeting

Different types of meeting

Since meetings take place within such a diversity of organisations and are used for so many different purposes, to arrive at a definition true for all types of meeting is virtually impossible, save in the broadest of terms.

Yet, the hostility which the calling of some meetings produces in those required or invited to attend often derives from an inadequate understanding of basics. If the meetings are poorly organised they quickly become 'a waste of time'; if they fail to result in action they are deemed 'pointless'; if the participants bring with them misconceptions about the 'terms of reference' which limit the powers of those attending a meeting, they are likely to become disappointed or embittered about the value or effectiveness of meetings. It is therefore important to define the nature of certain types of meeting, to appreciate the procedures and conventions which govern their conduct and then to evaluate their effectiveness in contributing to sound decision-making and good administration.

Definitions of meetings

Statutory

A legal definition of a meeting based on case law precedent is:

'the coming together of at least two persons for any lawful purpose'.

To embrace statutory meetings of companies and public institutions, this definition may be enlarged:

an assembly of persons meeting in accordance with legally defined rules and procedures to discharge business as required by law.

Executive

In the on-going administration of companies or local and central government many meetings take place which are participative – all present share in the making of decisions which leads to action being taken:

an assembly of people with common interests arriving at decisions and instituting actions through the process of an exchange of relevant views and information which leads to an agreement favoured by the majority of those present and subsequently supported by all.

Briefing

Some meetings are called, however, within organisations to relay decisions or information from a more senior level:

an assembly of people in a 'reporting to' position within an organisational hierarchy who are summoned to receive, accept and comply with the requirements of formulated decisions or to retain information for use relayed to them by a person in authority over them.

Advisory

In some organisations people meet to generate advice or to make suggestions for submission to a higher authority:

an assembly of people meeting to formulate advice, suggestions or proposals for submission to a higher, executive body for ratification.

Managerial

Many informal meetings occur (some arising spontaneously) between a manager and his subordinates or counterparts to exchange opinions, give advice or supply information as part of the managerial decision-making process:

a gathering of people within an organisation (but not necessarily restricted to the organisation) with clearly defined inter-personal relationships, meeting to exchange views, attitudes, or information with a view to making decisions and instituting actions.

Task force, working-party

A modern approach to solving an organisation's problems has been to bring together a group of people with varying responsibilities and from different departments to pursue a particular task or to resolve a specific problem:

an assembly of people drawn from various levels and sectors of an organisation, embodying different specialisms, brought together to find the solution to a problem by working outside the normal administrative structure.

Brain-storming, buzz-groups

Some informal meetings are called with the aim of generating a fresh approach or new ideas relating to organisational activities:

an informal assembly of people who aim to generate ideas, suggestions or approaches to organisational activities from an unrestricted interchange of views, opinions and attitudes.

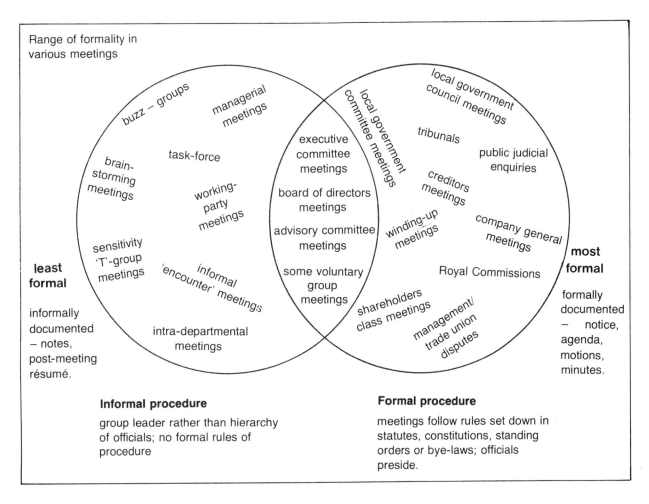

Range of formality in various meetings

least formal

informally documented – notes, post-meeting résumé.

most formal

formally documented – notice, agenda, motions, minutes.

Informal procedure

group leader rather than hierarchy of officials; no formal rules of procedure

Formal procedure

meetings follow rules set down in statutes, constitutions, standing orders or bye-laws; officials preside.

Formal structures and procedures

The preceding definitions and 'range of formality' diagram should be taken as guide-lines since the degree of formality with which a meeting is conducted depends not only upon the existence of a constitution, standing orders or rules, but also upon the climate or atmosphere generated within any organisation.

However, many formal meetings, especially those run by committees, follow broadly similar lines and share equivalent structures and procedures. Generally speaking there is a correlation between the degree of formality of a meeting and the importance of its decisions:

Policy-making **Executive**	affects entire organisation, usually made by a meeting of the board of directors made by senior or middle management probably affecting departments or divisions
Implementive **Routine** **Administrative**	day-to-day decisions made within departments

Structure of committee hierarchy

In complex organisations the structures of various committees are fixed in a hierarchy, and their ability to generate action is channelled and controlled:

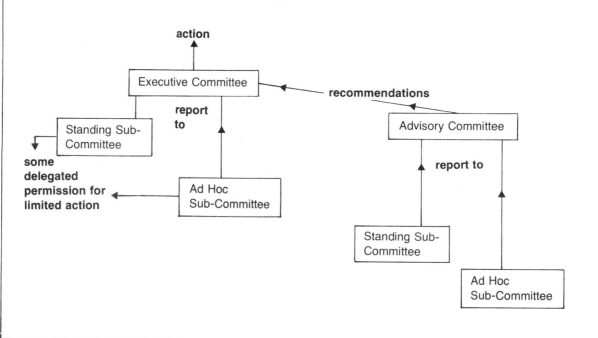

Executive committee	One which has the power to act upon decisions
Advisory committee **Consultative committee**	One which refers advice to a main, executive committee
Standing committee	One which meets during an indefinite period
Ad hoc committee	A committee constituted to carry out a particular task (from the Latin *ad hoc*: 'for this purpose')
Sub-committee	One performing for and reporting to a main committee
Policy committee	In large organisations, one which takes major decisions affecting future activities
Management committee	A form of executive committee which manages the important affairs of an organisation
Membership committee	Clubs, such as golf clubs, use such committees to vet and control membership

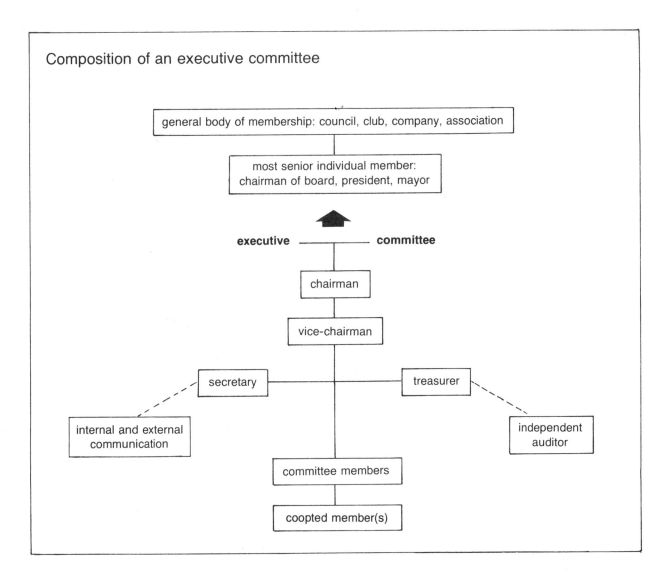

Composition of an executive committee

general body of membership: council, club, company, association

most senior individual member:
chairman of board, president, mayor

executive ——— **committee**

chairman

vice-chairman

secretary

treasurer

internal and external
communication

independent
auditor

committee members

coopted member(s)

The composition and functions of an executive committee naturally vary according to the type of organisation it is serving. The above diagram broadly represents a popular type of executive committee to be found in commerce, the public service or voluntary clubs. In large organisations the financial function may be integrated into an accounting department; the committee may be responsible through a board of directors to shareholders, or through a local government council to rate-payers.

Presiding member

Chairman

Vice–chairman

Secretary

Treasurer

Committee members

Coopted members

(Auditor)

In voluntary clubs particularly, a president or captain may act as a figure-head positioned between the executive committee and the club members, although the chairman of the executive committee is responsible for directing its activities and for presiding at its meetings. Some executive committees include a vice-chairman, usually a senior, experienced member, able to stand in for the chairman if need be. The secretary has a close relationship with the chairman in planning the business of meetings and generally administering the committee's work, while the treasurer keeps a watching brief and record of the committee's finances for an annual audit. The members of the committee may be elected or appointed by the general membership, serving for a pre-established term of office. Sometimes committees ask an expert or specialist to join them as a 'coopted member'; he or she may, or may not, be given the right to vote at committee meetings.

In the case of voluntary clubs and associations, the annual financial records, expressed by the treasurer in balance sheet form, are checked against receipts by an independently appointed auditor. In this way the general membership is reassured of the integrity of its committee.

The rules of the game

All meetings, whether statutorily called, run by company departments, or organised by local voluntary clubs are governed by rules. Sometimes the rules take the form of laws decreed by Act of Parliament, sometimes the form of company regulations lodged with the Registrar of Companies, and sometimes, in the case of a voluntary society, the form of a constitution. Even when no written rules exist – as may be the case in, for example, inter-departmental company meetings – there nevertheless exists a set of 'unspoken rules or conventions' which participants will have learned and which are just as effective in regulating activities.

The best piece of advice for all those whose work or whose leisure interests involve them in taking part in meetings, therefore, is:

It pays to know the rules of the game!

An inexperienced company director or county councillor may find him or herself outmanoeuvred or reduced to helpless silence by someone better versed in procedural technicalities – points of order or information – sometimes introduced to win a point or demolish opposition! Even in leisure or voluntary association committee meetings passions have been known to run high over the venue of the annual outing, and even here, it pays to know exactly what the club's constitution has to say on any particular point of procedure.

In the case of those meetings called within the confines of an organisation – a company or local government department – there may be no specific rules to guide procedure at a meeting, although it is held beneath the 'general umbrella' of local government or company law. Here it is much more difficult to grasp the rules of the game, since they are sometimes obscure and capable of change. Such meetings are largely controlled by those members possessing either status or assertive personalities.

In this type of meeting much will depend upon the quality of the chairman, who will need to be a leader, persuader, diplomat, tactician and healer rolled into one!

The inexperienced participator in meetings should, then, take the trouble to learn the rules, written or unspoken, and should 'play himself in' by listening to and observing his fellow-participants in action. Gradually he will perceive the responses and attitudes which motivate his peers, may discern where he will gain a sympathetic ear, and where a rebuff. He should also ensure that he has 'done his homework' before speaking, since if he is to sway his audience, he must first gain their respect. He should also bear in mind that *he* has to become acceptable to his peers before his ideas or suggestions are accepted.

Written rules affecting meetings

Companies Memorandum and Articles of Association:
Required by Company Law, the Memorandum and Articles define aims, activities and procedure of a company and are lodged with a Registrar of Companies.

Councils Acts of Parliament and Standing Orders:
Much council procedure is governed either by Act of Parliament – Local Government Act 1972, Public Bodies (Admission to Meetings) Act 1960 and approved rules in Standing Orders.

Voluntary bodies Written constitutions:
Voluntary clubs, associations and societies adhere to rules and bye-laws set down in a 'constitution', usually drawn up by founder-members: its rules also govern the composition of committees and meetings procedures.

9. THE COMMITTEE

The Committee shall meet at least once in each calendar month to examine the accounts and to arrange the affairs of the Society in accordance with Committee Standing Orders.

The Committee shall promote the interests of the Society and shall have the power to take and defend legal proceedings. Such power may only be exercised after a resolution has been duly proposed, seconded and carried in Committee by a majority vote of those present and voting. Any expenditure of funds for the purpose of litigation must be shown in the Society's accounts and be ratified by a simple majority of members in general meeting not later than the next Annual General Meeting after the termination of such litigation.

THE CHAIRMAN—shall have the power of vote in committee if he wishes to exercise it, but shall have a further and casting vote in the event of equal votes of those present and voting.

THE VICE CHAIRMAN—shall serve as a Committee Member and take the place of the Chairman at a Committee Meeting in the absence of the elected Chairman.

THE HON TREASURER—shall deal with all financial matters of the Society, keeping an orderly record of income and expenditure and prepare the books for audit at the end of each financial year, being March 31st. He shall receive annually an honorarium which shall be decided by calculation at 6½p per Society member.

THE HON SECRETARY—shall keep minutes of the business conducted at Committee Meetings and General Meetings and shall carry out instructions of the Committee, deal with general correspondence and other duties which from time to time shall be determined. He shall receive annually an honorarium which amount shall be decided by calculation at 6½p per Society member.

THE HON COMPETITION SECRETARY shall arrange and organise Society and inter-club competitions and visits to other clubs' waters. He shall receive annually an honorarium which amount shall be decided by calculation at 3p per Society member.

APPENDIX
BYE-LAWS

(1) **SUSSEX RIVER AUTHORITY** Each member of the Society shall make himself familiar with the Byelaws of the Sussex River Authority and regard them as additional to the Society's Byelaws.

(2) **BAILIFFS** The Committee shall be empowered to appoint Honorary Bailiffs as is deemed expedient, but members when elected shall undertake the voluntary role of Water Bailiff and will at all times endeavour to prevent poaching and unauthorised fishing on the Society's waters.

(3) **MEMBERS** Members shall at all times behave in an orderly manner or they will become liable for expulsion under the Society's Rule 8. All members are expected, where

(3) These Standing Orders shall take effect subject to any statutory provision for the time being in force affecting local authorities.

N.B. The main Standing Orders applying to Committees and Sub-Committees have been indicated by sidelines.

MEETINGS OF THE COUNCIL

Annual Meeting 2. (1) Each Annual Meeting of the Council shall be combined with an Ordinary Meeting and shall be held at the County Hall, Chichester, commencing at ten thirty o'clock in the forenoon, unless the Council or the Chairman shall otherwise direct.

Ordinary Meetings (2) Ordinary Meetings shall be held at the County Hall, Chichester, at ten thirty o'clock in the forenoon, unless the Council or the Chairman shall otherwise direct.

Minutes 9. (1) The Minutes of the business done at each meeting of the Council shall be printed and a copy sent to each member with the summons to attend the next meeting of the Council.

(2) As soon as the Minutes have been read, or if they are taken as read under Standing Order 10(3), the Chairman shall put the question "That the minutes of the meeting of the Council held on the   day of   be signed as a true record".

(3) No motion or discussion shall take place upon the Minutes, except upon their accuracy and any question of their accuracy shall be raised by motion. If no such question is raised, or if it is raised then as soon as it has been disposed of, the Chairman shall sign the minutes.

ORDER OF BUSINESS

Order of Business 10. The order of business at a meeting of the Council shall be:-

(1) To choose a person to preside if the Chairman and Vice-Chairman of the Council be absent;

(2) When required by Statute, to elect a Chairman;

(3) To read the minutes of the last meeting of the Council with a view to their confirmation as a correct record provided that, if so directed by the Council, the whole or any part thereof shall be taken as read;

(4) When necessary, to appoint a member of the Council to be Vice-Chairman;

(5) To deal with business expressly required by Statute to be done at the meeting;

(6) To deal with business specially brought forward by the Chairman;

NOTICES OF MOTION

Procedure 13. (1) Except as provided by Standing Order 15, every notice of motion shall be in writing, signed by the member giving the notice, and shall be delivered, at the office of the County Secretary, not less than nine clear days before the next meeting of the Council.

MEETINGS document cycle for monthly meetings

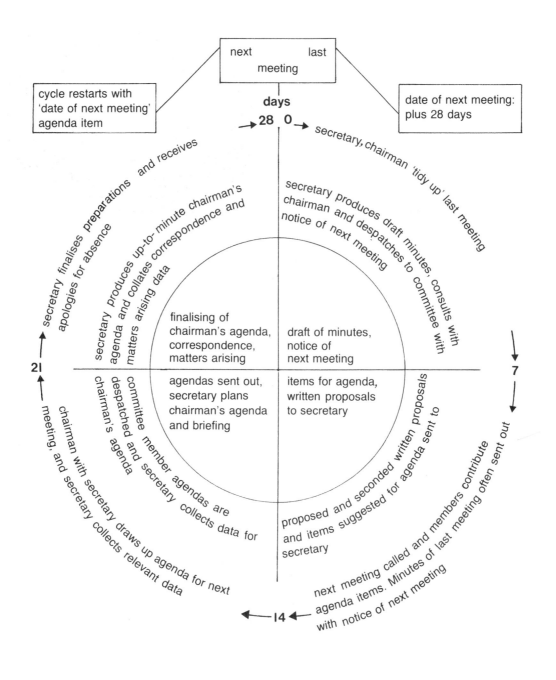

next   last
meeting

cycle restarts with
'date of next meeting'
agenda item

days
→ 28 0 →

date of next meeting:
plus 28 days

secretary, chairman 'tidy up' last meeting

secretary finalises preparations and receives

apologies for absence

secretary produces up-to- minute chairman's

agenda and collates correspondence and

matters arising data

secretary produces draft minutes, consults with

chairman and despatches to committee with

notice of next meeting

finalising of
chairman's agenda,
correspondence,
matters arising

draft of minutes,
notice of
next meeting

21

agendas sent out,
secretary plans
chairman's agenda
and briefing

items for agenda,
written proposals
to secretary

7

committee member agendas are

despatched and secretary

chairman's agenda   collects data for

proposed and seconded written proposals

and items suggested for agenda sent to

secretary

chairman with secretary draws up agenda for next

meeting, and secretary collects relevant data

next meeting called and members contribute

agenda items. Minutes of last meeting often sent out

with notice of next meeting

← 14 ←

Document sequence:

1 **Minutes**   agreed written record of business of a meeting
2 **Notice**   written 'invitation' to meeting's participants
3 **Proposals, agenda items**   business proposed for debate at meeting
4 **Committee agenda**   list of items of business for discussion
5 **Chairman's agenda**   similar to Committee Agenda, but includes helpful background or briefing notes prepared by Secretary.
Note: Advance notice   Some organisations require notices, proposals and agendas to be sent out and received by a fixed number of days in advance of the meeting to which they refer.

The participants

The chairman's role – helping members to make decisions. . . .

Profile of the chairman

There are as many different types of style of chairmanship as there are meetings. Where meetings are held without formal procedures or written rules, the chairman's role is often very loosely interpreted. He or she may do no more than provide the impetus for discussion and the interchange of ideas.

In formally structured meetings, however, the chairman's responsibilities become much more complex, requiring him to implement a code of written rules, adhere to long-established procedures and exercise sometimes discreet and sometimes explicit control over the participants at a meeting.

The following guide-lines indicate the broad areas of responsibility of the chairman presiding over meetings of the executive committee kind.

Authority

The chairman at meetings governed by the rules of Articles, Standing Orders or a Constitution has many responsibilities to discharge, all of which depend upon his authority, which will have been prescribed and written down. As the leader of a committee or working party, he will have as a principal duty the responsibility to ensure that all business is conducted fairly, according to the rules which obtain. For example, he may have to decide whether a speaker is 'out of order', or whether an item has been fairly introduced under 'Matters Arising'. In addition, he will, at times, need to use his initiative to solve problems not covered by precedent or covered in the written rules. Many aspects of procedure in formal meetings, such as addressing remarks to the chair, exist to reinforce the chairman's authority and so enable him more readily to control the meeting.

Social skills

Though many chairmen possess different styles in the chair, they all need to be skilled in handling people. Not only must meetings proceed according to rules, they must also generate a cooperative atmosphere or climate so that decisions of a good quality may be made from the active participation of all present. It is therefore the chairman's responsibility to see that all members are given a chance to speak or to reply, that no one speaker dominates, that private conversations or quarrels do not develop and that no-one 'switches off' out of boredom or frustration. Similarly, the chairman must ensure that the discussion remains relevant to the business in hand and that members do not meander down unproductive byways or parade their pet arguments. Equally, he may at times need to supply a résumé of the argument to help members crystallise their thoughts as they near the point of decision. And, while using such social skills, the chairman must avoid seeming to favour any particular group or party within the committee. Qualities of tact and diplomacy are therefore essential in exercising the duties of a chairman.

Administration

Although the secretary attends to much of a committee's administration, it is the chairman who has overall responsibility to ensure that the work of a committee proceeds smoothly. With the active support and assistance of the secretary, the chairman must ensure that accurate records in the form of minutes are kept, that committee members are kept fully informed of developments, that all financial matters are conscientiously attended to. In order to monitor delegated duties, the chairman will very often ask for reports to be made as a means of disseminating information and providing progress or status checks. Sometimes the chairman may decide to set up a sub-committee to deal with a particular problem or to organise an event.

Policy and direction

By adopting an impartial approach in meetings the chairman is able to keep in mind the wider objectives and perspectives of the committee, so that he may dissuade members from making commitments to untenable positions, or from taking extreme actions without heeding the wider issues or implications. Like the good manager, the good chairman achieves the committee's objectives through the active cooperation of other people – the committee members attending the meetings.

Profile of the secretary

The secretary is, perhaps, best regarded as the hub of the committee around whom its work revolves. The conscientious secretary undertakes much detailed work, frequently behind the scenes, to ensure that lines of communication between committee members and the organisation as a whole are kept open. In addition, the secretary has a duty to perform administrative tasks punctually and efficiently.

The chairman's 'right hand'

In terms of the seating arrangements of many a committee or working party, the secretary is to be found, quite literally, at the right hand of the chairman. Indeed, this physical proximity is symbolic of the full cooperation and rapport which must exist between chairman and secretary if the work of a committee is to be productive.

Very often, the other duties a chairman may undertake, either at work or in his local community, will mean that much of the routine and detailed work of the committee is left to the secretary. Nevertheless, the considerate secretary takes pains to ensure that his chairman is kept fully briefed at all times by means of the chairman's agenda, written briefings, or copies of documents and liaison between meetings. The chairman and the secretary will usually consult over the drafting of minutes, the compilation of an agenda and the calling of meetings.

During the meeting itself, the secretary will keep alert to come to the aid of his chairman, if need be, with detailed information, a helpful up-dating or confirmation of any late developments. Moreover, he must be careful to see that such supportive action does not detract in any way from the chairman's control or authority in the meeting but is proffered unobtrusively. Thus the relationship of the secretary to the chairman is largely supportive and it is not always easy for the secretary to accept the constraints which his role imposes. However, the good chairman and secretary realise that they are very much a team and the secretary generally derives much personal satisfaction from being at the centre of the committee's activities.

Administration

Though often enjoying much freedom of action, it is important to remember that the secretary's administrative duties are delegated to him and usually set out, for example, in a society's constitution or in the case of a County Secretary, the council's Standing Orders.

In broad terms, the secretary administers the committee's business. This responsibility includes keeping and distributing records of meetings in the form of minutes and keeping the regular cycle of meetings running smoothly. In this context, the secretary is responsible for producing the minutes of the last meeting to despatch to committee members often with notice of the next. In the case of formal meetings the secretary will accept written proposals from members of the committee to incorporate in a committee agenda, which members must also receive in good time before a meeting. The secretary must also compile a chairman's agenda and attend to any correspondence, written reports or briefings which the committee may need to receive. Before a subsequent meeting, the secretary very often needs to follow up any task delegated to him which may be referred to under 'Matters Arising' and will also need to collect any apologies for absence to pass on to the chairman.

In addition, it usually falls to the secretary to ensure that the venue of the meeting has been booked and that the meeting or conference room itself is fully prepared with a suitable seating arrangement, notepaper, and any further requirements or refreshments which may be needed. The thoughtful secretary also brings copies of relevant documents with him in case committee members arrive without them.

A further duty of the secretary is to see that any absent committee member is kept informed of the business of a meeting and that he receives copies of the appropriate minutes and other documents. As well as servicing the committee in this way, the secretary is also responsible for circulating papers or reports upon request to the organisation's membership and for maintaining any noticeboard which may display committee notices.

Lastly, the secretary has a duty to ensure that he supports the chairman in the sometimes demanding task of conducting a meeting's business in such a way that neither rancour, hostility nor boredom interfere with its work, and that attendance at meetings does not fall off as a result of low morale.

Profile of the treasurer

The treasurer has a crucial part to play in the work of any committee responsible for managing an organisation's funds. He not only keeps careful account of all income and expenditure during a financial year, but also acts as 'watch-dog', monitoring the financial implications of projects and activities, so that the enthusiasm of committee members does not outrun the organisation's financial resources.

Financial administration

The treasurer is expected to keep careful records of all financial transactions which a committee may make on behalf of its members, so that at the end of each year he is able to present a treasurer's report and balance sheet at an Annual General Meeting. Such a duty involves the keeping of all receipts, bills, cheque stubs, bank statements and petty cash records so that his accounts may be substantiated.

In time for the Annual General Meeting, the treasurer of a society will pass his accounts and records to an independent auditor who checks and passes them, so that the integrity both of the treasurer and the committee is preserved when the accounts are presented for the scrutiny of the membership. This function is mirrored in company practice in the work of the accounts or financial director and the company's chartered accountants.

Advisory role

In many situations, the decisions of a committee or working party may involve the spending of money. The treasurer is not only responsible for keeping an up-to-date record of the organisation's financial status – often to be found as an item on the committee agenda – but also to advise the committee on the financial aspects of proposed ventures, even though this may mean 'pouring cold water' on someone's cherished scheme! In this way, the treasurer maintains the solvency of the organisation – essential to almost every undertaking.

Talking point: In meetings chairmen and members tend to deserve each other.

Written documentation

If any committee, working party or convened meeting is to function effectively, it will need to pay careful attention to the range of written documentation it produces, whether a letter, report, agenda or minutes. Where meetings are concerned, written communications either prepare members for business, record business transacted or implement business decided upon. Broadly, the range of written documentation through which a committee will transmit much of its activities is:

1 Notice of meeting
2 Minutes of the last meeting
3 Committee members' agenda
4 Chairman's agenda
5 Chairman's additional briefing
6 Formal, written proposals; motions
7 Correspondence
8 Financial reports
9 Written reports

The secretary produces the first five items, and may ensure that members' proposals are framed appropriately. He or she will also attend to any necessary correspondence, while the treasurer is responsible for financial reports and statements, and the chairman of the committee may oversee the production of any committee report.

Note: There is sometimes confusion over the use of the terms Proposal, Motion and Resolution. It is perhaps helpful to regard the written submission of an item for discussion, before a meeting is held, as a 'proposal'. During the meeting, when the item is brought up for discussion, it is generally referred to as a 'motion'. Whether as a proposal or a motion the item will, in formal meetings, need to be sponsored by a proposer and seconder. If the motion is carried it thereafter becomes a 'resolution' which has been passed by a majority of voters.

The notice

Notices of meetings, despatched in advance according to standing regulations, may be written in one of several formats:
1   A form postcard
Such postcards are pre-printed and used to call routine, perhaps monthly, meetings. Spaces are left for the secretary to enter the committee member's name, and the day, date, time and venue of the meeting. Though there is less of a personal touch, they save the secretary valuable time and effort.

2   Centered notification
Some notices are produced on sheets of A5 landscape headed notepaper. The essential information is imparted in a centered paragraph.

3   Letter format
Sometimes formal meetings are called by means of a personally written letter from the secretary to each committee member on the organisation's headed notepaper.

4   Memorandum
In the case of meetings called by a company or public-service department, the format used is frequently the memorandum.

Agendas

As well as providing a kind of 'early warning system' to help meeting participants to prepare themselves for the topics to be covered, the committee members' agenda acts both as a 'running-order' schedule and time-table during a meeting. The adroit chairman will ensure that agendas are not allowed to become too long or ponderous. Similarly, careful thought may also be given to the position of an item of business on an agenda, where either 'the decks may be cleared' of less important items before a thorny problem is tackled, or where an important item of business is dealt with first, while members are fresh. It is in such instances that the acumen and experience of the chairman is invaluable.

'I didn't bother with an agenda this time – you know how awkward they get when they come prepared. . . .'

Thames Valley Cricket Club

NOTICE OF MONTHLY COMMITTEE MEETING

The next monthly meeting of the Committee will take
place on Wednesday, 3rd July 19-- at 7.30 p.m. in the
Clubhouse.

Items for inclusion on the agenda should be submitted
to me no later than Friday, 21st June.

signed:

John Richards,

Honorary Secretary

Wessex Association Of Licensed Victuallers

NOTICE OF COMMITTEE MEETING

The next Committee Meeting will be held on:

Day: *Wednesday*

Time: *8.00 p.m.*

I hope you will be able to attend.

Date: *16th March 19--*

Venue: *Dog and Duck, Hately.*

signed:

Joe Kemp

Honorary Secretary

MEMORANDUM

TO   All Regional Managers   REF   RGT/JF

FROM   Sales Manager   DATE   20th August 19--

SUBJECT   Quarterly Meeting of Regional Managers

The next quarterly meeting of Regional Managers will take place in
my office on Monday, 3rd September 19-- at 10.00 p.m.

I should be grateful if you would bring your region's sales documentation for the third quarter, together with a schedule of outstanding accounts of more than 60 days.

Mr R Williams, Regional Manager North

The committee members' agenda

As has already been outlined, committee meetings in particular subscribe to certain formalities. Thus the first three items on a routine agenda tend to be set out as follows:

1 Apologies for absence
Having declared the meeting open (while the secretary records the time) the chairman will announce the 'apologies', sent in advance to the secretary, of any member unable to attend the meeting.

2 Minutes of the last meeting
Here, the chairman will ask members, who generally will have received a copy of the minutes beforehand, whether they represent a true record of the previous meeting which he may sign. Discussion of this item will be limited to the actual wording of the minutes, which must be accurate in fact and fair in implication.

3 Matters arising
Some chairmen tend to dislike this item on the grounds that it provides an opportunity for controversial topics to be re-opened for discussion. There are numerous instances, however, when a situation may have developed, or where the secretary or a committee member may have pursued a particular item which arose directly from the last meeting and which should be reported.

Additionally, some committee agendas include as a fourth item, 'Correspondence'. Its inclusion as a regular feature of an agenda depends upon the frequency and extent of any exchange of letters between the committee and third parties.

These three (or four) items on the committee members' agenda represent a kind of ritual opening of the meeting, preserving the integrity and continuity of completed and on-going business before the fresh business which the meeting was primarily called to discharge, commences.

The new business is set out as a number of items in the middle of the agenda. At a meeting of a local branch of a professional institute they might appear as follows:

4 Publicity for new season's programme of events

5 Topic and speaker for meeting: 4th March 19—

6 Visit to business systems exhibition, Olympia

7 Proposal to levy an admission charge at meetings:
That an admission charge of 50p per head be levied by the Branch to cover the cost of coffee and biscuits and to contribute towards Branch funds.
Proposer: Mr J Pearson
Seconder: Mrs M Jenkins

Having debated and decided upon action for items 4–7 (for an explanation of proposals, motions and resolutions refer to page 14), the new business of the meeting will have been virtually concluded and the chairman will have delegated the actions to be implemented to members. There remain two items on the agenda to be dealt with:

8 Any other business

9 Date of next meeting

Some chairmen do not like to include item 8, since it allows members to introduce items without prior notice, may test the patience of members at the end of a meeting or may enable pet schemes and hobby-horses to be paraded for the 'umpteenth' time. On the other hand, such an item does allow a member to introduce a topic which he or she may feel has not been given sufficient attention, or which may have been overlooked entirely. If such a topic is sufficiently important, it may well appear as an item on the agenda of the committee's next meeting. The last duty of the chairman is to decide upon a date for the next committee meeting in consultation with the members. Thereafter the meeting is formally closed, and the secretary records the time.

Note: on some agendas 'Any Other Business' appears as the final item. The ordering of agenda items in this respect seems to be a matter of committee preference.

The chairman's agenda

The chairman's agenda is, essentially, an annotated version of the committee member's agenda. Both will carry identical agenda items in the same sequence. The chairman's agenda, however, will include after each item sufficient space for the secretary to insert background, briefing notes such as updating information, explanations of newly-developed situations, diplomatic reminders of past personality clashes and so on, to help the chairman to conduct the meeting both authoritatively and tactfully.

The chairman's agenda is particularly invaluable for the chairman whose prestige or status lends respect to the position he occupies, but whose other commitments may prevent him from retaining the detailed knowledge which the secretary readily absorbs from dealing with the committee's administration.

In this respect the attentive secretary may make an important contribution to the smooth progress of the meeting, although it is only the chairman who will fully appreciate such indispensable 'behind-the-scenes' work.

Special kinds of meetings

In addition to the regular and routine meetings, often held at monthly intervals, through which companies, public service departments and associations carry out their business, circumstances may arise which make it necessary to hold general or 'out-of-the-ordinary', termed 'extraordinary', meetings:

Annual General Meetings

Once a year all the members of an organisation meet to receive activity and financial reports and proposals for future developments and to elect or re-appoint officers.

Extraordinary General Meetings

Sometimes events occur which are sufficiently important and urgent to require the calling of a meeting of all members of an organisation, who may be asked to vote upon a particular matter or to grant special powers to an executive committee or board of directors to enable them to meet a specific contingency.

Creditors Meetings

When companies are unable to continue to trade by reason of insolvency, the official receiver will call a meeting of creditors to appoint a liquidator and arrange for the 'winding-up' of its activities.

Other types of special meeting include Shareholders' Class Meetings, Public Enquiries or occasional *ad hoc* meetings called to conduct business lying outside the normal routines and terms of reference of organisations.

A typical agenda for an Annual General Meeting of a voluntary society

1 Apologies for absence
2 Minutes of the last meeting
3 Matters arising
4 Chairman's report
5 Treasurer's report and presentation of accounts
6 Election of officers
7 (See note below)

Note: There are various ways in which an agenda for an Annual General Meeting may be concluded. For example, item 7 may take the form of, 'Revision of the constitution', or 'Vote of thanks to the president', who may be retiring. In other words, there may be specific business to conduct at any particular Annual General Meeting after more routine matters have been carried.

Some AGM agendas include items such as, 'Any other business' and 'Date of next meeting' to form the conclusion of the meeting. At other Annual General Meetings, however, 'Any other business' may be omitted and discussion and reporting limited to specific items such as those indicated above. Much depends upon the climate, precedents and the composition of constitution in the case of voluntary organisations, or upon the nature of the Articles of Association of a particular company and upon the inclusion, in the notice calling its Annual General Meeting, of additional items of business other than those required by its Articles or by statute.

In the case of Annual General Meetings of the companies governed by the Companies Acts, the usual business conducted includes the receiving of reports upon company progress and performance, the presentation of the company's accounts and dividends (if any are distributed) and the election or appointment of any directors if these are due.

The National Institute Of Computer Managers

Newtown Branch

The next Committee Meeting of the Branch will take
place on Wednesday 5th June 19-- in the Shelley Room
of the White Unicorn Hotel, 7.30 p.m. for 8.00 p.m.

COMMITTEE MEMBER'S AGENDA

1. Apologies for absence

2. Minutes of the last meeting

3. Matters arising

4. Publicity for new season's
   programme of events

5. Topic and speaker for meeting:
   Wednesday 4th March 19--

6. Visit to business systems

7. Proposal to levy an admission
   charge at meetings:

   That an admission charge of 50p per head
   be levied by the Branch as an admission
   charge to meetings to cover the cost of
   coffee and biscuits and to contribute
   towards branch funds

            Proposer: Mr J Pearson
            Seconder: Mrs M Jenkins

8. Any other business

9. Date of next meeting

Chairman: A J Lucas   Vice-Chairman: R T Nicholas

Honorary Secretary: M T Wilkins
Honorary Treasurer: H Jones

Committee Members: E W Booth, F C Carpenter, M Jenkins
                    G O F Nelson, J Pearson, K D Williams

Honorary Secretary's Address:

    'Appletree', Buxton Avenue, Newtown, Surrey, NE12 5AI
       Telephone: Business - Newtown 4571   Home - Newtown 46783

THE NATIONAL INSTITUTE OF COMPUTER MANAGERS

Newtown Branch

CHAIRMAN'S AGENDA

For the Branch Committee Meeting of Wednesday
5th June, to be held in the Shelley Room of the
White Unicorn Hotel at 8.00 p.m.

1 Apologies For Absence:
      Mr Booth will be visiting his wife in hospital.
      Mr Williams hopes to come but will be late -
      visit to London.

2 Minutes Of The Last Meeting:
      Mr Carpenter has intimated that he was not
      categorically against the change of venue for
      Branch Committee Meetings, and that his remarks
      as they appear in the Minutes of the Last Meeting
      have been misconstrued.

3 Matters Arising:
      Item 6: The manager of the Blue Boar has con-
      firmed that the Committee Room of the Blue Boar
      Hotel will be available on the third Wednesday of
      each month from 1st August onwards.

      Excelsior Printing Ltd. have promised the New
      Season's programmes by Friday 26th June at the
      latest.

4 Publicity For New Season's Programme Of Events:
      There does not appear to be any likelihood of the
      Newtown Chronicle repeating last year's price for
      the display advertisement. I spoke to the adver-
      tising manager on the 'phone last Thursday.

5 Topic And Speaker For Meeting: Wednesday 4th March 19--
      Lord Grenville has written respectfully to decline
      our invitation to speak. Copy of letter attached.

6 Visit To Business Systems Exhibition, Olympia:
      The Olympia management have confirmed that they
      still have vacancies for parties on Saturday
      25th September. 15% discount on admission
      charges for parties over 25.

7 Proposal To Levy Admission Charge At Meetings:
      As you will recall, John Pearson proposed a
      similar motion at last year's June meeting.
      His motion was defeated last year 6:2

      I understand Harold Jones is concerned about the
      Branch's ability to fund its activities in the
      programme for the New Season

Minutes

Producing the minutes of a meeting is probably the most demanding task assigned to the secretary or his counterpart. In the course of their production, the secretary needs to bear in mind not only that they should be a scrupulous record of the meeting's business, but he should also remember that members will be scrutinising them for any potential slights or reported inaccuracies. In addition, the secretary must appreciate the possible future importance of any set of minutes which may be used as a reference or source of precedent, and also that, while members may exchange mutual insults in the heat of the moment, neither they nor the chairman will thank the secretary for a verbatim report transcribed into reported speech for successive generations of committee members to wonder at!

Why minutes are so important is not difficult to appreciate. They incorporate a number of important functions, essential to the effective working of any meeting or committee. Firstly, the work of a committee or working party is largely evolutionary. Principles are progressively established; rules made and later modified; procedures and attitudes are developed and precedents formed. An ongoing set of minutes, therefore, provides both a source of reference and authority for chairman and members alike. A half-forgotten change made to a constitution which is recorded in the minutes may become crucial at a future date. Without such a source of reference, the work of any committee would be grossly impeded by a return to first principles whenever controversial business arose.

Closely allied to the reference aspect of minutes is their value in other ways as a written record. Human nature being what it is, orally communicated decisions have a way of being 'mis-remembered' when the occasion suits. The written record ensures, however, that democratically made decisions cannot be 'overlooked' or unilaterally abrogated by either chairman or caucus. When changes to the rules are sought, the minutes ensure that they are made through established procedures.

The minutes also render each participant at a meeting accountable for his or her utterances. The sure knowledge that an outrageous attitude, surly obstructiveness or domineering interjections are likely to find their way into distributed minutes frequently serves to hold less considerate committee

members in check. On the other hand, dissenting members are able to insist on having a particular point minuted either as a source for future reference or to indicate a strong disapproval of a matter at issue.

In some organisations the minutes record only the decision reached, and a veil is drawn over the preceding debate. Such minutes are 'resolution minutes', since a motion which is successfully carried in a meeting is thereafter referred to as a 'Resolution'. Such minutes may be variously expressed:

Resolution minutes:

RESOLVED: That the company's Eastbrook branch be closed with immediate effect.

or,

It was resolved that the company's Eastbrook branch be closed with immediate effect.

Alternatively, the chairman of a committee may prefer to have the interplay of various attitudes leading up to a decision included in the minutes. When the principal viewpoints of members are summarised in this way, the minutes are referred to as 'narrative minutes'.

Narrative minutes:

The chairman invited comment upon the steep decline in the Eastbrook branch's turnover during the past nine months. Mr Weston felt that the branch had always suffered a lack of sufficient advertising support. Mr Hopkins drew attention to the parlous state of the district as a result of urban renewal work.

While generally sympathetic, Mrs Peters alluded to the rapid turnover of staff – six sales assistants in three months. In citing the tendered resignation of the branch manager, Mr Watkins emphasised the gravity of the situation. In summarising, the chairman referred the meeting to company policy, which clearly stated that branch closure was an inevitable consequence of continued trading losses.

By a majority of 7–3, it was decided to close the Eastbrook branch with immediate effect.

The reasons for preferring either resolution or narrative minutes may be briefly summarised as follows:

Resolution minutes

In meetings where it is important for participants to maintain a united front and accept collective responsibility, for example boards of directors or senior officers in public service, then a preference is understandable for a minutes' format which publishes decisions reached, while concealing from junior levels of the organisation strong disagreements or conflicts. In addition, the minutes of formal meetings required by statute may be more appropriately recorded by means of a brief 'resolution statement'. There are also convincing arguments for employing a format which is, above all, succinct and which relates only that information which is necessary to enable decisions to be implemented.

Narrative minutes

On the other hand, there are many types of meeting for which it would be both more appropriate and, indeed useful, to have a summary of the main points of a discussion which precedes the reaching of a decision. For example, when management decisions are being debated, a managing director may well prefer to have the approaches, attitudes and judgments of his executives recorded in detail, so that individual accountability is recorded for given commitments or objections. In this way, a 'profile' of reliability and soundness of judgment may be identified, even when a single dissenter is in a minority at a meeting but subsequently proved right by a future turn of events. Thus managers, through narrative

minutes are persuaded to make responsible utterances and considered judgments.

Where voluntary bodies are concerned, narrative minutes provide a valuable psychological boost. When committee members give up their spare time to attend meetings, the extent of their motivation and the degree of their commitment may be enhanced by seeing *their* names and synopses of *their* contributions in print as contributions to the work of the club or association and to the decision-making process.

It is much more difficult, of course, for a secretary to write narrative minutes which achieve a successful compromise between terseness and long-windedness, and which report accurately without giving offence or glossing over points of conflict or deep-rooted disagreement.

In some organisations a compromise is achieved between the brevity of resolution minutes and the detail of narrative minutes. Where it is particularly important for executive decisions to be implemented swiftly, and where there is infrequent contact among participants between meetings, then the format sometimes referred to as **action minutes** may be employed. Here the proceedings are reported briefly and the name of the person delegated to act upon a particular item is entered in a column, usually on the right-hand side of the minutes page, opposite the reference to the item.

MINUTES:	ACTION BY:
5 MEMBERSHIP DRIVE The chairman referred to the decline in branch membership during the past six months and asked the membership secretary for a report. In view of the gravity of the situation, it was decided to institute an intensive recruiting campaign including an open meeting and visits to local companies. The membership secretary, John Watkins, was asked to submit a detailed strategy and programme for the next meeting.	John Watkins, Membership Secretary

Action minutes

The advantage of such a format is that it is very clear who has undertaken or been asked to do what. When minutes are circulated, it is immediately clear to a participant whether he has been required to act in any way, or whether he may read and file the minutes on an 'information only' basis. As the

minutes format is overtly directional, however, its use is, perhaps, better restricted to those meetings within organisations where there is an obvious 'line authority'. If used in the context of voluntary organisations, there is a possibility of members feeling that they are being coerced and 'driven' rather than wooed and 'led' by the chairman.

Format

There are a number of different ways in which minutes are set out on paper. In some instances, the minutes are numbered and given headings which reproduce exactly the sequence and numbering of the items as they appear on the agenda. In some organisations, however, each minute is numbered consecutively from the very beginning of the first numbered minute of the first meeting onwards. Thus the thirteenth committee meeting may discuss items 261 to 268 on the agenda. In some institutions, particularly in local government, a system is adopted frequently which gives an item on the agenda a number such as, 3.0 or 4.0 or 5.0, followed by its title or heading. Points which are minuted under such headings are then referenced 3.1, 3.2, 3.3 etc.

In the absence of any single, universally adopted format, the following points should be borne in mind:

1   The sequence of items on the agenda should be followed.

2   There should be an intelligent use made of spacing and indentation to help the reader to identify item headings and follow referencing systems.

3   Reported statements should be clearly attributable to identified speakers.

4   Care should be taken to use the correct names of speakers or to identify speakers by their designations – chairman, treasurer, etc.

5   Where names are recorded in lists (for example, of those present) the precedence of officers should be followed by an alphabetical list of members.

Reported speech
The techniques of writing reported speech are examined in detail in the 'Use of English' module. It is essential to master these techniques before embarking on the writing of minutes.

Resolution minutes

MINUTES OF THE BOARD OF DIRECTORS MEETING

Held at the Registered Offices of Delta
Business Systems Ltd on Thursday 16th
July 19-- at 10.30 a.m.

PRESENT: R K Baldwin (in the chair); P J Lewis, T A R Sheldon,
J T Talbot, H C Wilkinson, directors; N Cartwright,
Company Secretary

Apologies for absence were received from K T Frewin.

261 MINUTES OF THE LAST MEETING

The minutes of the last meeting, previously circulated, were
taken as read and signed as a true record.

262 MATTERS ARISING

There were no matters arising.

263 COMPANY LOGO, LIVERY AND CORPORATE IDENTITY

It was resolved that the R P Silverton advertising agency be
appointed to develop new company logo and livery designs as
part of the company's policy to revitalise its corporate
identity.

264 INTRODUCTION OF FLEXIBLE WORKING HOURS AT HEAD OFFICE

It was resolved that the system of flexible working hours
agreed be introduced in the company's head office with
effect from 1st September 19--.

265 RELOCATION OF SOUTH WEST REGIONAL OFFICE

It was resolved that the company's South West Regional Office
be relocated at 46-52 Tamar Road, Plymouth, Devon. The office
to be fully operative by 15th August 19--.

266 DATE OF NEXT MEETING

The date of the next meeting of the board of directors was
scheduled for Thursday 13th August 19--.

signed:

R K Baldwin
Managing Director

13th August 19--

Narrative minutes

THE NATIONAL INSTITUTE OF COMPUTER MANAGERS   NEWTOWN BRANCH

MINUTES

Committee Meeting of The National Institute
of Computer Managers, Newtown Branch, held
on Wednesday 5th June 19-- in the Shelley
Room of the White Unicorn Hotel at 8.00 p.m.

PRESENT   A.J. Lucas, Chairman, M.T. Wilkins, Hon. Secretary, H. Jones,
               Hon. Treasurer, F.C. Carpenter, M. Jenkins, G.O.F. Nelson,
               J. Pearson, K.D. Williams.

1   APOLOGIES FOR ABSENCE

    Apologies for absence were received from R.T. Nicholas, Vice-Chairman, and
    E.W. Booth.

2   MINUTES OF THE LAST MEETING

    Mr. Carpenter drew attention to item 6 of the minutes of the last meeting,
    Branch Committee Meetings - Change of Venue. He affirmed that his remarks
    had been misinterpreted and that he was not categorically against the
    proposed change of venue. By general consent it was agreed to substitute
    'had strong reservations about' for 'was categorically against' in item 6.

3   MATTERS ARISING

    The Secretary reported that in connection with item 6, the manager of the
    Blue Boar was able to offer his hotel's committee room on the third Wed-
    nesday of each month from 1st August onwards. The Chairman then requested
    the Secretary to confirm acceptance of the offer by letter.

    According to the latest information, the Secretary informed the meeting that
    Excelsior Printing Ltd. had promised the new season's programmes by Friday
    26th June. Mr. Nelson pointed out that it was essential for the programmes
    to be available by that date for distribution purposes. The Chairman asked
    Mr. Nelson to liaise with the Secretary to ensure that the promised delivery
    date was met.

4   PUBLICITY FOR THE NEW SEASON'S PROGRAMME OF EVENTS

    The Chairman, in referring to the branch's advertisements placed with the
    Newtown Chronicle, confirmed that the cost of such advertising was certain
    to increase. The Treasurer expressed his concern at any prospective increases
    in advertising expenditure in view of the agreed increases for speakers'
    expenses and mail-shots to members. After a wide-ranging discussion of the
    branch's expenditure on publicity, it was decided to place an order for six
    advertisements with the Newtown Chronicle instead of the customary seven to
    offset the anticipated increase in charges.

5   TOPIC AND SPEAKER FOR MEETING: WEDNESDAY 4th MARCH 19--

    The Chairman asked the Secretary to read to the meeting the letter received from Lord Grenville, who tendered his apologies for having to decline the invitation to speak on 4th March. Suggestions were then requested for possible alternative speakers. Mrs. Jenkins proposed that the Rt. Hon. Charles Hawkins, M.P. for Newtown East be approached, but it was generally agreed that M.Ps were subject to last-minute, unavoidable commitments in Westminster. Mr. Williams suggested Mr. John Farnham, Computer Manager for Global Computers, an acknowledged expert in developments in computer language. In the absence of any further suggestions, the Chairman requested the Secretary to write to Mr. Farnham inviting him to speak at the 4th March Meeting.

6   VISIT TO BUSINESS SYSTEMS EXHIBITION, OLYMPIA

The Secretary relayed to the meeting the confirmation from the Olympia management regarding existing vacancies for parties on 25th September 19--. A discount of 15% was offered on admission charges for parties over 25 in number. Strong interest was expressed by all present, and the Chairman asked the Secretary to order 30 tickets at the party rate. Mr. Williams offered to arrange the hiring of a motor-coach and was requested to report progress at the next meeting.

7   PROPOSAL TO LEVY AN ADMISSION CHARGE AT MEETINGS

The Chairman referred the meeting to Mr. Pearson's proposal on the agenda for the meeting. Before asking Mr. Pearson to speak to his motion, the Chairman reminded the meeting that the subject of admission charges to branch meetings had arisen during the previous season. It was a difficult matter and the financial status of the branch merited that it be re-examined. Mr. Pearson emphasised the rise in the cost of meetings and referred to the minutes of the meeting of Wednesday 17th October 19--, which recorded his prediction that events would prove him right about the need for an admission charge. He was advocating a levy of 50p, which he did not think would prove financially embarrassing to members and would not, in his opinion, result in falling attendances. Opposing the motion, Mr. Nelson felt strongly that members already paid a sufficiently large sum in annual membership fees to the Institute and that branch meetings should be funded from the allocation made to Institute Branches from Computer House. Mrs. Jenkins reminded the meeting that she had opposed the introduction of the charge when it was last debated, but felt that such a levy was the only fair way of keeping the branch solvent during the coming season. The Treasurer echoed Mrs. Jenkins' concern and stated that he was in favour of the motion. In view of the expression of conflicting views, the Chairman asked for a vote on the motion before the meeting. The motion was carried by 5 votes to 3.

8   ANY OTHER BUSINESS

Mr. Carpenter raised the matter of branch reports submitted to the Institute Journal. He had noted that for the past two quarters, no mention had been made of Newtown branch activities. The Chairman promised to look into the matter and to report back.

Mrs. Jenkins drew the meeting's attention to the new magazine, 'Computer Monthly'. She was personally acquainted with the editor and was able to recommend it to members without reservation.

9   DATE OF NEXT MEETING

The next Committee Meeting was scheduled for Wednesday 3rd July 19--

Terminology of meetings

Ad hoc from Latin, meaning 'for the purpose of', as for example, when a sub-committee is set up to organise a works outing

Adjourn to hold a meeting over until a later date

Advisory providing advice or suggestion, not taking action

Agenda a schedule of items drawn up for discussion at a meeting

AGM Annual General Meeting; all members are usually eligible to attend

Apologies excuses given in advance for inability to attend a meeting

Articles of Association rules required by Company Law which govern a company's activities

Bye-laws rules regulating an organisation's activities

Chairman leader or person given authority to conduct a meeting

Chairman's Agenda based upon the committee agenda, but containing explanatory notes

Collective responsibility a convention by which all committee members agree to abide by a majority decision

Committee a group of people usually elected or appointed who meet to conduct agreed business and report to a senior body

Consensus agreement by general consent, no formal vote being taken

Constitution set of rules governing activities of voluntary bodies

Convene to call a meeting

Executive having the power to act upon taken decisions

Extraordinary meeting a meeting called for all members to discuss a serious issue affecting all is called an Extraordinary General Meeting; otherwise a non-routine meeting called for a specific purpose

Ex officio given powers or rights by reason of office. For example a trades union convener may be an ex officio member of a works council

Honorary post a duty performed without payment – Honorary Secretary

Information, point of the drawing of attention in a meeting to a relevant item of fact

Lobbying a practice of seeking members' support before a meeting

Minutes the written record of a meeting; resolution minutes record only decisions reached, while narrative minutes provide a record of the decision-making process

Motion the name given to a 'proposal' when it is being discussed at a meeting

Mover one who speaks on behalf of a motion

Nem. con. from Latin, literally, 'no one speaking against'

Opposer one who speaks against a motion

Order, point of the drawing of attention to a breach of rules or procedures

Other business either items left over from a previous meeting, or items discussed after the main business of a meeting

Proposal the name given to a submitted item for discussion (usually written) before a meeting takes place

Proxy literally, 'on behalf of another person' – 'a proxy vote'

Resolution the name given to a 'motion' which has been passed or carried; used after the decision has been reached

Secretary committee official responsible for the internal and external administration of a committee

Secret ballot a system of voting in secret

Sine die from Latin, literally, 'without a day', that is to say indefinitely, e.g. 'adjourned sine die'

Standing committee a committee which has an indefinite term of office

Seconder one who supports the 'proposer' of a motion or proposal by 'seconding' it

Treasurer committee official responsible for its financial records and transactions

Unanimous all being in favour

Vote, casting when two sides are deadlocked a chairman may record a second or 'casting vote' to ensure a decision is made

Assessment questions

Types of meeting

1 What are the factors common to most meetings which help us to define the purpose of calling a meeting or of holding regular meetings?

2 List as many different types of meeting as you are able to recall.

3 In what circumstances do meetings tend to conduct their business

    a with written rules of procedure?

    b without written rules of procedure?

4 How would you define a formal meeting?

5 What is the point of a 'brain-storming' meeting?

6 Outline as many different reasons as you remember for calling meetings.

7 What do you consider the advantages and disadvantages of the meeting as a communications medium?

The structure of meetings

8 Illustrate by means of a diagram the relationship between the following: an executive committee; an advisory ad hoc sub-committee; an advisory committee and a standing sub-committee of an executive committee.

9 Explain the meaning of: 'ad hoc'; 'standing'; 'executive'; 'advisory' and 'coopted member'.

10 What are the functions of: a management committee; a policy committee; a membership committee?

The functions of committee officials

11 Explain the principal functions of: a chairman; a secretary; a treasurer.

12 What does an auditor do?

13 Outline the administrative programme followed by a committee secretary between one committee meeting and the next.

14 How would you justify the inclusion of a vice-chairman in a committee?

Rules and regulations

15 Explain the meaning of the following: a statute, a constitution, bye-laws, standing orders, Articles and Memorandum of Association. With what sort of meeting is each associated?

16 What is a quorum?

17 What do you understand by, 'a point of order' and 'a point of information'?

18 At what stages is a formal, written item for discussion at a meeting referred to as a 'proposal', a 'motion' and a 'resolution'?

The written documentation of meetings

19 List the main types of written documentation used in connection with meetings.

20 How does a chairman's agenda differ from a committee member's agenda?

21 List the items which comprise a typical committee member's agenda.

22 Identify the different formats suggested for the notice of a meeting. Suggest a type of meeting appropriate for each different format.

23 List the items of a typical Annual General Meeting agenda of a club or society.

24 What is the difference between resolution and narrative minutes?

25 When would you prefer to use narrative and when resolution minutes format?

26 In what circumstances would you advocate the use of 'action minutes'?

27 Identify three different ways of referencing minutes.

28 What advice would you give to someone about to become a committee secretary?

29 Why do some chairmen dislike 'Matters Arising' and 'Any Other Business'?

Terminology

30 Explain the meaning of: 'collective responsibility'; 'ex officio'; 'honorary'; 'lobbying'; 'nem. con.'; 'sine die'; 'casting vote'; 'extraordinary meeting'.

Written assignments, discussion topics

Notice

1 The chairman of the Middletown Traders' Association has recently expressed to you his dissatisfaction with the format of notices sent to committee members to call regular monthly meetings. Several members of the committee have expressed their concern at taking no part in the compilation of committee meeting agendas, despite their attempts to submit agenda items. The chairman has therefore asked you to design a suitable notice format for discussion at the next meeting. The committee has met for some years past in the Small Committee Room of the Middletown Town Hall, High Street, Middletown, Midshire, MI13 2AC.

Agendas

2 'Ah, Jim, come on in. I've been trying to sort out the items for inclusion in the agenda for the next committee meeting. I saw that written proposal from Jack Burton about changing the date for the Christmas Dance from Saturday 14th December to the 21st. Jack reckons there'll be more of a Christmas spirit nearer the day. You'd better put his proposal into the appropriate format. The seconder is Mrs Bignall. Then there's the complaints about the club-room bar prices. We must deal with that. Oh, and while I remember, I believe you said we've had a number of letters from fixture secretaries asking for dates for next summer's first team cricket fixtures. We ought to settle that one. As you know, I couldn't persuade Ken Palmer not to resign as Hon. Treasurer. You've had four nominations? Yes, well, it's most unfortunate but we can't afford to let the situation drag on. I'll ask Ken meanwhile to act as a caretaker. I think that's about it. Could you draft a committee members' agenda. You'd better give some thought to the running order. I'd help out but I'm late for a section meeting. Thanks a lot!'

As Honorary Secretary of the Lifelong Insurance Co, Ltd Sports & Social Club, Ashburnley Crescent, Richmond, Surrey, SU16 4TJ, draft the agenda asked for. The meeting is on Thursday 18th September, 19— at 8.00 in the Clubhouse Committee Room.

3 The chairman, Mr Peter Turner of the Lifelong Insurance Co Ltd Sports and Social Club has just telephoned you to say that he won't be able to take the chair at tomorrow's committee meeting. He has asked Mrs Kean, vice-chairman, to take the chair in his absence. As Mrs Kean is not as familiar with the background to the items on the agenda as he is, Mr Turner has asked you to prepare a chairman's agenda for her. The following are the points for her to keep in mind which Mr Turner has suggested:

J Burton proposal – problem of changing band booking – has Gordon Wilson already booked the Post House Hotel ballroom? Jack tends to go on at length when he warms to his theme.
Upset Miss Grainger at the last meeting – her suggestion to form Ladies' Soccer Team.
    Bar prices – main source of funds to run club-house – recent poor attendance by members mid-week – charges up by brewery – check Ken Palmer.
    Letters from cricket clubs – who is hon. sec. of cricket team? Harry Fielding will know – job needs delegating.
    Ken Palmer – resignation – tricky – have been criticisms of Ken's record-keeping – Harry Fielding keen to have office – not nominated – Ken fed up with sniping.

Correspondence

4 At the Lifelong Sports and Social Club committee meeting it was decided not to offer Albion Engineering Sports Club a cricket fixture next summer. After last season's match your clubhouse was left in a damaged state; repairs cost £23.50. Several ladies also complained of the language which was used during the evening at the bar.

As Honorary Secretary, you have been asked to write to the Cricket Club Secretary, declining their offer of a fixture. Coincidentally, Albion Engineering Ltd is a client of Lifelong Insurance!

Report

5 As a development of the Lifelong committee meeting's discussion of the Christmas Dance, it was decided to form an ad hoc sub-committee to arrange it under the chairmanship of Jack Burton. As the sub-committee's secretary, you have been asked to draft a report on the arrangements for submission at the next meeting.

Public Address, Narrative Minutes, Meeting Simulation

6 As Chairman of the Laystone College Students' Association, you are currently preparing your Chairman's Report for the forthcoming Annual General Meeting. The following are some of the events and topics you have to report upon. You may add others if you wish:

The number of active members has declined during the year – attendances at social events has generally declined.

Criticisms have been levelled at the committee – lack of decent events – programme curtailed – too autocratic.
But – members do not offer help or services – all is left to committee – Social Secretary – organised three discos singlehanded. Three resignations from committee during year – pressure of work – personality clashes.

Liaison with students' associations of neighbouring colleges – three meetings – little progress on joint approach to local accommodation problems – joint social committee formed to plan inter-college social events – starts next session.

Events: Christmas Dance – great success – thanks to Principal and staff for support; Sport – Ladies' Basketball Team won District League – Men came second in Regional Cup – Soccer Team hampered by lack of practice – won 5, lost 6, drew 2; Pram Race – collected £35 for charity – winners – Chris Parker and Susan Curtis; Summer Leavers' Ball – hope as good turnout as for Christmas – tickets still available from Social Secretary.

Financial situation – leave to Treasurer but say balance of £434.28 – thanks to Treasurer and Committee's good management.

Future – emphasise unless better support many facilities and events will die – which now taken for granted – questionnaire being sent out to ask for suggestions for preferred future programme.

Thanks – thank all college staff and committee for help during year – too many to name – wish success to successor.

a Tape-record or write out in direct speech the chairman's report based on the above topics. Your aim should be to structure the speech logically and to place suitable emphasis on important points.

b Write out in narrative minutes form the Annual General Meeting's agenda item: Chairman's Report, using the direct speech report in Assignment *a*.

c Compose a suitable AGM agenda for the meeting of the Laystone College Students' Association and then role-play the meeting. Assume that relations between the Committee and the general membership have deteriorated and that some noisy dissatisfaction is voiced from the floor.

d Write the minutes of your simulated Annual General Meeting in narrative minutes form.

Resolution Minutes

7 Write in resolution minutes form minutes appropriate for a board of directors' meeting for the following:

a decision to introduce the post of Communication Co-ordinator into the management structure

the decision to terminate the company's laundering contract with Speedy Cleaning Services Ltd currently due for renewal.

8 Organise a brain-storming meeting aimed at establishing a methodical approach to studying. Produce a study-guide for distribution to new students.

Discussion topics

1 'Decisions take too long to reach in committees and when they are arrived at invariably they take the form of harmless compromises.'

2 'Too much store is set by the traditional formal procedures by which some meetings are conducted. All too often they become the means by which the expert "bamboozles" the layman.'

3 'The most important decisions are usually made before the meeting starts.' Is the practice of lobbying fair? Should it be stopped? Could it be? Does it matter?

4 'If the cost of holding meetings was calculated more frequently, there would soon be fewer of them – and better ones at that!'

Case studies

Mending the cracks in Plastimould

Plastimould Ltd is a company manufacturing a range of household utensils from a chemical base – bowls, buckets, pipes, brushes etc. For the past six weeks it has had a serious industrial dispute on its hands. One of the stages in the production process has been declared 'unsafe' by the unionised factory staff.

This stage concerns the cleaning out of vats which have contained the material for moulding into the various products in the company's range. It is accepted by both management and union representatives that it is possible during the cleaning process for fumes to be generated which are dangerous to the skin and which under no circumstances should be inhaled.

Recently three men have collapsed not long after working on the cleansing of the vats and they are still off work sick. After the third man had fallen ill, the union decided after a full meeting of the factory union membership to ban any of the union's members from working on the vat cleansing process. The effect of this ban was to halt production completely.

The union want an independent enquiry into the dangers and effects to health stemming from the cleansing process. For their part, management have declared that the cleansing process is perfectly safe, provided that the protective clothing and equipment provided is worn and used as specified in company regulations.

The union's position is that the clothing is old-fashioned, having been designed more than ten years previously, and that no-one to their knowledge has carried out any recent tests to confirm the effectiveness of its protection. The men have complained that it is too hot to wear, and that its bulkiness makes it impossible to work in the more inaccessible parts of the vats. The respirators are also, according to the men, inefficient, especially when any physical exertion is required.

Management has pointed out that the protective clothing and equipment conforms to the safety specifications laid down for such work in the relevant section of the industrial safety legislation. The men, says management, have been cutting safety corners to boost bonus earnings by not wearing all the equipment and clothing when there is a clear need to. If there have been instances of men becoming sick, which management will not accept as being a direct consequence of the cleansing process, then it must be the result of contributory negligence.

The union regards this last attitude of management as totally hypocritical. It claims that in the past management has turned 'a blind eye' to total adherence to factory safety regulations. Only now that the company is faced with a law-suit for damages arising from the medical condition of the three workers currently sick in hospital has the accusation of 'contributory negligence' arisen. In any case, the company has failed in its obligation to inform its factory staff adequately of the potential dangers involved in the cleansing process, and now, 'caught red-handed', was trying to prevent an independent enquiry from being set up.

The latest rejoinder from management is that unless a formula can be decided to re-start production with immediate effect, there may well be a possibility that the parent company of Plastimould will divert its production to another factory in another country, thus causing wide-spread redundancy. The union is inclined to see this as bluff, although some members concede that the six-week lay-off must have had crippling effect on the company's financial position.

Assignments

1 Form the management or union team, prepare your case for a 'return-to-work' negotiating meeting and then simulate the meeting. Observers or a team member should take notes and produce narrative minutes.

2 Depending upon the outcome of the meeting draft either a 'joint communiqué' or separate statements for circulation to Plastimould staff.

3 As an individual student write an essay on the problems implicit in the case study and suggest how you think the management and the union would resolve their differences.

Frosty climate at Arctura

Recently, your company, Arctura Refrigeration Ltd has been experiencing a serious problem affecting both its export sales and production departments. The company manufactures a range of refrigerators and freezers, many of which are sold abroad. Of recent months relations have deteriorated between the Export Sales Department and the Production Department. The root of the problem lies in the failure of the company's production department to meet production targets and deadlines for refrigerators and freezers ordered by customers in Middle and Far Eastern markets.

The Export Sales Manager, Mr K D Mears, is receiving letters daily from customers and agents complaining bitterly about broken promises over delivery dates and emphasising the danger of loss of business and the closing of accounts. Until some three months ago, the company's overseas order book had been full, but as a result of the recent poor performance in production, there has been a decline in repeat orders. This situation has been reported by the Export Sales Manager, who drew the Managing Director's attention to the fact that competitors were exploiting the situation to the full.

The Production Manager, Mr J D P Jones, has recently been critical of the poor communications existing between the Export Sales and Production Departments. Orders have been taken he affirmed, which did not take into account the company's overall production capacity and the production commitment to a more profitable home market. There had also been a spate of late modifications to individual product specifications which had made it impossible to plan an efficient production schedule. Batches of both refrigerators and freezers were being stored because they had not met a modified order requirement.

A further complication lies in the current 'work to rule' being followed by the factory's operatives, members of the Metal Workers' Union, in pursuit of an improved bonus scheme. Talks with the company's management team, headed by the Personnel Manager, Mrs K Wheatley have broken down over agreement on a revised basic rate of pay and hourly output targets upon which bonus rates are based.

The following are the company's personnel involved principally in the problem:
Mr A Hartley, Managing Director
A N Other, Personal Assistant to the M.D.

Mr K D Mears, Export Sales Manager
Miss A Jameson, Assistant Export Sales Manager
Mrs P Nielson, Export Sales Order Co-ordinator

Mr J D P Jones, Production Manager
Mr R V Kershaw, Assistant Production Manager
Mr N P Oliver, Work Progress Officer

Mrs Wheatley, Personnel Manager
Miss K Bright, Personal Assistant to the Personnel Manager

Mr P R Grimshaw, Works Convener, Metal Workers' Union
Mr J K Briggs, Shop Steward
Mrs R Roberts, Shop Steward

Assignments

1 As Personal Assistant to the Managing Director, you have been asked to draft a memorandum report for Mr Hartley, outlining an approach aimed at solving the problem by 'getting people round a table'. You have been asked to specify the type and number of meetings you would suggest, who should take part and what procedures should be followed in any given meeting.

2 In order to develop this case study further, it is possible to provide additional background and briefing notes for each interested group and then to proceed to a role-playing simulation of one or more meetings. Secretaries may be appointed to *each group* to take minutes of any meeting. Each set of minutes may be produced and circulated to all participants. It may well be instructive to compare the various sets of minutes of the same meeting drawn up by groups with different aims and outlooks. Remember, however, that it is customary to produce only one set of minutes in normal circumstances.

Multi-media assignment

Newbourne Knights – rescued from distress!

Background

The Newbourne Knights is a voluntary charitable society of Newbourne citizens, whose charitable activities are mainly concerned with raising money to provide outings, entertainment and treats for local underprivileged old people and children. Its committee meets monthly in the Committee Room of the Old Town Hall, High Street, Newbourne at 7.30pm. As a member of the committee, you receive the following telephone call from Mrs Jean Carson, chairman:

'Sorry to trouble you, but Harold Johnson (Hon Sec.) has just gone down with 'flu. Do you think you could take over as Acting Honorary Secretary to organise the next committee meeting on the 21st? You'll need to get a notice out as soon as possible – and ask for any agenda items as well, to be sent to you by – well, you fix a deadline.'

A week later, you have a discussion with Jean Carson about the items to be included on the committee agenda. The following points emerge from your conversation:

'It's time we made a date for the annual senior citizens' outing – and I think we'd better set up a sub-committee again to organise it.

  'Jack Peters says he'd like to make a Treasurer's Report and also provide a **breakdown** on the cost of the children's Christmas party – I gather he's a bit fed up because some committee members haven't yet given him their raffle ticket money.

  'Mrs Simpson rang to say she's annoyed because her suggestion for holding an Easter Bonnet competition was omitted from Item 6 in last meeting's minutes – Future Programme. Don't forget that we need her support in laying on the refreshments for the Spring Holiday Fete, which we ought to start discussing now.

  'Oh, and I mustn't forget to thank Mrs Hargreaves for her recent donation under AOB.

  'By the way, here's a letter from the vicar of St Peter's offering his garden for the Spring Bank Holiday Fete again.'

  Assume that the committee meeting duly takes place and that its items of business are as indicated on the committee agenda above. Unfortunately, the day before the meeting, Mrs Carson rang you to say she couldn't attend as a relative was seriously ill and she had to visit her. She asked you to prepare a chairman's agenda for Mr John Dickinson, Vice-Chairman, based on the committee agenda, to enable him to chair the meeting.

  With Mr Dickinson in the chair, with you as Acting Secretary, and with eight other committee members attending, the meeting proceeds. Amongst other matters agreed, a sub-committee is formed to organise the annual senior citizens' outing.

  The selected sub-committee, formed to plan the senior citizens' outing, has been asked to investigate suitable ideas for it, locations, costs, transport, refreshments etc.

Assignments

1 Notice
Draft a suitable notice to call the next committee meeting.

2 Committee agenda
As she was in a hurry to visit the matron of the Newbourne Nursing Home, Mrs Carson has asked you to draw up a committee agenda based on the points raised above, and has asked you to use your discretion in forming a running order of items.

3 Chairman's agenda
Prepare the chairman's agenda requested by Mrs Carson for Mr Dickinson, based on the above committee agenda produced.

4 Meeting simulation
Simulate the committee meeting, having produced and circulated the relevant documents and prepared notes etc.

5 Minutes
Produce narrative minutes of the meeting.

6 Report
Draft a report of the sub-committee's outing plans to submit to the next committee meeting.

People and Communication

Oral and Non-Verbal Communication

Desmond W Evans

Contents

Acknowledgments

The author and publishers have made every effort to trace the
ownership of all copyright material and to obtain permission from
the owners of copyright.
Thanks are due to the following for permission to reprint the
material indicated:
Professor Alec Rodger and NFER Publishing Co for the N11P
Seven Point Plan, p17.

PITMAN EDUCATION LIMITED
39 Parker Street, London WC2B 5PB

Associated Companies
Pitman Publishing Pty Ltd, Melbourne
Pitman Publishing New Zealand Ltd, Wellington

© Desmond W Evans 1978

First published in Great Britain 1978
Reprinted 1979, 1980

Text set in 10/12pt Sabon
printed and bound in Great Britain
at The Pitman Press, Bath

ISBN 0 273 01246 0 (bound book)
     0 273 01247 9 (module pack)

Introduction

Our lives are moulded by the way we communicate in speech with others and man's highest artistic and technological achievements derive from his ability to communicate orally with his fellow man.

In the modern business world, the spoken word is used far more frequently in shops, offices and factories as a communication channel than are the written, numerical or visual media. In many organisations oral communication may take up 60–70% of the manager's or secretary's working day in a host of different situations:

face-to-face conversations
interviews, meetings
telephone-calls, briefings
customer reception
public address.

But, in spite of the varied and extensive use of the spoken word at work, the techniques which enable people to speak and listen effectively are often taken for granted – until something goes wrong:

'I could have bitten my tongue off!'

'Better let Harris handle the negotiations – Smith's likely to speak first and think afterwards.'

Such comments are heard all too frequently in organisations, where the inability to use the spoken word with precision, tact or persuasion may cause unintended slights. Of course, being human, everyone is bound to make occasional mistakes – what *is* important is to learn from them by studying how to use the spoken word tactfully and effectively.

What, then, are the principal skills of effective speaking and listening?

Any message passes through six stages, from sender to receiver, from being conceived, encoded and relayed, to being decoded, comprehended and acknowledged. What characterises oral communication particularly is the rapid interchange between being a speaker and a listener when two or more people talk together. In addition, the whole process is amazingly subtle. The way in which the spoken word is transmitted and understood may be affected by a wide range of factors – expression, gesture, intonation, choice of words, the background to the situation, the relationship of sender to receiver and so on.

Also, the extremely rapid exchange of ideas in dialogue or conversation means that people need to 'think on their feet'. They have to consider the likely effect of what they are saying, or about to say, upon the recipient of the message and to listen actively to what is being said. In other words, oral communication requires a conscious effort, both in judging in advance the impact of what is about to be said, and in monitoring the receiver's feedback to assess how the message is being received.

The following table illustrates the skills of oral communication which the speaker and listener need to acquire:

Speaking skills
Mastery of the mechanics of speech
Logical structuring of the message
Choice of an appropriate style
Effective delivery
Awareness of the message's context
Understanding of the recipient(s)

Listening skills
Active concentration when listening
Correct interpretation of visual
signals – expression, gesture
Sending of feedback signals

An ancient Chinese proverb runs:
'Open your mouth, that I may know you.'

Are you revealing the best parts of yourself every time you speak?

The voice in action

The process of speaking

The physical process of human speech is the result of millions of years of evolution. It requires co-ordination of the muscles and nerves controlling diaphragm and lungs, tongue, palate, lips, teeth, nose and 'mouth box'. Air is forced out of the lungs, past vibrating vocal chords and expelled through the nose and mouth. The sounds produced by the vibrating vocal chords are then 'moulded' into the components of human speech by a complex series of positions of lips, tongue, palate, teeth and cheeks, working together to produce vowel sounds like 'eh', 'uh', 'ooh', or consonants like 'tuh', 'buh', 'guh' or 'kuh', and so on. The process relies upon air being expelled from the lungs during speech.

Articulation and pronunciation

The process of learning to speak is imitative – babies absorb and mimic the sounds they hear around them, first from their mothers and then from their families. Later, as children, people tend to imitate the speech they hear in the streets or playgrounds they play in.

It is only in later life that we become aware of different modes of articulating or pronouncing words or expressions. Indeed, the whole topic of spoken English is a controversial one, since we naturally defend and hold to the speech patterns most deeply embedded in our consciousness. It is always the other person who has 'a plummy voice', 'speaks all lahdidah' or suffers from 'lazy speech'.

What matters more than the variations in pronunciation, however, is that people's speech should be understood – not just by a close, local circle of family and friends – but by people from geographically distant national regions, and, where the language is common, from other countries.

Thus clearly articulated expression *does* matter – not from any misapplied sense of snobbery which one social group may have for another, but simply, and essentially so that, for example, two participants in a long-distance telephone-call may understand each other and carry out actions, instructions or requests unambiguously!

The language of childhood:

S'mine! 'T'ain't!
Gotny swee's?

or its adult extensions:

Skay spoz
Thernks orfly

will, inevitably, contribute to oral communication breakdowns if personal speech habits allow words to become badly slurred, syllables clipped or omitted or vowel sounds completely modified.

Accent

One of the glories of English is the range of accents with which it is spoken internationally. Few can resist the lilt of the Scot, the soft brogue of an Irishman or the musical rhythms of the English-speaking African or West Indian. The English language would be infinitely poorer without the modifying influences of place and time which maintain English as a living language.

It is important, however, for the effective oral communicator to realise that a strong local accent which is perfectly intelligible in his own community may be extremely difficult for a colleague to understand who lives and works five hundred miles away. By the same token, it is a perceptive and sensitive communicator who restricts the use of his accent's dialect words to those who share and know them.

The area of articulation, pronunciation and accent is indeed a sensitive one. Adults tend to assume that anyone who does not share their mode of expression will not share their views and there are historical and sociological reasons why groups with different speech patterns may view each other, if not with hostility, then with caution.

Perhaps the best advice to the oral communicator in this area is to speak with his natural accent and internalised patterns of pronunciation, as long as he is sure that he is being understood and satisfied that his attachment to his way of speaking is not a cover for maintaining bad habits of speech which ignore the needs of his listeners.

Consider, for example, two versions of a receptionist paging an employee on the company's public address system:

'Will -ah Mistyeah Seempsone plee- yerse com-ah teyew re-ah-cerption-ah. Mistyeah Herndcock would-ah laik a word-ah wiyath heem.'

or,

'Wu' Mister Sums'n plees cum ah reception. Smisterancock'd lika wordivim.'

On the one hand there is the artificial, imagined accent of 'posh speech' and on the other an ugly and slurred habit of speaking. Neither is pleasant to the ear, and both would be lucky if Mr Simpson ever arrived at reception!

Intonation and speech rhythms

Effective speaking relies, not only upon the clear articulation with which words may be pronounced, but also upon the way in which we raise or lower our voices as we speak and upon the pace of our words – whether we say them slowly and deliberately or quickly and cheerily.

Whether a spoken message is understood at all, and the way in which it is interpreted depend a great deal upon the emphasis and intonation given to its component syllables.

Consider, for example, the simple sentence:

I don't know him.

Its meaning is apparently clear and simple, yet by emphasising any one (or two) of the four words, the sentence takes on quite different shades of meaning:

a I don't know him.
b I don't *know* him.
c I don't know *him*.
d I *don't know* him.

In *a* the implication may be that, 'whoever does, I certainly don't, (and have no wish to). While *b* may imply that, 'while I have met him, I do not accept that I know him and do not wish to be involved in any commitment.' The emphasis in *c* may be that 'I do not consider him worth getting to know'. And *d* strongly refutes, after being pressed on the matter, any suggestion of the speaker knowing 'him'.

Moreover, by stressing the word '*know*' and raising the voice on the word 'him', the statement has not only been turned into a question:
e I don't *know* him?
but also carries the sense that the speaker not only knows 'him' well, but that notion of his not knowing 'him' is incredible.

The subtleties which intonation, and emphasis may bring to conveying the meaning of the spoken word are clearly evident in this one example. And, as we shall see later, such subtleties may be further enlarged by the addition of non-verbal signals such as facial expression or gesture.

One of the fascinating aspects of the spoken word is the way a speaker builds up his phrases or expressions into units of speech. Users of direct speech build up a bank, not of single words, but rather of expressions or phrases which occur frequently and which may precede or follow other such units:

. . not at all. . . .
. . . wonder if you would mind . . .
Excuse me, please. . . .

. . . it's a matter of. . . .
. . . come straight to the point . . .

Such units of speech help to link ideas and also, because of their very familiarity act as 'pauses' while the speaker frames his next idea. Sometimes stock expressions are used by a speaker as a substitute for a sincere conversation contribution:

. . so long as you've got your health and strength . . .
. . . none of us getting any younger. . . .
. . . takes all sorts . . .

In such circumstances these stock expressions are called clichés and are usually irritating to the listener.

In order to test the effect of intonation, emphasis, voice level and pauses upon the spoken word, consider this example:

I was térribly sórry | to hear the

news | of yóung Jím's ¦cár áccident.||

How ís he?|| I dó hópe | it isn't

ánything ¦ sérious.

Key: ⌣⌢ rise and fall of voice

¦ | || length of pause

____ emphasised words

/ highly stressed syllables

Much depends upon how we express ourselves in direct speech. As the above example indicates, key words and phrases are intensified by the use of emphasis, stress and a rising voice level, while the endings of speech units and sentences are indicated by the voice falling. Questions are signalled by a rise in the ending of the sentence and pauses are used partly to identify speech units, partly for breathing spaces and partly to signify the end of one sentence and the start of another. Failure in any of these areas may be interpreted as a lack of concern, or even hypocrisy in the example of Jim's accident. The human ear is extremely finely attuned to pick up inappropriate voice levels or emphases, especially when these are accompanied by facial expressions which do not match the situation.

It is not an over-statement to say that intonation, emphasis and phrasing are crucial to effective oral communication. One speaker may be described as, 'dynamic', 'a real enthusiast', 'extremely persuasive', 'very authoritative'; while another is regarded as 'dull as ditch-water', 'lacking in conviction' with the ability to 'bore the pants off' people.

Un .. a .. cust .. omed ..... as .... I .. am to ...
pub .. lic .... speak .. ing ......

Such judgments are accorded, not only about what someone has to say for himself, but how he says it. And indeed, unless the speaker wins his listener's attention with the 'how' from the outset, he may never create the climate in which to convey the 'what'!

Projection

Those people, like actors, lecturers or public speakers, who regularly communicate to large groups in theatres or auditoriums, soon feel the need to project their voices. Ensuring that one's voice carries over a wide area requires a correct posture to enable the diaphragm to function properly, an 'open' position of the head and throat to allow the voice to carry readily, and a voice pitch which helps the voice to travel. Successful voice-projection also involves taking the accoustics of hall or room into account, and in some cases will require accentuated articulation. The shy speaker must avoid speaking too softly into his chest, while the extrovert must learn to speak more slowly and take care not to batter the listeners' ears with harsh, grating tones.

Effective voice projection is particularly important in business – it is often the speaker whose voice commands attention at, say, a meeting, who frequently wins the day. Having something worth saying is one thing. Reaching one's listeners compellingly is quite another!

Practice pieces

1 Check the clarity of your vowels, diphthongs and consonants by tape-recording the following sentences by yourself:

Blue Skies Tours mean fine, warm days!

Mining underground often requires working in confined spaces.

Tempered steel displays both strength and elasticity.

Strict adherence to company regulations is essential.

Advertising is quickly becoming an integral part of people's lives.

Picking grapes is a popular choice for a working holiday.

Baking bricks is a back-breaking business!

Play back your recording and check that:
the open vowels are really open
-ed, -ing endings are not clipped
'h's' have not been omitted
's' and 'z' sounds are clear
syllables have not been slurred
consonants are clearly sounded

2 Study the following extracts from three different work situations. Consider how you would use intonation, emphasis, pauses and voice-levels to make them as effective as possible when spoken. Re-write them using the key signs employed in the 'Jim's car accident' example. Then record them on to tape and submit your version for evaluation by your group:

'I wanted to speak to you about a personal matter as you know I have been with the company now for eighteen months as far as I know my work has always been satisfactory and I feel that I have been a conscientious employee I should therefore like to ask you for an increase in my salary'

'I have called you in to discuss a most serious matter with you during the past three weeks I have received a number of complaints from customers upset by your apparent rudeness while serving them I propose to outline the circumstances of each complaint from the customer's point of view and then to ask you for your own account of what allegedly took place.'

'Charlie we're in trouble Johnson's have just phoned a large order in but they must have it by tomorrow morning I told them I couldn't promise anything until I'd spoken to you is there any chance of your fitting in another production run I'd certainly appreciate it if you could use your influence.'

3 The following passage is the closing section of a managing director's address to his Annual Sales Conference. Study it carefully and then record it on to tape for play-back analysis. Your aim should be to fire the sales representatives with enthusiasm during a difficult period:

'I know – and you know – that the company, and indeed the country, have been going through a difficult trading period. Equally, I know that the strength of Allied Products lies in its ability to meet a challenge. It hasn't been easy, and I can give you no guarantee that it will get better at all quickly. What I do know is that if anyone is going to lead the company into a better tomorrow, it is you, its sales representatives. And so my closing message to you all is: the company is proud of what you have done during a difficult year and will back you all to the hilt in the coming months; but it will only be your determination and enthusiasm which will turn the corner during the next year. I know I can rely on you!'

Check the recorded versions for the following:
audibility – clarity
delivery – pace, emphasis
commitment – sincerity
ability to enthuse
Where any version may be considered to have fallen short, try to decide the reasons for its lack of success.

Non-verbal communication

'So what went wrong? . . .'

'Good morning, may I help you?'

'Here's the crucial point.'

'Search me.'

'Hi, Joe, what'll it be?'

Non-verbal communication either reinforces the spoken word or acts in place of it

Kinesics

Facial expressions
smiles, frowns, narrowed eyes transmitting friendliness, anger or disbelief etc.

Gestures
pointing fingers, 'thumbs up' sign, shakes of the head, transmitting an emphasising focus, congratulations or disagreement etc.

Movements
quick pacing up and down, finger-drumming, leisurely strolling, transmitting impatience, boredom or relaxation.

Proxemics

Physical contact
shaking hands, prodding with the forefinger, clapping on the back, transmitting greetings, insistence or friendship.

Positioning
keeping a respectful distance, looking over someone's shoulder, sitting close to someone, transmitting awareness of differing status, a close working relationship or relaxed mutual trust.

Posture
standing straight and erect, lounging, sitting hunched up, leaning forward, spreading oneself in a chair, transmitting alertness and care, self-confidence (or even over-confidence), nervousness or ease.

Para-linguistics

feedback sounds of surprise or agreement of annoyance or impatience –
'uh-uh', 'whew!', 'oops!', 'tsk', 'tut-tut' etc.

Non-verbal communication (NVC) is a fascinating area of study. It concerns the many ways in which people communicate in face-to-face situations, either as a means of reinforcing or of replacing the spoken word. Sometimes people employ non-verbal communication techniques consciously, at other times the process is carried out unconsciously. In many instances, the response is involuntary. A sudden shock, for instance, may result in someone draining in facial colour, opening his or her eyes wide and becoming slack-jawed.

Non-verbal communication may be divided into three main areas, with rather technical labels for readily observable activities or responses:

A heightened awareness of what people are 'saying' non-verbally greatly assists the manager or secretary to read a situation and to act – perhaps to head off a personality clash or to calm an irate customer.

NVC and effective communication

Working successfully in an organisation requires that staff develop human relations skills by becoming more aware of how other people are reacting or feeling. Specifically, it requires the ability to 'read' a situation quickly and correctly. Though information and attitudes may be readily conveyed by means of the spoken word, the constraints of courtesy and staff relationships may result in the spoken message masking how someone is really feeling or relating. At other times, a correct interpretation of NVC signals may allow the interpreter to act positively.

For example, the sales representative who recognises that the nods, smiles and approaching movements of his prospective customer mean that he is won over, is able to proceed confidently to close the sale. Equally, the secretary who correctly interprets her principal's frowns, toe-tapping and fist-clenching as he reads a report, may rightly decide to postpone until a more favourable moment her request for a salary increase! Moreover, the receptionist who recognises annoyance in the hurried approaching steps of a member of staff who bursts into her office, eyes narrowed, chin jutting forward and mouth down-drawn will have the commonsense to ensure that her opening words are calming:

'I'm very sorry, Mr Jones is out at the moment. Is there anything I may do to help meantime?

rather than exacerbating:

'Mr Jones is out. I'm afraid you'll have to call back.'

Thus the ability to recognise NVC signals and to modify responses in their light is essential to the maintenance and promotion of good human relations within an organisation as well as being a valuable tool in helping the manager, secretary or clerk to achieve objectives involving direct personal contact with others.

Facial Components	A Range of Responses
Forehead – upward and downward frowns	ACCEPTANCE REJECTION
Eyebrows – raising or knitting, furrowing	ENJOYMENT DISLIKE
Eyelids – opening, closing, narrowing	FRIENDSHIP HOSTILITY
Eye pupils – dilating	INTEREST
Eyes – upwards, downwards gazing, holding or avoiding eye contact	DISINTEREST ANGER LOVE SYMPATHY
Nose – wrinkling, flaring nostrils	JEALOUSY ASSURANCE
Facial muscles – drawn up or down, for grinning, teeth clenching	NERVOUSNESS AGREEMENT DISAGREEMENT ATTENTION
Lips – smiling, pursing, drawn in	BOREDOM ACCEPTANCE
Mouth – wide open, drawn in, half-open	DISBELIEF SURPRISE FEAR
Tongue – licking lips, moving around inside cheeks, sucking teeth	IMPATIENCE FRUSTRATION ENVY EMPATHY
Jaw/Chin – thrust forward, hanging down	EASE DISCOMFORT ALERTNESS
Head – thrown back, inclined to one side, hanging down, chin drawn in, inclined upwards	STUPOR PAIN PLEASURE ECSTASY TORMENT SATISFACTION DISPLEASURE

Though the above check-list of responses may not, perhaps, be manifested in every office or factory, it does indicate the incredible range of emotions and feelings visible in the human facial expression!

Expression, gesture and movements

Facial expression

The human face is capable of conveying a wide range of expression and emotion. Various parts of the face are used to convey signals:

Assignment

Choose a number of varying responses from the above check-list and, from the list of facial components, make out a description of how the individual parts of the face would act together to form the particular expression for each response.

Gesture

Apart from actors, politicians and public speakers who may rehearse a telling gesture to emphasise a point, many of the gestures which people employ as they speak or listen are used unselfconsciously. When the speaker becomes excited, for example, sweeping movements of the arms or the banging of a fist into an open palm may act to reinforce what is being said. Alternatively, the propping of the head upon a cupped hand may signal that what is being said is boring and failing to interest.

Of course, some gestures are consciously and deliberately made. The car driver who points a finger to his head with a screwing motion is demonstrating what he thinks about the quality of someone's driving!

The range of gestures which utilise head, shoulders, arms, hands, fingers, legs and feet is indeed wide. Though frequently supporting the spoken word, gestures may either be used, consciously, to replace speech, as, for example, with the finger placed in front of the lips urging silence. Unconscious signals from the listener – the brushing of the hand across mouth and chin may be 'saying', 'I'm not sure that I go along with what is being said'. On the other hand, someone may seek to calm a meeting which is becoming heated by consciously patting down the air with both open palms which transmit the sense of, 'Steady on, let's not lose our tempers over this!'

Commonly used gestures

The following gestures are seen regularly in daily life, either reinforcing or substituting for the spoken word:

Head
nodding sideways to urge someone along
nodding up and down
shaking sideways
inclined briefly
cradled in one or both hands

Arms and hands
widely outstretched
jammed into trouser pockets
firmly folded across the chest
holding the back of the head with fingers laced
making chopping movements with the side of the hand
hands pressed together in 'praying' position
one or both hands held over mouth
flat of hand patting desk-top
hand brushing something away in the air
both hands placed open upon the chest

Fingers
running through the hair
drumming on table-top
stroking mouth and chin
stabbing the air with forefinger
clenched into a fist
manipulated in an arm-wave
patting the fingertips together with the fingers of both hands out-stretched
rubbing the thumb and fingers together

Legs and feet
leg and foot making kicking motion
foot or toes tapping the ground
moving legs up and down while seated

Posture

The way people 'arrange their bodies' as they stand or sit may also be extremely communicative. The candidate at interview, for example, who sits hunched into a chair with arms tight, hands clenched, and legs and feet pressed and folded together is probably 'saying' very 'loudly' to the interviewers, 'I am feeling extremely nervous.' By the same token, the interviewee who lolls and sprawls in the chair may be revealing an unpleasant over-confidence and familiarity. As a general rule, the body frame is more widely spread in a relaxed position, whether seated or standing, when someone feels at ease, and is more tightly held, with arms and legs together when discomfort, nervousness or tension is being experienced.

The ability to interpret such signals and to act as necessary to disarm or reassure is invaluable in promoting good human relations.

Assignment

Add to the above examples of gesture and posture and then describe the sort of messages sent through each example and identify the contexts in which they may be seen.

Communicating face to face

'I've come because your letters don't give me the same, mysterious uplift I get from your misty, blue eyes, Miss Ponsonby. Now, about the tax rebate. . . .'

Face-to-face communication is the oxygen in the life-blood of business and public service organisations. Despite the efficiency and speed of modern telecommunications – essential in their way – there is no totally acceptable substitute for people talking and reacting in close, direct contact. How often at work are sentiments expressed such as:

'Pop into my office and we'll talk it over.'

'I'm sure we can thrash this out round a table.'

'I'm glad I've bumped into you, Jane, I'd like your opinion on . . .'

Communicating face-to-face embraces a wide variety of situations:

private discussions in offices
encounters in corridors
conversation over lunch in staff restaurants
taking part in meetings
selling across the sales counter
explaining on the factory floor
discussing in the large open office
speaking at conferences
questioning at interviews

Also, the context of the dialogue may render it formal or informal. A 'natter' over lunch will be expressed in words very different from those used at a formal appointment interview. Also, the way in which a dialogue develops will depend entirely upon its context and the relationship of its participants, who may be conversing with the aim of directing or requesting, informing or persuading, congratulating or disciplining.

Whatever the circumstances, the reason why most people prefer most of the time to communicate face-to-face is that such a medium best provides them with 'a total impression' in a way that written communication or telephone calls do not. This impression derives not only from what is being said, but from the whole manner of a person's delivery, including non-verbal communication factors. Moreover, the medium permits instant feedback, the means of asking snap questions and of, sometimes, obtaining prompt answers!

In face-to-face contact many 'tools' of communication are working in concert: intonation of the voice, facial expression, gesture, posture and movement, all of which provide a much fuller and often more accurate indication of the import of any given message.

Factors affecting face-to-face communication

What, then, are the most important factors which affect and influence direct personal contact? Whether the context is formal or informal and whether there has been an opportunity to plan beforehand will clearly make a difference. The following check-list includes some of the main ingredients necessary for effective face-to-face communication:

Check before you speak!

1 *Plan beforehand* – have supporting notes and documents to hand
2 *Explore opposing points of view* – look at the situation from the other point of view and have counter-arguments ready if needed
3 *Check out the location* of the contact – it helps to be familiar with surroundings, whether for a meeting or interview.
4 *Exclude interruptions and distractions* – frequent telephone-calls or staff interruptions prevent concentration.
5 *Consider the person or people you will be seeing* – it pays to be as well informed as possible about colleagues, associates or customers, and to know 'what makes them tick'.
6 *Select a mode of speaking appropriate to the situation* – being over-familiar and 'chatty' or reserved and formal may prove blocks to effective communication, depending upon the context of the dialogue.
7 *Check your appearance* – dress is another way of signalling what we represent, or how we wish to be accepted.

Courtesy

The effective communicator is always courteous. Avoid:
interrupting,
contradicting,
'showing off' to impress others,
making someone 'look small',
losing your temper,
being condescending,
showing boredom or impatience.

Listening

Failing to listen to someone is not only a grave discourtesy, but also may result in your looking silly or making a *faux-pas*.

Pay attention, consider the implications of what is being said. Look at the speaker, provide him with feedback to show you are following.

Styling

Strive to ensure that the manner in which you speak is appropriate to the circumstances.

Choose your words and expressions carefully, mindful of the personalities and backgrounds of others present.

It is easy to give offence but difficult to overcome its effects.

Thinking

It is vital to think before you speak – once a statement is uttered it may be difficult to retract.

If you agree with a point, try to develop it constructively; if you disagree do not become over-assertive. Show that you can see more than one point of view.

Remember, it is better to say a little which is considered, than a lot which is superficial.

Mannerism

Avoid irritating, unpleasant or discourteous mannerisms of speech, gesture or posture.

Do not distract by 'fiddling' with a pencil, doodling or indulging in other distractions.

Timing

Choose the right moment to speak; sometimes it is better to let others have their say first.

Listen for the drop in a person's voice, look for a smile or nod which may indicate that someone has finished making a point.

Be alert for the signs a person makes when he wishes to end a conversation or interview.

Know when you have won and leave promptly!

Structuring

If others are to follow your argument and value what you say, it is important that you structure your points logically, and express them in connected phrases and sentences.

It is also essential that you do not speak for too long at a time; people will quickly reject what you have to say if you deprive them of the opportunity to have their say too!

Reacting and contributing

One of the quickest ways of alienating others is to show no reaction to what they have said. Enthusiastic agreement or determined disagreement both indicate that there is an interest and commitment present.

Ensure you make some positive contribution to the dialogue – if you have nothing to say, people will assume that you have nothing of value to contribute and may assess you accordingly.

Interviews

The interview is used in organisations to meet the needs of many, quite different, situations. Some interviews are extremely formal affairs, where a candidate for a post may be examined and evaluated by a board or panel of interviewers. Others are conducted in a much more relaxed atmosphere, in a 'one-to-one' relationship, between, say, a manager and a subordinate.

In point of fact, it is very difficult to establish where conversation ends and the interviewing process begins in the work situation. A working definition of an interview may follow these lines:

Working definition

An interview takes place when two parties meet to satisfy pre-determined objectives by mutual interrogation.

The process is characterised by the posing and answering of questions, or by the giving and receiving of directions, instructions or advice.

In particular, both parties have specific aims to achieve by directing questions and answers to an end known usually to both interviewer and interviewee.

According to the above definition, an interview may, in effect, be taking place far more frequently than we may realise. When, for example, a manager calls a subordinate into his office, invites him to sit down and then says,

'How have things been going, lately, Jim? You've been looking rather unsettled . . .'

a counselling interview is probably about to take place to enable the manager to get to the root of a problem.

So it is that the interview process is employed to obtain information and responses in a wide variety of areas, from sales performance to accounts collection, from disciplinary proceedings to promotion selection, from counselling on personal problems to personnel appointments. The following table indicates some of the principal areas in which the interview is commonly used:

Main applications of the interview

Job application
Resignation – debriefing
Performance assessment
Counselling
Disciplining
Promoting
Information seeking
Instruction giving

It is therefore important for the members of any organisation to regard the interview not as an intimidating process to be endured, but rather as a tool of communication from the use of which the interviewee has as much to gain as the interviewer. The truth of this observation becomes much more apparent if the interviewee in particular stops to consider that the process *is* two-way.

Consider, for instance, the job application interview. Careful preparation and probing questioning on the part of the interviewee may result in his declining an offered post with a company which is performing poorly and where job prospects exist in theory rather than in practice. It is important, therefore, at the outset to interpret the term, 'interrogation' as 'a two-way channel for finding out'.

Applying for a job

Preparing for the interview

Before attending for interview, **THE APPLICANT** will have:

* Researched the organisation for performance, prospects and personalities.

* Compiled and duplicated a *curriculum vitae* under the suggested headings of: Personal details, Education, Qualifications, Work experience, Interests and Circumstances.

* Made and kept a copy of the returned application forms for reference.

* Made a check-list of anticipated questions and considered their answers.

* Compiled a list of questions to ask on topics such as: organisation's performance, job prospects, conditions of service, duties, salary etc.

* Assessed the nature of the work location if possible.

* Ensured that personal appearance is smart without being over-dressed.

* Arrived at the interview location in good time.

Before calling applicants for interview **THE INTER-VIEWER** will have:

* Carefully assessed the needs to be met through the job.

* Assessed the qualities required in the successful applicant.

* Screened applications against requirements.

* Obtained references and scrutinised applications.

* Drawn up a check-list of questions to assess the candidate: specialist abilities, working qualities, potential, personal disposition, interests and circumstances.

* Examined his own attitudes to ensure that interviews are objectively approached.

* Arranged for interviews to proceed without interruption.

The job selection process

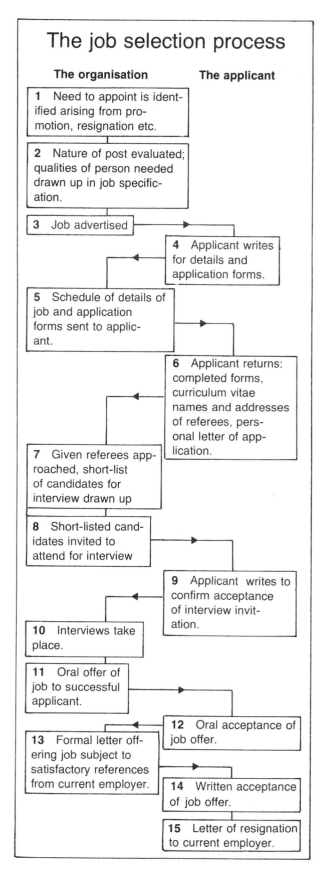

The organisation   **The applicant**

1   Need to appoint is identified arising from promotion, resignation etc.

2   Nature of post evaluated; qualities of person needed drawn up in job specification.

3   Job advertised

4   Applicant writes for details and application forms.

5   Schedule of details of job and application forms sent to applicant.

6   Applicant returns: completed forms, curriculum vitae names and addresses of referees, personal letter of application.

7   Given referees approached, short-list of candidates for interview drawn up

8   Short-listed candidates invited to attend for interview

9   Applicant writes to confirm acceptance of interview invitation.

10   Interviews take place.

11   Oral offer of job to successful applicant.

12   Oral acceptance of job offer.

13   Formal letter offering job subject to satisfactory references from current employer.

14   Written acceptance of job offer.

15   Letter of resignation to current employer.

Note: Some applicants also send open testimonials from past employers; discussion of job application with current employer is at the discretion of the applicant; prospective employers do not normally contact applicant's employers for references without applicant's permission.

The interview

When interview techniques are being discussed, it is usually the formal interview which is considered. It is important to remember, however, that even in informal interview situations the guide-lines which follow will still hold true in principle, if not in detail.

In any interview, the interviewee will be assessed, either directly or indirectly in these areas:

appearance, deportment, manners, speech, intelligence, judgment, values, commonsense, initiative, resourcefulness, assurance.

Basically, the interviewer will be seeking reassurance or information in line with the questions:

How does the interviewee project himself?

What has he to offer in terms of specialist skills or knowledge?

What has he to offer in terms of personality?

What potential to develop does he display?

Appearance, manners, deportment

As an interviewee, whether as job applicant or employee, your personal appearance matters! Rightly or wrongly other people will make judgments about you, which will be influenced by your appearance. Looking smart and well-groomed is an asset in any situation and is nowhere more important than at an interview.

The way you hold yourself, move and gesture will also affect the way people regard you. In professional and business life attractive people are those who temper assurance with modesty, and who behave calmly, with due consideration for others. On entering the interview room, for example, take care to do so politely but not over-hesitantly, and wait to be proferred a hand to shake or to be invited to take a seat. Once seated, avoid the tendency to slouch or lounge and assume a posture which is comfortable, but alert. Also, it is sensible to hold the hands in the lap, and to return them to this position between any gestures.

It is also important to master any feelings of nervousness. Feeling nervous is natural during an interview and you may be sure that the interviewer is aware of this fact and that he will go to some trouble to set you at your ease. Nevertheless, allowing nerves to take over, and displaying signs of tension by hunching into the chair, wringing hands, twisting rings or biting lips not only impairs your performance, but transmits a sense of unease to the interviewer as well. The result may be that you do not do justice to yourself and that you leave doubts about your capacities in the mind of the interviewer.

Listening before speaking

Once the interview is under way, perhaps the best advice is to *listen*! It is all too easy as an interviewee to attend with only half an ear to what is being said or asked. Moreover, you will need to employ all your faculties and to keep extremely alert to ensure that you anticipate, for example, where a sequence of questions is leading you, or to see the probing which may be going on beneath an apparently harmless question!

Listening attentively will also help you to prepare your answer while a question is being framed. It is amazing how fast the brain works in such situations.

Looking at the questioner

Rightly, the ability to 'look someone squarely in the eye' has always been regarded as a sign of honesty and assurance. It helps in any case, during an interview to look at a speaker posing a question since facial expression, gesture or posture often provide valuable insights into what is in an interviewer's mind, and shows that you are paying attention.

Similarly, when providing an answer you should make eye-contact with the questioner, but not to the extent of boring into him with a transfixing stare!

Think before you speak!

This well-worn truism is still excellent advice to the interviewee. Blurting out a nonsense or 'gabbling' on because of nerves are traps into which the unwary often fall. Moreover, it is not possible in an interview to escape from being assessed and both the words you utter and the way in which you express yourself will reveal much about your intelligence, judgment, commonsense and *nous*.

In order to answer questions successfully and in so doing to create a favourable impression, you should ask yourself these questions both before and during your answer:

Have I understood the question?
Do I appreciate what it is driving at?
Are there any traps or pitfalls present in the question?
Can I draw on my own experience to illustrate my answer?
Am I speaking clearly and convincingly?
Have I covered the ground and said enough?

Thinking *while* speaking

Just as the practised reader's eye travels ahead before he reads a phrase aloud, so the practised interviewee's mind will be thinking ahead and monitoring what is being said. Additionally, the interviewee's eyes will be looking hard at the interviewer for signs of a favourable response to what is being said.

Sometimes the way in which the spoken word is constructed into phrases or sentences allows for 'rest' or 'pause' expressions to be uttered while the brain composes the next important point:

.. as a matter of fact I . . .

. . . I accept the truth of that but . . .

. . . although my initial response might be to . . . in this case I would . . .

Also, there are means of delaying arrival at the explicit answer point of a difficult question by means of a sort of delaying tactic:

I suppose it depends to a large degree upon how the term X is interpreted. . . .

I don't have an easy or quick answer to that question, but on reflection I . . .

It should be noted that interviewers are only too aware of how much easier it is to pose questions than to answer them, and make natural allowances for initial hesitancy. A word of caution, however: if an interviewee displays a frequent inability to answer questions directly, he is bound to sow in the interviewer's mind seeds of doubt regarding integrity, honesty or, quite simply, lack of knowledge.

Measure what you say

Interviewers are skilled at posing questions which cannot be answered by a simple 'yes' or 'no'. For example, a question would not be phrased:

'Did you enjoy your previous job'

but rather,

'What did you find most satisfying about your previous job?'

In this way the interviewee is invited to expand a reply rather than to offer monosyllabic answers, which inevitably cast doubts upon fluency, knowledge and assurance. It is common, however, for inexperienced interviewees to speak rapidly at great length, as if the assessment were based on words spoken per minute and the range of unrelated topics covered! You must therefore ensure that what you

'I was rather hoping you would ask me that. Yes . . . and no. I think it really depends on how one views the broader implications. Looking at it objectively, what was the question again? . . .'

are saying is relevant to the question and forms a summary of the main issues as you see them. It is good practice to pause after having made what you consider an adequate number of points to allow the interviewer either to ask you to continue or to ask another question. Try to strike a happy medium. Saying too little prevents you from demonstrating your knowledge and ability. Saying too much reveals a disorganised and 'butterfly' mind.

Ask your questions

Whatever the interviewing situation, the interviewer largely has control of the interview. Nevertheless, you should ensure that you make an opportunity to ask the questions you have framed. In the context of an application for a job, you wish to establish whether you want the organisation equally as much as it may wish to decide whether it wants you! Such opportunities tend to occur at the end of the interview but clarifying questions may be put throughout.

Useful information for the interviewee

The NIIP Seven Point Plan

The following headings summarise an assessment system used in selection processes by interviewers and as a basis for personnel specifications:
Physical make-up
Attainments
General intelligence
Special aptitudes
Interests
Disposition
Circumstances

The application form

The following information is generally required on an application form for a job:
Name
Address
Telephone no.
Age: date of birth
Status: married, single
Maiden name if married woman
Education
Qualifications
Current, previous experience
Present designation or title
Name and address of employers
Details, with dates, of employment since leaving full-time education
Details of salaries in each appointment
Outline of hobbies, interests
Names, addresses and occupations of referees
Date of availability
Signature and acknowledgment of accuracy of data provided

The curriculum vitae

A *curriculum vitae* may be composed by using the following framework:
Personal details
Full name and current address
Telephone number
Age, status – married, single
Nationality
Dependents – wife, husband, children
Education
Secondary school(s)
College(s) ⎱   with
University ⎰   dates
Post-graduate institution
Main subjects taken
Activities, interests
Post(s) of responsibility

Qualifications
Examination passes indicating grades, dates and examining boards.
Work experience
Usually expressed by starting from immediate past and working backwards.
   Name of organisation, location, job designation, range of duties, extent of responsibilities, reasons for leaving.
Interests
Leisure activities, hobbies, indicating posts of responsibility – e.g. Honorary Secretary of Drama Club – where appropriate.
Circumstances
Period of notice required to be given.
   Mobility – car-ownership, any limiting commitments.

A *curriculum vitae* is usually set out schematically, with appropriate dates and chronological structures.

A golden rule for interviewees

Be yourself!

Pretence or affectation may land you in a job, or with responsibilities which may hang, like the proverbial albatross, around your neck! Hold to what you believe in – it will almost certainly give you a happier and more fulfilled working life.

The telephone

Using the telephone sometimes has a dehumanising effect on people. . . .

Telecommunications systems in general, and the telephone in particular have become indispensable tools for communicating the spoken word in business today.

Indeed, the range of telecommunications services now offered to the businessman is amazingly wide and still growing fast!

People and organisations are now linked nationally and globally by networks of satellite, radio, undersea cable and land-line which provide telephone, telex, computer and video conference links. The near future will almost certainly bring a video-telephone service to business and domestic users.

For some time to come, however, the oral-aural telephone network will continue to be the most widely used of the telecommunications systems, and a mastery of telephone techniques is essential for those planning a career or already working in industry, commerce or government.

The first, and indeed principal factor to be borne in mind by the telephone user is that the medium is oral and aural but *not* visual! As has been already discussed in the section on non-verbal communication, one of the main benefits of face-to-face communication is being able to see facial expression, gesture and posture which help enormously to convey the significance or implications of what is being said.

Telephone users, however, often refer to the 'disembodied voice' which is much more difficult to understand and which may be prone to communication breakdowns for a number of reasons including:

the spoken message is inaudible
the spoken word is misheard
the spoken message is misinterpreted because required feedback is not forthcoming

To become an effective user of the telephone, therefore, requires the acquisition of specialist skills ranging from distinct articulation of the spoken word to expertise in handling sophisticated telephone equipment. Such skills are particularly important in view of the dehumanising effect which using the telephone may have on people who cannot see the person they are talking to!

The following check-list indicates the principal skills which using the telephone successfully involves:

Knowing how to make and to receive telephone calls greetings, identifications, message-taking, obtaining confirmation, providing feedback, closing the call, passing messages on.

Using the spoken voice effectively articulation, clarity, warmth, friendliness, courtesy, charm, persuasiveness.

Employing telephone reception techniques routing, filtering, message-taking, appointment-making, relaying information.

Planning telephone calls organising the message, having supportive documents to hand, being aware of time and costs, synthesising essential information, ensuring the transmission and receipt of all required information.

Being fully conversant with the equipment and systems in use within the organisation – use of internal and external telephone directories, switchboard facilities etc.

Techniques of using the telephone

Making a telephone call costs time and money. It can also be an extremely frustrating experience if undertaken without forethought and preparation. The following guide-lines will help you to make effective use of the telephone in your working life and to use its advantages to their fullest extent:

Before telephoning:

Familiarise yourself with the main telephone systems in use. It helps to know how, say, PMBX or PABX systems are used in organisations, and will save you from starting your message several times before reaching the appropriate recipient of your call.

Plan carefully what you aim to achieve from your call and what you wish to say, whether you are seeking or providing information, requesting assistance or confirmation or endeavouring to convince or persuade.

Identify what action you seek from the recipient of your call and ensure you have worked out in advance any relevant deadlines.

Organise your material. Make a checklist of what points you wish to make for instant reference and to guard against any omission – especially important when telephoning long-distance. Locate and have to hand any files or documents to which you may wish to refer. Nothing is more irritating or calculated to lose the thread of a conversation than having to break off to rummage for a letter or report.

Check the sequence of your points. Does your explanation follow a logical order? Is your approach tactful? Does your effort to persuade culminate with the most telling arguments?

Know who you need to speak to. Valuable time may be lost and frustration experienced if you are 'shunted' around a large organisation because you do not know who deals with your specific enquiry. Although this process is inevitable at times, keeping your personal telephone directory and noting both names and extension numbers will prove invaluable and save time at the switchboard.

Make sure that your call will not be affected by interruption or distracting noise which will interfere with the flow and audibility of your call.

Dial the required number carefully, or relay it to your operator clearly. Expense is often incurred by obtaining a wrong number through mis-dialing or misreading directories.

When contact is made

Bear in mind whether you are likely to be connected to a telephone directly or via a switchboard.

Wait for an identifying greeting from the answering recipient. Return an offered greeting and identify yourself and, if appropriate, your organisation:

'Good morning, Mr Ford of Britco Ltd speaking, I'd like to speak to Mr Jones, please.'

If you are being connected via a switchboard, the operator will ask you to hold:

'Just one moment, please, Mr Ford,'

and will then contact the relevant extension. If Mr Jones is available to speak to you, the operator will say:

'Putting you through now,'

and you will be in contact either with Mr Jones, or his secretary. If Mr Jones has a secretary, one of her duties will almost certainly be to filter his calls, and so you should not be put off by a polite request from the secretary asking you to state the nature of your call. If it should be confidential, you may reply to such a request with a courteous:

'I should like to speak to Mr Jones personally upon a confidential matter.'

Sometimes the person you would like to speak to may be engaged or out. A decision must then be made whether to ask an assistant or secretary to pass a message on, or whether to call back later.

Once connected to your desired contact, keep the following in mind:
Do not rush your message. The recipient may be taking notes of your points.

Remember the nature of the medium. Ensure that you speak clearly and make good use of intonation and emphasis to impart friendliness, warmth, cooperation or goodwill.

Spell out any proper names or trade names. Repeat any number series or codes.

Pause fairly frequently for responses confirming that your message is being understood. Seek such feedback if it is not forthcoming:

'Have I made that clear?'

Check your notes as you speak to avoid errors or omissions.

Make notes of any arising information you receive.

Emphasise the action you desire, any urgency or deadlines to be met, at the end of your call, but remain courteous. Using the telephone effectively means retaining the goodwill of the recipient.

Seek confirmation at the end of your call that its main points have been understood.

Be brief. Using the telephone is expensive, so do not allow your call to become protracted. (Remember the times when telephoning is cheaper and make your calls during that period whenever possible.)

Always check before ringing off that you have made a note of the identity and telephone number of the person to whom you spoke. This information is invaluable if your requested action is not progressed and you have to make a follow-up call.

Be polite. Remember to thank the recipient of your call for his time, help or interest. In this way the future calls and requests you will make are much more likely to be met with cooperation.

After the call has been made

Check your notes and expand them if necessary before becoming involved in anything else. Inform any interested colleagues of any developments or results of your call. Make a note in your diary to check on any progress relevant to your call.

The ability to take an incoming telephone call efficiently is one of the most important aspects of oral communication.

'Trying to connect you.' . . . Eeny, meeny, miny . . . mo! . . .

The nature of the medium makes demands upon the call-taker which do not arise in face-to-face contact. Your voice and manner, for example, may provide a prospective customer with his first – and perhaps only – impression of your organisation. It is therefore of the utmost importance that you develop a professional approach to answering the telephone, so that, whatever the circumstance, you are unfailingly courteous, helpful and efficient. After all, you never know who may be making the call!

Before taking a call

The roles of the switchboard operator, secretary and manager differ widely in terms of call-taking. Broadly, the operator provides a routing service, the secretary a filtering and assisting role and the manager a decision-making role, though there is, of course, a wide area of overlap in the secretarial and management functions.

Nevertheless, the following guide-lines will help you to develop a good telephone-answering technique – essential to effective communication in organisations:

Organise your working area so as to enable yourself to handle telephone calls quickly and efficiently. This means having to hand:

telephone message pad
writing implement
internal telephone directory
appointments diary

Having to hunt for a pencil and writing messages on scraps of paper is not only time-wasting, but can be potentially disastrous if important messages go astray.

Ensure you are thoroughly familiar with the telephone equipment in use within your organisation. Cutting someone off because you do not know how to transfer a call creates a bad impression and is avoidable:

As far as possible, try to ensure that when your telephone rings there is no distracting level of noise around you. In addition, you should always ensure that confidential conversations take place in confidential surroundings – even if it means calling someone back.

During the call

Anyone taking calls direct from outside lines should have a courteous identifying greeting for the caller:

'Good morning, Gourmet Restaurants, may I help you?'

It is good practice – and many firms insist upon it – that the greeting is standardised and is neither too curt nor too involved.

Staff within an organisation employing a PMBX system will know that an initial greeting has been given from the switchboard, and should offer name, designation and department in whatever combination is most appropriate:

'Mr Brown's personal assistant speaking.'

'Miss White, sales manager's secretary.'

'Johnson, County Surveyor, speaking.'

Sometimes only departments are identified:

'Accounts Department'

but it is an elementary courtesy to let a caller know to whom he is talking. Some call-takers deliberately avoid providing their identity on the assumption that if anything goes wrong they are shielded by anonymity. Such tactics are, however, quite indefensible and demean their user.

It is important to identify the caller, and in many instances his organisation. Secretaries performing filtering duties may also need to ascertain diplomatically the nature of the caller's business. Such information may then be relayed to a principal who may, or may not decide to be 'available'. Additionally, if the call is routine, it may be dealt with by the secretary, thus saving the principal's time. Over-zealousness should, however, be avoided in this regard, since it may become a prime cause of a communication block that both principal and caller may justifiably resent.

When taking the details of the call, it is vital to listen attentively. Some telephone messages are extremely important and may require instant action – after all, speed is one of the main advantages of the telephone system.

Do not hesitate to slow the caller down, to ask for spellings or to request that a point be repeated:

'Could you spell that name, please.'

'I didn't catch your last point, would you mind repeating it – it sounded important.'

Ensure that you have a telephone message pad handy and that you make it an unbroken rule to use it consistently. Organisations design their own pads or obtain them from stationery suppliers. The illustration on this page shows the information generally included in such message pads.

TELEPHONE MESSAGE

Time: 10.30   Date: 14.6.7-

Message For: Mr. Dixon

Caller: Mrs Jean Mills

Address: Bella Boutiques Ltd.
14 King Street,
LONDON WC2A 4ND

Tel No.: 01-642-9461   Ext: 242

Message: Unable to make 11.00 appointment tomorrow. Will ring back at 2.30 p.m. to arrange another day.

Message Taken By: John White

Some message pads also contain boxes to be ticked to save time for routine message-taking situations.

TELEPHONED		WILL CALL BACK	
CALLED TO SEE YOU		PLEASE CALL HIM	
WANTS TO SEE YOU		URGENT	

Noting names and addresses as well as telephone numbers is important since the recipient of the message may wish to write to the caller rather than telephone back.

As the caller relates his message, make sure that you provide him with reassuring feedback:

'Yes. Quite.' . . . 'I see.' 'Oh no, it won't be any trouble' . . . 'I'm not sure I agree entirely' . . .

Remember that the caller cannot see you and needs, therefore, spoken signals to enable him to continue his message in the knowledge that it is being understood.

When you are speaking, always remember to talk clearly and distinctly. Telephone lines are sometimes bad and it is easy for words to be confused. Adopt a helpful and alert approach and use your voice to impart warmth or charm. Avoid using words or expressions which are over-familiar or slang:

'Yeah. Okay.'

'Geddaway! You're kidding!'

Keep in mind, too, that it is very easy on the telephone to become more aggressive, brusque and rude than in face-to-face situations; similarly, there is a greater tendency for the person at the other end of the line to take what you say amiss, since he or she is only *hearing* what you say.

Never allow someone near you to distract you with a gesticulation, whispered instruction or by putting some papers in front of you. Not only are such actions discourteous to you, but may result in your missing a vital point.

Do not keep the caller waiting on the line unnecessarily. Such behaviour creates a bad impression, the more so because your organisation is not paying for the call.

At the end of the call, check that your telephone message is correct by briefly repeating the main points to the caller. Bear in mind that what seems elementary in telephone technique theory is easily overlooked in practice. Moreover, once the call has been concluded, it is embarrassing to have to telephone the caller back to ask for a piece of information he has already given but which you overlooked or could not decipher from your notes. Similarly you will appear rather ineffectual to your principal if you noted a name but not an address or telephone number or time:

'There's a Mr Smith coming to see you tomorrow from a firm in Birmingham. I forgot to ask the name. . . . anyway, it's definitely tomorrow. . . .'

After the call has been made

Check that the message is clearly taken down without omissions. Pass it *directly* to its recipient or ensure its delivery by placing it prominently on his desk if he is out and remind him on his return.

Carry out any additional duties connected with the call by entering, for example, an appointment in a diary or fetching out files or documents needed for your principal to make a call on his return to the office.

Dictate or draft any memorandum or letter arising from the call, if time and priorities permit, as soon after the call as possible, while matters are still fresh in your mind.

Make a note, if applicable, in any forward planning system to ensure that progress is checked or initiated actions carried out. In this context it is important to keep in mind that most telephone calls are made to instigate action on the part of the receiver. Your own personal reputation and the image of your organisation will suffer if any expected follow-up is slow in coming or not forthcoming at all.

'Just a minute . . .'

A customer once telephoned the book department of a large store to enquire whether a particular text has arrived which had been on order for some weeks. A young voice answers,

'I'm afraid Miss Stanshawe's at lunch.'

The caller then asked if there was any means of checking – from a goods in or order processing ledger – whether the book in question had arrived, but was met with the same response,

'Well, you see, Miss Stanshawe's at lunch.'

Whereupon the caller asked if the sales assistant would mind having a look to see if there was any sign of the book. The assistant said,

'Just a minute . . .'

After about ten minutes of waiting, the caller heard a second, young voice whisper,

'Go on. You can put the 'phone down now. He's bound to have rung off!'

What does the above situation reveal about the inadequacies of the book department's and store's management?

Telephone situations

The following telephone situations may be used as the basis for role-playing simulation exercises or developed for group discussion and analysis purposes.

It is helpful to tape-record simulations for subsequent evaluation, or to duplicate dialogue transcriptions, for members of the group.

1 Mr Jones, an impatient, but important client, calls to speak to Mr French, sales manager, who is out. His secretary takes the call.

2 An irate customer succeeds in being connected to the General Manager of Home and Leisure Departmental Stores Ltd. He proceeds to complain vehemently about a defective television set he purchased from his local branch and the company's failure to rectify matters.

3 A prospective applicant rings in response to the current advertisement for a shorthand typist in the Office Administration Department. The personnel manager's secretary takes the call. Her principal is at a meeting.

4 You receive an urgent 'phone-call, as personal assistant to the managing director, from the personnel manager wishing to inform your principal that important negotiations with trade union negotiators have just broken down. The officers of the union are about to recommend an immediate strike with official backing if their demands for a new bonus incentive scheme are not met. The managing director is with a client company discussing a new product.

5 The personal assistant of the County Treasurer receives a telephone call from one of the Treasurer's personal friends who insists on speaking to him. He is at an important meeting and has left instructions that he does not wish to be disturbed. The friend maintains that he wishes to speak to him upon a personal and confidential matter and will not, apparently, be put off.

6 The secretary of the chief buyer of Smartahomes Building Contractors Ltd, receives a call from a sales representative wishing to speak to the chief buyer about a new line. The buyer tells you, his assistant, to handle the call.

7 As the manager of a selling organisation, you are engaged upon the telephone with an important but extremely long-winded customer. What techniques could you adopt to end the call without seeming discourteous?

8 You are trying to obtain a number to make an urgent call but you keep getting a wrong number. What do you do?

Oral aspects of meetings

The way in which organisations have developed over recent years has resulted in the meeting being used much more frequently for decision-making and problem-solving. This has come about largely because of the pressures imposed upon business and government to adopt more participative and open styles of management and employee involvement.

Some managers feel that meetings are a poor way of arriving at decisions, preferring the process of consulting individuals and then making up their own minds. The opponents of 'management by meetings' would point to the extensive use of people's time – often with little to show for it, the cost in terms of the combined salary total per hour of those present, and the poor quality of decisions made, based on consensus and compromise. They would also refer to the tendencies of some meetings to deepen rifts between people and departments rather than to heal them. There is more than a little truth in such points of view.

Nevertheless, most organisations consider that the advantages outweigh the disadvantages. Meetings *do* tend to improve communication between people and departments by 'keeping people in the picture'. They also help people to feel involved, and to consider that their contributions matter. Moreover, when it comes to implementing decisions, those who have shared in the decision-making process are much more likely to use their influence and authority to help put into practice what has been decided in principle.

Meetings, then, both formal and informal, are used as a communications medium to:

plan future policy, strategies
design systems, regulations, processes
analyse past performance, activities and problem situations
develop new products, promotions, structures
negotiate salaries, conditions of service, work methods
persuade motivate personnel, explain changes

Progressive organisations also use the meeting to bring together different departments and staff to solve problems in a way which serves to integrate companies or departments and to break down traditional, sectional interests. Thus meetings may take place under the group title of:

working party
task force
study group
management committee
negotiating panel

Whether the meeting is formal and inter-departmental or informal and within a departmental section, it is likely to have aims to meet and to require the active participation of all present. In addition, although the process may not be specifically referred to, the meeting will, if it is to be successful, result in the modifying of the opinions and attitudes of at least some of those present.

Thus there is present in all types of meeting an element of persuasion or 'winning over'. This means that the participant must develop a number of skills and professional practices if he is to make a positive and effective contribution:

Being informed
It is essential that all relevant 'homework' is done before the meeting – reading minutes and reports, obtaining briefings, researching files and documents, appraising situations. Appearing misinformed or 'behind the times' invalidates the force of any contribution.

Being aware of other participants
Very few people attend meetings with entirely open minds; people may have hobby-horses, pet projects, confirmed attitudes or 'axes to grind'. They may also have 'soft spots', susceptibilities. If they are to be won over, or their support gained, then consideration will need to be given to 'where they stand' and 'what they stand for'.

Being ready for opposition
For any contribution to be accepted it must be able to withstand challenge and opposition from those with conflicting points of view. Views, standpoints and positions must therefore be critically examined and the ground prepared for answering criticisms.

Being an effective speaker

The ability to speak effectively is nowhere put to a more rigorous test than in a meeting. The following rules-of-thumb illustrate areas involving such skills:

Listen first Each meeting develops its own climate. Its temperature may become boiling or frosty. By listening and waiting, you will be able to assess not only the general climate, but also the moods and attitudes of individuals. Test the temperature first, before diving in!

See where the land lies Most meetings tend to comprise sub-groups or caucuses allied to achieve common objectives. While speaking or providing feedback, others may reveal where sympathies or antipathies lie.

Timing   If your contribution is to be effective, then timing the moment to speak is all-important. Personal judgment is important here to perceive when a developed argument proposed by another is failing, or when the ground has been prepared and participants are sympathetic or amenable.

Succinctness   More good ideas fall by the wayside by being 'oversold' in protracted explanations than are dismissed by reason of their brevity. Keep your points short and simple. Use any previous arguments to support your opening statement, justify your points with generally appreciated examples and stress your main contention when closing.

Involving others   If other participants have shown a like-minded point of view, ensure you make reference to their contributions. In this way you will broaden the base of your approach and may win helpful allies.

Overcoming counter-arguments   When people are behaving reasonably and rationally, the most convincing means of persuasion is the use of a superior argument. If, therefore, your approach seems more logical, rational and justifiable, then the opposing arguments must be analysed and shown to be inferior.

It is in this situation that human relations skills are at a premium. No one likes to see his own argument demolished or derided. Moreover, such an argument may well be the 'sheet anchor' of four people out of a committee of ten. The whole process requires, therefore, the capacity for 'gentle persuasion' rather than the brutality of the battering ram!

Loss of face   One of the hurts which goes deepest and which people least forgive is when someone causes them to 'lose face' in the company of associates or colleagues.

It is deceptively easy to make someone 'look small' by treating what they have said with scorn, contempt or heavy sarcasm. Additionally, the hierarchical structure of an organisation may make it difficult for them to reply in the same vein. Some actions may make an enemy, or at least an opponent, for long after the meeting – even though nothing further may be said! Consideration for others and the ability to construct 'face-saving' formulae, approaches and remarks is one of the most important skills which those who take part in meetings need to acquire.

Integrity not obduracy   Holding to a point of view generally challenged by others may require a great deal of courage and integrity, and, in general, commands respect. It is important, however, that you look objectively at your attitudes in such circumstances. Stubborn resistance to persuasion may indi-

cate a closed mind, pettiness or even spite. The mark of the mature person is that he has the strength of personality to defer to a superior argument – graciously!

Courtesy   Each participant at a meeting is inevitably being assessed by his peers. People are quick to label behaviour as boorish, arrogant or rude. Bad habits in this regard are easy to acquire by:

Interrupting someone by 'talking over them'.
Exchanging leers, winks or grins with a neighbour as a means of criticising what is being said.
Showing annoyance by 'switching off' or sulking silently.
Showing boredom by lounging or doodling.
Engaging in a conversation while someone else is talking.
Losing your temper.
Belittling others when speaking yourself.
Failing to show the chairman due respect.
Monopolising the proceedings by being long-winded.
Failing to pay attention, and then showing it.
Looking constantly at a clock or watch.

Good manners displayed by attentiveness, politeness, consideration of other points of view and respect for the rule of procedure are the hall-marks of the effective participator.

Being an effective note-taker and relayer of information

The business of any meeting is only partially concluded when it closes. For decisions to be effective, participants may either be expected to implement actions themselves, or to relay information back to their own sections or departments. Thus it is essential that the main points of the meeting are noted clearly. From such notes you may be required either to deliver an oral report to your superior, or to disseminate information informally to colleagues.

One attitude to guard against: participation in meetings provides automatic membership to a small, perhaps even élite group within an organisation. Such membership may also result in your acquiring information not generally known. It is a natural tendency, therefore, to keep such information to yourself or to release it in small portions, while enjoying the status which goes with having knowledge not given to others. Of course, some meetings deal with confidential matters and expect that members respect the fact. However, your membership of a meeting group may be to act as an information disseminator. Hoarding information is a common cause of communication breakdown, is resented by those around you and reflects insecurity rather than efficiency.

The following diagrams illustrate different ways of organising the seating of participants at meetings:

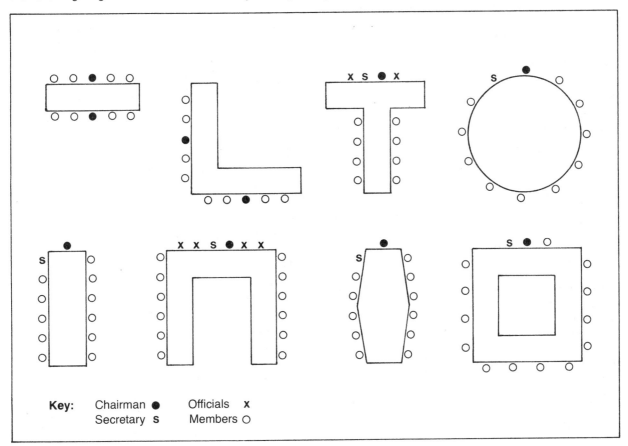

Key: Chairman ●   Officials x
       Secretary s   Members ○

Assessment questions

The spoken word

1 Make a list of situations in which oral communication commonly occurs in organisations.

2 Outline the principal skills involved in speaking and listening effectively.

3 Explain briefly the physical process involved in the act of speaking.

4 Explain the importance of the following in using the spoken word successfully:

    a articulation, pronunciation

    b accent

    c intonation, emphasis

    d voice levels.

5 What is voice projection? How is it achieved? When is it necessary?

Non-verbal communication

6 What do you understand by the term 'non-verbal communication'?

7 What NVC activities are involved in:

    a kinesics

    b proxemics

    c para-linguistics.

8 What is the connection between non-verbal communication, speaking and listening?

9 Outline briefly the NVC signals you would associate with:

    a nervousness

    b anger

    c impatience

    d boredom.

The interview

10 How would you define an interview?

11 List as many uses of the interview in organisations as you can recall.

12 Make a check-list of the preparations made before a job application interview by:

    a the interviewee

    b the interviewer.

13 What is a job specification?

14 What advice could you give to an interviewee about being interviewed?

15 What does the interviewer seek to assess or establish during the job application interview?

16 What headings would you use in a *curriculum vitae*?

The telephone

17 What are the main differences in communicating by telephone as opposed to communicating face-to-face?

18 Find out the difference between PMBX and PABX.

19 What advice would you give to someone new to an organisation

    a in taking calls

    b in making calls.

20 Explain the difference in greeting a caller

    a by a switchboard operator

    b by an internal extension user.

21 Why is feedback especially important in telephone use?

22 What do you understand by the term 'filtering'?

23 List the component parts of the telephone message pad.

Oral aspects of meetings

24 What are the advantages to organisations of oral communication through meetings?

25 How does the process of communication differ between a group meeting and a one-to-one face-to-face interview?

26 What advice would you give to someone whose new job will involve him in taking part in frequent meetings?

27 What constitutes discourteous behaviour at meetings?

28 What obligations does a participant of a meeting have after it is over?

29 Summarise a 'golden rule' which you think all oral communicators should follow.

Assignments, discussion topics

1 Make a tape-recording of members of the group discussing one of the Discussion Topics. Analyse the tape for evidence of irritating speech mannerisms. Consider how the manner of delivery of any points could be improved.

2 Enact the following situations in role-play simulation:
    a a door-to-door salesman selling brushes or polishes
    b a sales representative selling office stationery
    c a sales assistant selling cosmetics.
First, make notes on product details, selling benefits and prices, then sell the products to a sceptical consumer. Record the transaction on tape and then analyse the language used for persuasiveness and effectiveness.

3 Deliver a short talk to the group on one of the following topics:
    a How to address a group
    b Taking part in meetings
    c Using the telephone effectively
    d Coping at interviews.
Two or more members of the group may deliver the same talk. Listening group members should assess each talk for subject-matter, organisation, delivery and effectiveness.

4 Assume that you work in your local careers office. Design a brochure to be given to school-leavers which offers them practical advice on how to be successful in an interview for their first job.

5 An employee in your company is persistently late in arriving for work. Several warnings have had little effect. Simulate the disciplinary interview between manager and employee called to resolve the matter. The employee is aware that others are also late in the mornings.

6 Morale in your organisation is low. Working conditions have deteriorated because of lack of investment. Managers are hard-pressed and irritable. Staff turnover is high. Productivity is low. A meeting of departmental heads has been called to suggest solutions. Simulate the meeting.

7 Two members of staff have been at loggerheads recently over what each considers as an intrusion of the other into his job. One orders office stationery, while the other supervises secretarial staff and ensures they are equipped to work efficiently. Each accuses the other of inefficiency. Matters come to a head and the manager decides to sort the matter out. Simulate any resulting interviews and analyse your solutions.

8 Your organisation recently advertised for a personal secretary for the accounts manager. Good shorthand and typewriting speeds were required, together with some ability with figures. Draw up a job specification, compile the display advertisement and arrange for members of the group to apply for the position. If possible, duplicate a schedule describing the post and also, application forms. Form an interviewing panel to interview short-listed applicants and then simulate the interviews, recording each one for subsequent analysis.

9 Make contact with a large local organisation. Find out what types of meeting it conducts, how frequently and in what areas of work. Summarise your findings in an oral report to your group.

10 Interview members of your organisation on their attitudes to taking part in meetings. (It will help to design a small questionnaire.) Collate your findings and report back orally to your group.

11 Select one of the Post Office Telecommunications services. Research the service and then write an article for your organisation's house journal describing the range of the service and its current costs.

12 Find out about the Post Office's Confravision service. When you have gathered your material, draft a memorandum to be sent to senior staff outlining its advantages and how the service may be obtained.

13 Assume you work for an organisation using a PMBX system with 10 external lines and 40 extensions. Find out how the system operates and then compose a leaflet to be given to new junior staff explaining how they should use the system and practise good telephone techniques.

14 Recently you have received a number of letters from customers unhappy about the way they have been treated on the telephone when making a complaint about your firm's products. You have called a meeting of all staff to explain to them your company's new procedure for handling telephone complaints. Draft the procedure in notice form. Explain its principal points orally to assembled staff.

15 An irate customer telephones to complain about the non-delivery of goods promised faithfully two days ago. The delay has been caused by an unofficial 'go-slow' in the factory. Simulate the telephone call.

16 Examine the diagrams of seating arrangements for meetings. Decide which plan would be most appropriate for which sort of meeting. Suggest any short-comings in any of the seating plans illustrated. (See p25.)

17 Simulate a committee meeting of your student association. Any of the following agenda items may be discussed:
    a Increasing student participation
    b Extending the scope of activities
    c Voluntary help in the community
    d Organising a special event for charity

18 Tape-record one of the discussions from the Discussion Topics list. Analyse the progress of the discussion and its conclusions. Establish how far arguments were rationally based and how far emotionally biased. Try to establish the quality of the conclusions reached. Make notes of the proceedings. Deliver an oral report to someone who was not present; ask him or her to validate it against the taped transcript.

19 Write an article for the *Receptionists' Quarterly Journal* about non-verbal communication and how the ability to recognise and interpret NVC signals can help receptionists in their work.

20 Hold a discussion with your whole group. Seek to establish what the group considers to be the most important factors influencing the ability to use the spoken word successfully. Produce a report of the discussion.

Discussion topics

1 Effective oral communication techniques tend to be overlooked because people are loath to admit – even to themselves – that they are less than expert in any aspect.

2 The way a person speaks is a highly personal matter. People are best left to 'sort things out' for themselves.

3 Studying the way people communicate non-verbally is rather like hitting them below the belt.

4 Too much consideration of oral communication techniques destroys natural, unselfconscious rapport between people.

5 The interviewing process, since it is quite artificial, rarely arrives at any meaningful conclusions.

6 In the interview situation, there is, inevitably, a conflict between truth and self-projection.

7 The interview process is loaded against the reserved, quiet and introverted. Yet more often than not they may be better in the job than the brash, assertive or plausible candidate.

8 The telephone is an interrupting inconvenience in organisations far more frequently than it is a time-saving helpmate.

9 There's far too much mystique preached about using the telephone – you just pick the thing up, make contact and talk!

10 The ability to use the telephone is generally taken for granted. Yet the national bill for its misuse and abuse must run into millions.

11 Meetings are usually little more than opportunities for people to confirm their innate prejudices to each other.

12 Nothing is achieved through meetings that couldn't be done more quickly, cheaply and with much less fuss by a series of individual conversations.

13 Contributing effectively at meetings has more to do with listening than with speaking.

14 Meetings are for bureaucrats. The doers are usually out of the office, busily doing!

Case studies

Professor Arnold's breakdown

Today is the day of Auto Components Ltd's Annual Sales Conference, which has been organised by Mr Charles Dutton, sales director. The conference is to follow this programme:

Auto Components Limited
Annual Sales Meeting

0930—1000	Assemble in coffee lounge
1000—1015	Opening Address by Mr G. Rose, managing director
1015—1100	'Profitable Retail Marketing' Professor James Arnold
1100—1145	'Better Selling Techniques' Mr Paul Hendrix
1145—1230	Open forum
1230—1400	Lunch
1400—1530	Study groups
1530—1545	Tea
1545—1630	Plenary session

The Annual Conference is taking place in the company's Conference Room at its Head Office. The time is 0935. Mr Dutton is already in the Conference Room making final arrangements with Mr Hendrix. Professor Arnold has not yet arrived.

At this moment the telephone rings in the office of Mr Dutton's personal assistant. It is Professor Arnold, ringing from a public telephone box opposite the Hare and Hounds, Barringford, a rural village some 23 miles from Head Office. When the personal assistant takes the call, Professor Arnold explains that his car has broken down; he sounds agitated and proposes to walk down into the village to see if he can find a garage or a bus.

Assignment

Either:
Discuss what action the personal assistant should take.
Or:
Simulate the telephone conversation and any ensuing telephone calls or actions.
Auto Components has a modern, extensively installed PMBX switchboard system.

'A little something I dreamed up!'

Hotex Furnishings Ltd is a company which manufactures and sells a range of furniture and fittings to hotels and restaurants. The firm was founded by Sir Alfred Gaskin, a forthright and determined person and a confirmed entrepreneur. Much of the company's success has been due to his efforts.

The personal secretary to Mr John Chesterton, managing director, has, among her responsibilities, the job of looking after bookings of the directors' dining suite, which seats 10 people, has its own drinks cabinet and is serviced by Mrs Rosina Carter, an extremely capable but rather temperamental staff restaurant manageress.

Today, Mr Chesterton has called a working lunch meeting in the dining suite for eight of the company's marketing executives at 12.45 p.m. At present he is holding an important meeting with accounts staff preparing for the annual audit.

The time is now 11.30 a.m. The telephone rings in the personal secretary's office of Mr Chesterton's suite. It is Sir Alfred on the line:

'Hello, Carol? Sir Alfred here. I'm at the Phoenix Hotel. I've been selling the directors here our new line in dining tables and chairs, and I'm pretty sure I've won them over. But it needs a few final touches. So I want you to contact Mrs Carter straight away and tell her I'm bringing six guests and myself over for drinks and lunch at about one. I shall need the dining suite, of course. You know the drill. I realise it's a bit short notice, but this could mean a really big order if they buy for their chain. See if you can get Mrs C. to pull something out of the bag. Must go now or I'll be missed!'

Assignment

Either discuss how the personal secretary should resolve the situation.
Or:
Simulate any subsequent arrangements made over the telephone.

Pulses race over communications at Pulsar!

A meeting has been called at Pulsar Electronics Ltd to discuss the proposed appointment of a Communication Officer, whose job would be to coordinate company communications. Present at the meeting are: John White, managing director and chairman; Kay James, Personnel Manager; David Kean, Sales Manager; Lawrence Carr, Marketing Manager; Caroline Brooks, Office Manager; Harry Brent, Production Manager; Jean Bates, Company Secretary and Peter Short, Accounts Manager.

Chairman:
Right. Everyone's here. I think we should start. As you know, I have called this meeting to discuss the proposed appointment of a Communication Officer. The company's growth and dispersed buildings have made internal communication more difficult. It has therefore been suggested that someone working full-time to coordinate communication would improve the situation. Who would like to start the ball rolling?

Harry Brent:
I'm going to lay my cards on the table. I think the idea, though fine in principle, will never work in practice. I remember when we tried employing a trouble-shooter in the Works. The thing was a flop because the operatives still went through their union channels and management went up the traditional line.

Lawrence Carr:
Just a moment, Harry, I'm not sure a Works trouble-shooter and a Communication Officer are quite the same thing. As I see it, this new post will enable someone to coordinate areas like the house magazine, notices, internal publicity generally and to act as an advisor to senior staff – like yourself.

Peter Short:
That's all very well, Larry, but I think Harry's got a point. Without sufficient authority this new Officer will be a loose floater. Departmental heads will still keep control of any important communications.

Kay James:
Peter and Harry are both right – to a degree. As I see it, this new post is a natural for Personnel Department. After all, we already run the house magazine and are deeply committed to personnel communications.

Harry Brent:
Oho! Another lieutenant for Kay's Commandos in the pipe-line! Do I detect a take-over bid?

Chairman: (cutting in)
That was uncalled for, Harry. I wonder though whether attachment to any particular department would be appropriate in this case.

Kay James: (ruffled)
Well, so far all we've had from some quarters (looking hard at Harry) is a completely negative attitude. At least mine was a *constructive* proposal. . . .

David Kean:
In my view, I think we're all looking at this from too personal a position. Larry's right. There are a number of important functions going by the board because none of us has the time to devote to them. Obviously the job would call for tact and initiative, and clearly there would be overlap in, say, Personnel and Training. But surely the value of a new post would be to have an expert, independent and with no departmental axe to grind. I see no reason why he or she could not report to the M.D.

Caroline Brooks:
I've been sitting here listening, because I had no fixed views when I came in. If you don't mind my saying so, everything seems to be proceeding a little too fast. Surely the best approach would be to establish whether departmental heads are for or against in principle – since their cooperation would be essential – and then to draw up a job specification and description which 'a' would work and 'b' other heads would accept.

Harry Brent:
Never underestimate a woman! If *you* don't mind my saying so, Caroline, I think you're trying to push us into a quick decision before we've even had time to have a proper exploratory discussion. How can we decide in principle before we've had a chance to examine the situation fully. It's a big decision. I don't think we should rush into it. . . .

Assignment

Assess the contribution of each member.
Comment on the Chairman's role.
Suggest how you think the meeting *a:* would end and *b:* should end.
Carry on the meeting by role-play simulation.

Interview simulation

Assistant required for office administration manager . . .

This simulation is designed to involve the whole group. The interviewing panel may comprise up to three members. Authentic roles would be: managing director, personnel manager, office administration manager. Three candidate profiles are outlined below, but more candidate roles may be devised to provide a larger short-list if required. Other members of the group should be divided into two sections – observers of the interviewers and observers of the interviewees. They should meet to decide upon what they will assess and design a check-list to note performances. Each group of observers should report its assessments after the interview simulations have taken place. Interviewers and interviewees should then be asked for their reactions and impressions.

The situation
A post has recently been advertised for an assistant to the Office Administration Manager of Reliant Employment Bureau Ltd. The company has 30 branches throughout the country placing secretarial, clerical and junior management personnel both in full-time and temporary positions.

The job
The duties of the assistant will mainly involve relieving the Office Administration Manager of some of his work-load. Specifically the post will include:

reponsibility for the company's stationery supplies, maintenance of existing administration systems, records, filing etc. drafting of correspondence, memoranda, reports, composing advertisements, taking part in meetings, telephone reception. Commercial experience is not essential as training will be given. Shorthand and type-writing skills would be advantageous.

	Candidate A	*Candidate B*	*Candidate C*
Age:	18	27	38
Status:	Single	Married (no children)	Divorced (boy 15, girl 10)
Education:	Park View Comprehensive and West Park College of Further Education	Westerham Grammar School	Hightown College and Cumbria University (left after one year to get married)
Qualifications:	4 'O'-levels BEC National Award in Business Studies; including Shorthand/Typewriting option	6 'O'-levels 2 'A'-levels Shorthand/Typewriting speeds: 90/40	5 'O'-levels 3 'A'-levels Read English at University
Commercial:	Part-time Holiday Jobs One job as 'Temp' in busy office	4 years in local tax office 2 years as cabin crew member in airline: grounded with blood-pressure: later joined engineering company – made redundant	Housewife until 25 divorced at 30 succession of part-time jobs; refresher shorthand/typewriting course at local College just completed

Physical Appearance   ⎫ Candidates should decide upon these factors and play a role. For example, hesitant or assured,
Interests, Circumstances: ⎭ social or solitary, flat renter or mortgagee etc.

Note for candidates:
Use the above information to provide the basic framework for your 'personality', background and career. Ensure that you have prepared your ground sufficiently.

Note for observers:
Every observer should have a full brief of each candidate's background, including any 'skeletons in cupboards' deliberately 'planted' by candidates for interviewers to discover!

Multi-media assignment

All out at Alumix?

Before attempting this assignment you will need to research the following: Dismissal and Grievance Procedures; Summary and Unfair Dismissal; Industrial Tribunal Procedures.

Situation

For the past three weeks, the wife of Mr Fred Jackson, a machine operator at Alumix Alloys, has been seriously ill. Fred has been very worried about her and is currently on a course of tranquillisers prescribed by his family doctor, but is still at work.

Fred operates a machine that needs constant attention, and Alumix's company regulations state that a relief operator must be summoned to take over temporarily if the machine is left for any reason. If left unminded, the machine could cause serious injury to other factory workers, and three weeks ago, Alumix had issued a works reminder about the dangers.

Feeling rather agitated, and in need of a smoke, Fred leaves his machine, thinking he'll only be away 'for a few minutes', and goes into the staff restroom. He has only been there a minute or two when he is startled by the appearance of Mr Alfred Parker, the foreman for his part of the factory. Fred becomes extremely upset and is unable to express himself very clearly. Mr Parker is known as a strict but fair man.

Mr Parker reports the absence of Fred from his machine to the assistant works manager. Both consider Fred to have been in breach of company regulations.

The management of Alumix take a serious view of the situation. Fred is summoned to the works manager's office, and following the company's procedures is summarily dismissed for negligence.

Fred returns to his locker in a very upset state, claiming to his friends that he was not given a chance to state his side of the case. At this stage the shop steward of Fred's trade union, the Allied Workers' Association, arrives and asks Fred to put him in the picture. The shop steward's view is that Fred has been 'unfairly dismissed', and he determines to take the matter to his branch.

Meanwhile, word of Fred's summary dismissal has spread round the factory like wildfire! The factory staff have decided to take matters into their own hands and are threatening an unofficial walk-out, claiming that Fred is being victimised. Extremely concerned, Mr Parker tries to telephone the works manager, but obtains no reply. He therefore, determines to ring Mr French, the company's personnel manager. He is out, but his personal assistant, Miss Sally Barnes takes the call.

The following day, the Works Committee, including trade union representatives, seeks and obtains a meeting with the management of Alumix to try to sort out the problem.

Several weeks pass (you may at this stage assume that the meeting between the Works Committee and management was unsuccessful). Both Alumix and the Allied Workers' Association think they have a strong case, and Fred's dismissal is taken to the local Industrial Tribunal for judgment.

Assignment

1   Face-to-face encounter
Simulate the encounter between Fred and Mr Parker. Two of Fred's friends, taking a legitimate break enter the restroom and join in.

2   Dismissal interview
Simulate the interview between Fred and the works management personnel.

3   Briefing conversation
Simulate the conversation between Fred and the shop steward, Mr Tom Harris.

4   Telephone call
Simulate the call between Mr Parker and Sally Barnes, and any subsequent action taken.

5   Meeting
Simulate the meeting between the Works Committee and management.

6   Hearing
Having prepared a case, a management and union team simulate the hearing before the Industrial Tribunal panel.

People and Communication

Use of English

Desmond W Evans

Contents

Acknowledgments

The author and publishers have made every effort to trace the ownership of all copyright material and to obtain permission from the owners of copyright.
Thanks are due to the following for permission to reprint the material indicated:

Invalid Children's Aid Association for the extract from 'Spelling for the Dyslexic Child', *Winter Bulletin* 1966, G C Cotterell and A D Ballantyne, p19.

R Grant, Advisory Teacher Reading (Secondary), West Sussex Council, for his advice on p19.

PITMAN EDUCATION LIMITED
39 Parker Street, London WC2B 5PB

Associated Companies
Pitman Publishing Pty Ltd, Melbourne
Pitman Publishing New Zealand Ltd, Wellington

© Desmond W Evans 1978

First published in Great Britain 1978
Reprinted 1979, 1980

Text set in 10/12pt Sabon
printed and bound in Great Britain
at The Pitman Press, Bath

ISBN 0 273 01246 0 (bound book)
     0 273 01247 9 (module pack)

Introduction

'Put those semaphore flags away Jenkins! Good grief! There must be an easier way of confirming Hotchkinson's order . . .!'

The ability to use English correctly and effectively is an essential skill which all those working in business or the public service must seek to master.

Many people speak or write English intuitively. They do not realise that often the most effective use of the language is the result of much conscious effort and practice.

Guesses at spellings or 'stabs' at punctuation will not satisfy the conscientious communicator. Neither will rambling sentence-structures nor the inappropriate use of slang find a place in the professional's use of English.

English is the medium through which objectives are achieved, people motivated and productive human relations strengthened. It is therefore essential for the manager, secretary or clerk to appreciate how important it is to speak or write in a way which will achieve positive results.

For example, a business letter may be the only form of contact between a retailing company and a potential customer. The manner in which a friendly and courteous receptionist takes a call may make all the difference to an important buyer. The carefully judged recommendations of a report may have far-reaching consequences. A persuasive sales letter may produce thousands of pounds' worth of orders.

For everyone, then, using English effectively is a vital skill well worth the pains taken to acquire. Like any craft, expertise in English requires a committed apprenticeship. When words are the 'tools of the trade', the good communicator must learn to build structures which are not merely purpose-built but also pleasing and elegant!

Though such skills may take time, patience and effort to secure, the rewards which they bring will be well worthwhile and last a lifetime.

Using English effectively

Syntax and grammar

Understanding the rules which govern the structuring of ideas into accepted sense-groups or patterns of meaning.

Spelling and punctuation

Reproducing words in their accepted form and linking them together clearly and unambiguously.

Vocabulary

Developing a reservoir of general and specialist words and expressions which permit the accurate and effective transmission of the spoken or written word.

Sensitivity and discrimination

Acquiring a feeling for the nuances and shades of meaning which words convey within their contexts.

Style

Appreciating the different effects which various combinations of words, expressions and structures will impart and developing the ability to express ideas in informative, discursive or persuasive ways.

Critical faculties

Being prepared to look critically at what is to be said or written, to measure consciously its likely effect and to modify it where necessary.

Awareness of the recipient

Establishing a rapport with the recipient so that he is receptive to the message.

Grammar

The parts of speech

What is a noun?

Nouns are the naming words in English which act as 'labels' for objects, ideas, people, places, works of art and so on. Nouns which name real, physical things such as 'letter' or 'pen' are called **concrete** nouns. Nouns which express thoughts, ideas and feelings such as 'efficiency' or 'communication' are called **abstract**.

Sometimes nouns are sub-divided into the following categories:

Common: everyday objects or concepts – book, speed, garden

Proper: names for people, places, works of art – John, Pitman 2000, London, the Mona Lisa

(Notice that proper nouns are given capital letters.)

Collective: names for groupings or collections – team, jury, class

What is a pronoun?

Pronouns are also naming or identifying words which can replace nouns. They may refer to people:

I, you, him, her, mine, ours

or to things:

Where is *it*? I don't agree with *that*.

Sometimes they are used in questions:

Who is coming? *What* did you say?

or to complete meanings:

I cut *myself*.

In addition they may be used to introduce further information about a noun:

This is the gentleman *who* earlier wished to see you.
The report, *which* concerns office reorganisation, will be ready tomorrow.

What is an article?

Not to be overlooked are the hard-working definite and indefinite articles: *the* job, *a* report, *an* idea.

What is an adjective?

Adjectives are essentially describing words which extend the meaning of nouns or pronouns:

The secretary typed the *important* letter.
A *good* manager looks after *his* staff.
It's only *little* me!

Sometimes adjectives are used to denote possession:

my desk, *their* pay, *your* turn

or to identify a particular object or idea:

this suggestion, *that* idea

or to introduce questions:

What price did you agree?
Which way did he go?

As a general rule, adjectives in English usually come immediately before the noun or pronoun they qualify. But not always:

The office will be *busy* tomorrow.

What is a verb?

Verbs are the words which 'do' –that is, convey actions, identify thought processes or denote states of being:

She *typed* the letter and *posted* it.
He *considered* his next move carefully.
The manager *was* aware of the problem.

Verbs are used in two principal ways:
actively when verbs directly express the actions of the doer:

The manager *dictated* the letter.

or **passively** when the structure of the sentence is changed to make the doer become the agent by which something is done:

The letter *was dictated* by the manager.

Using verbs passively tends to make the message more impersonal and one trick of its use is that the agent is sometimes omitted:

Your services *are* no longer *required* (by me).

The passive is used in this way as a means of conveying unpopular news, where its communicator pretends not to have been involved.

What is an adverb?

Adverbs are used to extend the meaning of verbs or adjectives:

She can type *quickly*.
He spoke *slowly* and *carefully*.
We need an *extremely* fast duplicator.

Adverbs indicate: How? When? Where? To what extent? How many? etc.

Most adverbs are easily recognised by their -ly endings.

What is a conjunction?

Conjunctions are the linking words which are used to join ideas together:

The report was concise *and* had been clearly constructed. The letter was brief *but* it included the main points.

Some conjunctions – and, but, next, then, yet – are used to link ideas together which could stand independently of one another:

The report was concise. It had been clearly constructed.

Other types of conjunction are used to link together a main and a dependent or subordinate idea:

They decided to repeat the advertisement, *although* the cost had risen sharply.
He decided to answer the letter immediately *because* it was so important.

In order to vary the way in which ideas are presented, conjunctions introducing dependent ideas sometimes begin sentences:

As you have worked so successfully, I have no hesitation in recommending you for promotion.

Conjunctions frequently used to introduce dependent ideas are:

when, where, why, what, as, since, because, although, though, even though, if, whether, so that, in order that, with the result that, after, unless, as soon as.

Some conjunctions are used as paired sets: either . . . or, neither . . . nor, both . . . and, not only . . . but also.

What is a preposition?

Basically, prepositions are locating words and come immediately in front of nouns or pronouns:

under the blotter, *across* the road, *up* the ladder, *of* him, *to* me

Sometimes they are used to form parts of verbs:

to get *down to*, to stand *up to*

What is an interjection?

The interjection is a part of speech which transmits a sense of feeling or emotion: Whew! Ouch! Oh! Ah!

Used most frequently in direct speech, the interjection may express relief:

'Whew! That was close!'

or delight:

'Ah, that's beautiful!'

What is the point?

What, then, are the practical advantages of being able to identify the various parts of speech?

Firstly, with knowledge rather than intuition comes self-confidence in recognising the different components or 'building blocks' of English. Constructions and sense groups appear far less intimidating as the writer begins to feel master of the medium.

In addition, such knowledge has distinct, practical value once the writer has developed the ability to recognise the function of each part of speech. If, for example, he had written or was editing this sentence:

The paint spreads quick and even

he would recognise that 'quick' and 'even' both modify the verb 'spreads' and so need the -ly ending of an adverb

The paint spreads quickly and evenly.

Syntax

Constructing sentences

Just as there is a practical value in being able to recognise the parts of speech, so it is also important to be able to understand the various ways in which sentences are constructed.

How, for example, does the writer come to recognise that

With reference to your letter of 21st February.

is not a sentence? Intuition may create in him a sense of unease, but there is no substitute for knowing and therefore being able to correct it:

I refer to your letter of 21st February.

'You know, Carter, there are times when I think there's a lot to be said for the intuitive approach!'

What is a sentence?

A useful definition of a sentence is:
A group of words which conveys a complete meaning.
Sentences comprise two basic components:

a subject +	a predicate
Mr Brown	arrived early.
I	am not going.
The last train	has already left.
You	have not signed this letter.

All sentences require a subject – a word which is a noun or a pronoun or a longer group of words which has the force of a noun – and a predicate.

What is a finite verb?

All sentences require a finite verb – a verb which carries out the 'action' of the 'doer' or subject word. Finite verbs need to meet three requirements. They must possess:

A number   singular or plural
A person   first, second or third
A tense   past, present, future or conditional

The verb 'arrived' in the above example is singular, in the third person and in a past tense.

Thus basic sentences need to contain a subject and a finite verb:

He awoke. The visitor left.

When sentences contain a single subject and a single finite verb they are called simple. When more than one subject and finite verb are used in linked sense groups they are called complex.

What is a predicate?

A predicate may include not just a finite verb, but also words which enlarge the verb's meaning:

He awoke *early*.

or which provide more information about the subject:

The manager felt *irritable*
Mr Brown is *our chief buyer*

Some finite verbs need an 'action receiver' or object to complete their meaning:

I have bought *a new typewriter*.

Simple sentences, then, may be constructed as follows:

a **Subject + finite verb**
b **Subject + finite verb + enlargers**
c **Subject + finite verb + object**

Useful definitions

A phrase

A phrase is a group of words which are related in sense and are often introduced by a preposition:

at the moment, on his way to the office, in the ledger

or conjunction:

after a busy day's trading, as soon as possible

Phrases do not include finite verbs, but may be introduced by participles:
Turning the corner he saw the factory ahead.

A clause

A clause is a group of words which forms a component of a sentence and possesses both a subject and a finite verb. Clauses are linked in sentences by conjunctions:

He caught the train although *he arrived late at the station.*

A main clause

Main clauses may form complex sentences by being joined together by what are termed coordinating conjunctions:

He stopped and *he called his secretary on the intercom*, then *he resumed drafting the report.*

A dependent clause

Dependent clauses cannot stand alone and are linked by subordinating conjunctions to main clauses in complex sentences:

It is impossible to reach a decision   <u>because</u> we lack sufficient information.

<u>As</u> the market is so sluggish,   we shall have to reduce our prices,   <u>even though</u> it may mean a reduction in our gross profit.

A sentence

A sentence is a group of words which conveys a meaning complete in itself. Every sentence must possess a subject and a finite verb and conventionally they begin with a capital letter and end with a full stop.
(Note that phrases like:

Down in the mouth? You need Fizz, the fun drink!

and,

Rocky and reeling. That was the sad state of Monolithic Enterprises following rumours of a takeover bid.

are accepted conventions of advertising and journalism but such techniques are best avoided until the more conventional techniques of sentence-writing have been mastered.)

A simple sentence

A simple sentence is one which contains a single subject and a single finite verb in its predicate.

A complex sentence

A complex sentence is one which comprises two or more clauses which may be main or dependent. It must, however, contain at least one main clause.

Table of verb tenses

Infinitive to write
Present participle writing
Past participle written

Tenses

	Active	*Passive*
Present	She:	The letter:
simple	writes	is written
continuous	is writing	is being written
Past		
simple	wrote	was written
continuous	was writing	was being written
Perfect		
simple	has written	has been written
continuous	has been writing	
Past perfect		
simple	had written	had been written
continuous	had been writing	
Future		
simple	will write	will be written
continuous	will be writing	
Future perfect		
simple	will have written	will have been written
continuous	will have been writing	
Conditional		
simple	would have written	would have been written
continuous	would have been writing	

What is a subject?

Subjects are the 'doer' words or groups of words which control or govern the actions of finite verbs. They may be common or proper nouns:

The report is on your desk.
Miss Jenkins is in Scotland.

or they may be pronouns:

They thanked him for his help.

In addition they may take the form of a whole phrase:

Complaining about the poor service got him nowhere.

or even a clause:

That you were ignorant of company regulations is no excuse.

(The terms 'phrase' and 'clause' are explained on the previous page.)

In English, subjects normally come immediately before the verbs they govern. Sometimes, however, additional ideas about the subject are inserted between it and its verb:

Miss Johnson, *a most efficient member of staff*, will look after you.
The sales representative, *who was experienced*, soon made the sale.

How are verbs used?

As we have seen, finite verbs in sentences are governed by subjects and need to possess a number, person and tense.

When verbs literally convey ideas of action they are easy to identify:

She *cut* the paper on the guillotine.
Jack *drives* carefully.

Many verbs, however, express abstract ideas:

He *motivates* his staff well.

and some verbs consist of more than one word:

I *shall have left* for Bristol by the time you arrive.

In order to recognise verbs successfully a knowledge of their tenses is necessary, as well as an understanding of their active and passive use.

Active and passive

Verbs which take objects, when used actively, convey the action of the subject or doer on to an action-receiver or object:

Miss Johnson   typed   the report.
<u>subject</u>   <u>finite</u>   <u>object</u>
                 <u>verb</u>

The same idea may, however, be expressed passively, where the object becomes the grammatical subject of the sentence and the active subject becomes an agent in the passive:

The report   was typed   by Miss Johnson.
<u>subject</u>   <u>finite</u>   <u>agent</u>
              <u>verb</u>

The passive structures of verbs are formed by using the verbs 'to be' and, when necessary the verb 'to have' as well with the past participle of the verb:

is being typed, was typed, has been typed

Verb forms as adjectives and nouns

There are two parts of the verb which are used in sentences, not as verbs, but as nouns or adjectives. Present participle as an adjective:

The *driving* rain obscured the wind-screen.

Past participle as an adjective:

The *typed* letters are ready to sign.

Present participle form as a noun (gerund):

His *going* surprised us all.

What is an object?

Objects in sentences receive the action of the verb. Certain verbs which need objects to complete their meaning are called transitive. Verbs which are capable of conveying a meaning without the need for an object are called intransitive.

It is sometimes helpful to think of objects as answering the question 'What?':

The manager	arranged	a meeting
<u>subject</u>	<u>finite</u>	<u>object</u>
	<u>verb</u>	

(What did the manager arrange?)

Some objects take the form of word groups:

The personnel manager wrote *a long and difficult letter.*

Objects may sometimes take the form of clauses:

The inspector detected *what appeared to be a flaw in the casing.*

Remember that when transitive verbs are used in the passive, the object of the active voice of the verb becomes the subject:

A *long and difficult letter* was written by the personnel manager.
What appeared to be a flaw in the casing was detected by the inspector.

As will be seen later, there are a number of uses to which the passive voice of the verb may be put.

Enlarging intransitive verbs

When verbs are used intransitively (when they do not need an object), adverbial words or expressions may be used to extend their meaning:

He awoke *with a start.*
The meeting continued *for quite some time.*

What are complex sentences?

So far we have considered sentences which are called simple – they contain a single subject and predicate. Many sentences are constructed, however, which are composed of two or more clauses with the following relationships:

main clause + main clause
She worked hard on the report
and
she did not finish until 7.30 p.m.

main clause + dependent clause
He asked her to stay late
because
he needed the report for the next day.

Main and dependent clauses may be combined by using conjunctions in a number of different ways:

Dependent	Although it was not entirely convenient,
Main	she did not mind working late
Dependent	because she realised the importance of completing the report.

Ideas are frequently linked in this way to form complex sentences which provide interest and variety for the reader and which also serve to indicate the relationships between ideas. Remember that dependent clauses cannot stand alone. They need to be accompanied by main clauses. Also, all clauses, whether main or dependent, must possess both a subject and a finite verb.

One of the problems of writing complex sentences is that it is easy to lose control of the meaning by stringing clauses together ungrammatically:

The young typist, who wanted to make a good impression when she arrived for work on her first day, although she was feeling nervous because the surroundings were unfamiliar, despite the friendly greeting she received from the commissionaire when she entered the lofty office block.

Here we wait in vain for the main verb to follow 'the young typist'. It is much better to shorten the structure of the ideas by constructing two sentences:

The young typist wanted to make a good impression when she arrived for work on her first day. She received a friendly greeting from the commissionaire when she entered the lofty office block, but was feeling nervous because the surroundings were unfamiliar.

Practical assignments

Parts of speech

Identify the parts of speech underlined in the following sentences:
1 I asked him to read it.
2 The large envelopes are in the top drawer.
3 The invoices have been checked.
4 He read the report slowly and made his notes methodically.
5 I am pleased to announce that Amalgamated Steel has made extremely good progress during the past year.
6 His instructions were clear.
7 An elderly man carrying a bulky briefcase arrived at reception.
8 Although its price was competitive, the new product sold poorly.
9 Either we increase production or we turn down firm orders.
10 I shall have finished checking the draft by the time you return and then it will be ready for typing.
11 The meeting will require my staying late at the office.
12 'Oh! I never expected such a smart retirement present!'

Syntax

Identify the subject, finite verb, object or adverbial verb enlarger in the following sentences:
1 The last train leaves at ten o'clock.
2 'You have designed a masterpiece!'
3 An increase in output is urgently needed.
4 I followed his instructions precisely.
5 Everyone heard what he said.
6 What he said echoed loudly.
7 The speaker should have arrived last night.
8 The office party has been postponed indefinitely.
9 The performance of the energetic sales force was praised by the managing director.
10 The art of management requires achieving objectives.

Clauses and conjunctions

Identify the main and dependent clauses in the following sentences and state which words are the linking conjunctions.
1 If you do not arrive more punctually, I shall be obliged to take further action.
2 Whatever the market research may forecast, the board is determined to go ahead.
3 We shall have to cancel the project as public response has been totally hostile.
4 When he had finished interviewing the last candidate, he reluctantly began to scan his notes because he knew he would not have time tomorrow.
5 As soon as you have time, Mr Jones would like you to see him in his office, which is on the fifth floor.

Sentence structures

What defects in syntax can you find in the following sentences:
1 Hoping to receive your reply without delay.
2 Unless we hear from you in the meantime.
3 However much we would like to help you.
4 Please let me know as soon as possible.
5 Despite our repeated reminders regarding non-payment of your account, which is long overdue.
6 The prices of our range of kitchen utensils, which, as you know, have not increased, despite the pressure of the increased cost in raw materials.
7 Further to your recent request for samples of our new range of fabrics.

'He seems to have found a whole new purpose in life.'

Usage: helpful hints

Remember also that collective nouns may, on occasions take either a singular or a plural verb depending upon the sense – whether the components of the collective noun are seen as a single unified unit or as separate sub-groups:

'*Has* the working party found a solution?'
'No, the working party *are* divided into two distinct camps at present.'

Many writers experience problems with grammar, syntax and usage in the course of composing written documents. Such errors spring from a variety of sources – haste, a failure to read through and check a draft or from simply having missed learning a particular form of accepted usage.

Some of the most frequently encountered problems of usage are as follows:

Agreement

Remember that a plural subject requires a plural verb:

The sales assistant who sold it and the engineer who installed it ~~is~~ *are* responsible for the customer's complaint.

Remember also that pronouns should be used consistently and not changed because of an oversight:

I am
~~We are~~ sure you will be pleased with the new model and I look forward to hearing from you.

Incomplete sentences

Incomplete sentences are usually written as a result of haste or a failure to check a draft:

With regard to your recent order for 100 boxes of carbon paper.
Further to your letter of 14th June.

Remember that all sentences require both a subject and a finite verb:

Further to your letter of 14th June, I am pleased to inform you that your order has now been despatched.

Each everyone nobody all

Notice that the following generally take singular verbs:

Each is hand-made.
Everyone is present.
Nobody is willing to stand.

but that 'all' usually takes a plural verb:

All are agreed that the decision should be deferred

Misrelating the participle and the noun

When beginning sentences with participle constructions care should be taken to ensure that they are not misrelated to the noun immediately following:

Walking along the road, the tile hit him on the head.
Having typed half the letter, the telephone rang insistently.

Clearly, tiles cannot walk and telephones do not type! Such sentences need restructuring to provide the correct subject of 'walking' and 'having typed':

As he was walking down the road, a tile hit him on the head.
Having typed half the letter, the secretary heard the telephone, which rang insistently.

Mixing metaphors

Linking two quite distinct metaphors is often the result of muddled thinking and sometimes produces humorous results:

'You must put your foot down with a firm hand.'
'As long as we all keep our shoulders to the wheel, we'll have a smooth flight'.

Using words wrongly

Some words are frequently used wrongly as a result of confusion over their meaning:

illegible
This faint copy is quite ~~unreadable~~!

Placed as he was in a neutral position, he was able to

disinterested
voice an opinion which was quite ~~uninterested~~.

affected
He was quite ~~effected~~ by receiving so many letters of

encouragement.

Who or whom?

Some writers find it difficult in certain sentences to decide whether 'who' or 'whom' is correct: as in

The umbrella belongs to the customer who I served.

A simple rule of thumb will solve this particular problem. In cases of uncertainty, substitute who(m) by either:
he she they = who
or, him her them = whom
in the relevant part of the sentence: I served him. (Clearly it cannot be, 'I served he'). Thus the correct version in the above sentence is, 'whom'.

Overloading verbs

In some constructions verbs are sometimes overloaded by being required to express two tenses at once:

Property values have and always will rise in an inflationary economy.

Here, the writer has tried to make a false economy by expecting 'rise' to serve not only as a future tense – 'will rise', but as a perfect tense as well – 'have (risen)'. The sentence needs reconstructing:

Property values have always risen and will always rise in an inflationary economy.

Verbs in their noun forms

When verbs are used in their noun forms as gerunds, they are preceded by the possessive form of the personal pronoun used adjectivally:

'I hope you didn't mind me leaving before the end of your talk.'

The absence of Mr Brown will require you taking the chair at the meeting.

Avoiding the cliché

Clichés are expressions which have suffered from over-use. As a consequence they transmit a tired, stale and sometimes irritating meaning:

It has come to my notice
I am writing . . .
with regard to
with reference to
I note that

Most people resort to the cliché occasionally but the effort to express an idea simply and freshly is always well worthwhile since it helps to maintain the reader's interest.

Practical assignment

The following sentences contain errors of usage. Rewrite them correctly, changing the sentence-structure as little as possible:

1   So long as you don't object to me going, I would be glad of an opportunity to revisit my home town.

2   Regarding your letter of 21st March 19— concerning the delivery of a defective calculator.

3   As the consignment is already three weeks overdue, I would be grateful if you would ensure prompt delivery.

4   On entering the office late, the busy hubbub stopped and all eyes turned towards her.

5   The secretary who I recently employed is proving most conscientious.

6   Who's coat has been left on the coat-stand?

7   His consistent effort led to him winning the 'Salesman Of The Year' award.

8   Though I have not met the buyer who you refer to, I do know the sales manager.

9   Whatever sales approach one employs, the basic requirement is to get the customer on your side.

10   Every time he opens his mouth, he puts his foot in it!

11   The deeds had laid, undiscovered, for over fifteen years in the trunk.

12   We acknowledge your letter of 28th September and are also in receipt of your order for a Summit adding machine.

Punctuation

The system of punctuating written English is perhaps best viewed as a means of ensuring that any message is transmitted both clearly and unambiguously. The system does more than this, however, by providing occasional breathing spaces and by conveying not only what has been written, but, sometimes, the feelings of a writer or speaker.

Basically, there are some eleven major punctuation marks in general use:

. the full stop
, the comma
; the semi-colon
: the colon
' the apostrophe
( ) brackets
? the question mark
! the exclamation mark
- the hyphen
– the dash
" " or ' ' direct speech marks or inverted commas

● The full stop

The full stop has two principal uses. Firstly, it is used to signify the end of a sentence:

He considered his next move carefully. He would call a meeting of his regional managers at the earliest opportunity.

Sometimes a succession of short sentences may be used to obtain a certain effect:

He scanned the memorandum. It told him nothing. He dismissed it entirely.

Although too frequent a use of the above technique may prove irritating, it is generally sound advice to keep sentences short rather than to allow them to ramble. Some researchers have found that constructing sentences with more than 25–30 words leads to comprehension problems on the part of the recipient, particularly if the vocabulary used is multi-syllabic. A useful motto, then, is, 'When in doubt, finish the sentence and start another'.

The other main use of the full-stop is to indicate that a word has been abbreviated:

Mr. Rev. Dr. St. i.e. e.g. etc.

It should be borne in mind, however, that some current practices in typing letters embody 'open punctuation' in their format. This format omits full-stops (and commas) in those parts of the letter other than its body. Similarly, some abbreviations are currently accepted without full-stops, provided that the use is consistent:

OBE Ltd HMS OHMS Mr Mrs

Sometimes abbreviations such as 'a.s.a.p.' are used in messages to indicate 'as soon as possible', but such abbreviations should be avoided in formal documents. Lastly, remember that each sentence begins with a capital letter.

❦ The comma

The comma is used within sentences to indicate a pause between sense-groups of words:

Reaching the corner he stopped, looked both ways, then crossed.

The comma is also used to separate words (or phrases) put into a list:

The drawer contained paper-clips, rubber-bands, pencils and paper.

Another use of the comma is to show that an enlarging or modifying idea has been inserted between a subject and its verb:

The answer, which had been quite unexpected, took them by surprise.

Note, however, that when such an inserted clause defines a preceding noun, no comma is used:

'The book which you ordered is out of print.'

As a general rule, commas are not needed before conjunctions like 'and', 'or', 'but' or 'then' which link main clauses:

He spoke quietly and they listened intently.
'You must hurry or you will be late.'
The visitor was late but his host displayed no sign of irritation.

Some writers use the comma to separate a dependent clause from a main clause when a sentence is started with the former:

Although he worked at a slow and methodical pace, John could be relied upon to keep going when others wilted.

But this usage is by no means universal:

When he had finished he rang for his secretary.

The use of the comma in such constructions perhaps coincides with the need for a breathing space in longer sentences.

There are a number of words in frequent use which are employed with one or more commas:

Lastly, the report indicates that . . .
It proved, however, to be of major importance.
Nevertheless, I should be grateful if . . .
The mistake was, moreover, extremely costly.

In direct speech, the comma may be used to indicate an element of hesitancy on the part of the speaker:

'Oh, and another thing, don't forget to ring when you arrive.'

As outlined above, the comma is used to separate lists of words. Sometimes writers employ several adjectives to describe a single noun:

The report was marred by a loose, rambling, disjointed and careless structure.

Heaping such adjectives together may be a deliberate ploy to create a certain effect, but the inclusion of several adjectives before a single noun smacks of 'overkill' rather than good style.

Some writers, though in a minority, insist, and that is not too strong a word, on using the comma, not just when occasion demands, but indiscriminately, with the effect that sentences limp, totter and stumble along, which can be very irritating, and is quite unnecessary!

As the above sentence amply illustrates, the comma should be used sparingly to assist rather than to impede the reader's understanding of what is written.

The semi-colon

Many writers today tend to shy away from using the semi-colon and it is not used as much as it used to be. It indicates a pause which is longer than the comma but shorter than the full-stop. Most frequently it separates main clauses in the following manner:

The sales campaign had been brilliantly conceived; it caught our main competitors completely unprepared.

In such constructions the semi-colon is particularly effective in securing a dramatic pause before the ensuing statement which thus gains in impact. Notice that such a use of the semi-colon requires that the two ideas expressed in the main clauses are closely related and could, if need be, stand as sentences. The semi-colon in the above example could be replaced by 'and' or 'it caught' by 'catching'. The effect, however, would be to lose the emphasis the semi-colon supplies.

The colon

The colon used to be employed as a stronger stop or break than the semi-colon to separate clauses in a manner similar to that illustrated above. Nowadays it is primarily used to introduce an example or quotation:

I have always found the advice of Polonius in *Hamlet* to be sound: 'Neither a borrower nor a lender be'.

or to preface a list. The list may be set out vertically, as in the notice of a bonus award:

The following members of staff won this month's bonus award:
    Mr J Harris
    Mr T Jones. . . .

Alternatively, the list may be set out in sentence form:

The exhibition will include: typewriters, duplicators, accounting machines, adding machines, audio-dictating equipment and telephone systems.

The inclusion of a dash with the colon :– is now obsolescent.

The apostrophe

The apostrophe has two major uses. The first, used in conjunction with the letter 's', denotes possession:

The secretary's note-book. . . . The manager's report

Notice that when the possessor is *singular* – 'of the secretary', 'of the manager', the apostrophe comes *before* the 's' which should be separated from the rest of the word.

To show possession in the plural the apostrophe is positioned immediately *after* the 's' which is added to most nouns to indicate their plural form:

the representatives' calls
the books' prices

Some nouns, however, change in their plural form:

child   children
woman   women

The apostrophe for such nouns is placed immediately after the final 'n' which is followed by an 's':

women's coats
children's shoes

A very useful rule of thumb is: put an apostrophe at the end of the word and add an 's'. If the word already ends in 's' in most cases the second 's' is omitted.

In addition, there are a large number of nouns ending in 'y' which changes to 'ies' in the plural. Such nouns show possession in this way:

ladies' fashions
secretaries' meeting

In cases of uncertainty, a simple test may be applied to a word suspected of needing an apostrophe 's'. Try to substitute 'of the' followed by the word in question in the sentence or phrase:

the fashions of the ladies
the meeting of the secretaries
the shoes of the children
the report of the manager

If the wording still makes sense, then the apostrophe is needed!
Remember: that when 'its' means 'of it' the apostrophe is not used.

The other use of the apostrophe is to indicate that a letter (or letters) has been omitted from a word which has been contracted:

do not . . . don't
it's . . . it is
telephone . . . 'phone

Such contractions are very frequently used in spoken English but should not be used in any formal, written documents.

( ) Brackets

Brackets are used to separate what is often a secondary or additional idea from the rest of a sentence:

A shortcut (though this is not recommended for beginners) would be to leave out the second step.
He decided to try (although his chances of succeeding were remote) and entered his name on the list.

Sometimes the brackets enclose a source of reference or information:

The results obtained (Appendix C refers) indicated a distinct preference for the blue colour.

? The question mark

The question mark is placed at the end of the sentences which are structured to form direct questions:

'How many did you sell?'
'When does he leave for London?'

As the above examples illustrate, the stop of the question mark serves to replace any other form of sentence-ending punctuation mark. The following practices should be avoided:

'What did he say?.'
'What did she call you?!'

Sometimes speakers introduce questions known as rhetorical questions into speeches. Such questions are used for effect and do not expect any answer. Nevertheless, they require a question mark:

'An entirely new approach is needed. And who among us would deny that a thorough review is long overdue? Once this need is accepted . . .'

Indirect questions, however, do not require a question mark:

He asked if he might be excused.
She enquired whether the train had left.

! The exclamation mark

Exclamation marks are used to indicate feelings of surprise, astonishment, sarcasm, approval or enthusiasm:

Incredible! No other word would do justice to the performance of the new Magiscribe electric typewriter.
'Are you going to the meeting?'
. . . 'You can't be serious!'
'So this is the new model. It's beautiful!'

Some writers endeavour to increase the element of surprise or approval by placing several exclamation marks together. Such a practice is an accepted convention in comic books, but has no place in serious writing. Lastly, the exclamation mark suffers from over-use and is best used sparingly.

— The hyphen

The hyphen's function is to link together either words or parts of words. When it is employed to link words together it does so because they have become so closely connected in meaning that they are almost one word:

leap-frog
master-at-arms
turn-table.

Some words, however, have been used in conjunction for so long that any hyphen has been dropped: racecourse, turnover, mouthpiece. It is difficult to know for certain when to run words together and when to hyphenate them and in cases of uncertainty the dictionary must be the arbiter.

The other use of the hyphen is to join parts of words together which must each be pronounced separately:

co-edition
co-existence
pre-emptive.

Some current writers are tending to drop this use of

the hyphen and run such words together, but its use is certainly helpful.

The hyphen is also used in typing and printing to indicate the continuation of a word which starts at the end of one line and finishes on the next.

— The dash

The dash is used in a way similar to that of brackets. It signifies that some utterance or additional statement has been inserted or added:

'I'll come straight to the point – oh, but forgive me I see your glass is empty –.'
The sales of accessories – in fact the entire sales performance – has been extremely satisfying!

‘’ Direct speech marks/inverted commas

The use of direct speech marks is restricted to showing exactly which words were spoken by a particular speaker:

'I don't know,' he said, 'but I'll find out.'

When a second speaker is introduced, the spoken words begin a new paragraph. The punctuation of the direct speech is all placed *within* the direct speech marks.

Double or single inverted commas are nowadays used to indicate a quotation or a title:

'Look before you leap' is still good advice.
'Have you read "The Efficient Secretary"?'

Remember:

Punctuation is an essential aid to understanding and interpreting the written word correctly. Similarly, the spoken word is conveyed more readily if pauses and intonation are employed to provide oral punctuation.

Practice pieces

1 Set out the following recipient's name and address as it would appear in a business letter employing closed punctuation:

j a crossman esq m sc a m b i m sales manager sentinel security ltd 14 kings road maidenhead berks mb142ap

Now set it out according to open punctuation rules.

Punctuate the following:

2 he skimmed rapidly through the article he had found in his morning paper there was nothing on plant bargaining although the articles title had led him to suspect there would be

3 choosing his words carefully the chairman of the management committee who was clearly anxious to avert a head on clash expressed his desire for a calm rational and productive discussion

4 the equipment however proved more costly than the production managers estimate

5 however hard it may be keeping the customers goodwill is essential in any business

6 the first design which the advertising agency submitted was rejected by the marketing manager

7 if you dont tell him i will avowed john parker the sales manager angrily its ridiculous to set such an impossible target

8 the directors meeting will take place on wednesday 3rd July at 930 am in the boardroom

9 the sales performance for the last quarter has surpassed all expectations turnover has risen by no less than twenty five per cent

10 the following branches exceeded the January sales targets portsmouth aberdeen chester norwich and bath

11 the distribution of the companys branches map page 12 refers now provides a comprehensive nationwide coverage

12 he asked whether he could be heard at the back of the hall

13 i realise your problems and dont forget that i too began as a sales representative and i want to resolve them as quickly as possible

14 is there anyone here at this meeting tonight who seriously believes that such complex problems can be simply solved i very much doubt it

15 Using the closed punctuation system, set out the following typescript section of a business letter in an appropriate format:

your ref fj mg our ref jtd mdf 21st october 19— mrs fiona jackson ba dms personnel manager futura fabrics ltd queens house wellington place london wc2a4tg dear madam personnel management the next decade thank you for your letter of 16th october enquiring about the publication of the above book recently publicised in our autumn catalogue i very much regret that the publication date of gordon richardsons book has been delayed it is however anticipated that it will be available by the end of next january should you experience any difficulty in obtaining a copy from your local bookshop please do not hesitate to contact me in the meantime i enclose a copy of our current personnel management publications catalogue for your consideration please let met know if i may be of any further assistance yours faithfully jean davis mrs assistant sales manager enc

Spelling: some guidelines

The ability to spell correctly is particularly important for the manager or secretary since composing and distributing a wide range of written documents form a central part of their daily work. Moreover, adverse value-judgments are often made about an organisation if documents are received which are marred by spelling errors.

Though the English language is not the easiest to spell, patience, a handy dictionary and the following guide-lines will certainly help in overcoming some of the more common problem areas. It is extremely helpful to keep a record of any irregular spellings or exceptions to spelling rules.

The 100% rules

1 q is always followed by u
2 no English word ends in j
3 no English non-colloquial word ends in v

Plurals

Most English plurals are formed by adding s to the singular:

books   posters   aches

But there are exceptions:

potatoes   brushes   fuzzes

and foreign words with plurals which need to be learnt:

bureaux   stimuli   bases
formulae   stadia   aquaria

(though stadiums is now often seen).

Some words possess irregular plurals:

child/children   ox/oxen   woman/women

Words ending in y in the singular mostly drop the y and add ies in the plural:

secretaries   ladies   hobbies

If the y is preceded by a vowel then the usual s is added.

Note that words ending in: s x z sh ch ss in the singular add es to form the plural:

batches   crosses   mixes

Some words ending in f in the singular discard it for ves in the plural:

scarf scarves   leaf leaves   loaf loaves

Prefixes

An especially helpful rule is that adding a prefix to a word does not alter its basic spelling:

dis/appear un/necessary ig/noble
dis/seminate pro/claim

Note that some prefixes are connected to the base word by a hyphen:

pre-emptive   co-edition

Suffixes

The adverbial -ly ending is added quite straight-forwardly to most words:

lively   freely

even those which already end in l:

principally   critically

The -ing ending is also added straight on to the ends of words, except those which end in e, where the e is dropped:

moving   scraping   serving

Another very useful guide-line is that when a word ends in a consonant preceded by a vowel, the final consonant is doubled:

fit fitting   tip tipping

This rule is also true of -er, -ed and -est endings:

big bigger   occur occurred   omit omitted

Note that where many verbs end in t, a noun is formed by dropping it for the -sion ending:

convert conversion   divert diversion

The suffix -ness is normally straightforward, but note that when the base word ends in y, it is frequently replaced by an i:

happy happiness   lovely loveliness

Some endings which simply have to be learnt stem from various Latin roots for which the suffixes are: -able or -ible

commendable   infallible   unavoidable
incomprehensible   divisible

Homophones

The English language abounds with homophones – words which sound the same but which are spelled differently:

air heir   threw through   bite bight   course coarse what watt

It helps to collect these, to learn their spelling by heart and then to recognise them from the context in which they are used.

Rules of thumb

The soft g sound in a word means that the letter g (or gg) will be followed by: e, i, or y:

impinge   dingy   intelligent

The letter i comes before e, except after c:

conceive   ceiling   deceive

If a word ends in a single l, preceded by a single vowel, then the l will double before any further suffix is added:

typical typically   crystal crystallise
actual actually   unravel unravelled

A word ending in t which has more than one syllable *and* has the accent on the last syllable doubles the t before any further letters are added:

permit permitting

If you are not sure about a word beginning with f or ph, remember that the ph sound stems from Greek, so that it is likely to introduce such word components as:

phil   phono   phen   phal   phos   photo   phys

One further helpful rule of thumb is that a single vowel preceding a double letter consonant is very often short, but when the vowel sound is long, it is very often a single consonant:

fŭnnel fūneral   hămmer lion-tamer

scrăpping scrāping   fĭlling fīling

spĭnning dīning   ŏtter pōtato

Lastly, in syllables other than the first in a word, the sh sound is most likely to be either: ti, ci, si

spacious notion confusion

'There, there, Miss Lightbody, I *like* the way you spell. It gives my letters – character!'

Check list of trouble makers

The problem pack

The following words have caused spelling problems for generations of English-writing people. Study them carefully checking especially the parts which have been underlined, since this is where most people go wrong:

accessible
accessory
accommodation
acquiesce
acquire
address
aggressive
analysis
appalling
argument
beneficial
benefited
changeable
chargeable
committed
committee
conscious
contemptible
deceive
deferment
deferred
definite
develop
disappear
disseminate
embarrass
equipped
exaggerate
existence
foreign
fulfil
gauge
government
grateful
honorary
humorous
illegible
immovable

inconsistent
insistent
intelligible
irresponsible
maintenance
manoeuvre
miscellaneous
mischievous
necessary
negligible
noticeable
occasion
occurred
omission
omitted
parallel
precede
procedure
profess
psychology
receive
recommend
referred
regrettable
resistant
secede
separate
sincerely
skilful
succeed
supersede
technicality
temporary
tragedy
unnecessary
untouchable
woollen
wreath

Assignment

Compose a sentence illustrating the use (or different uses) for each of the words displayed as pairs.

Once you have used them correctly, you will be well on the way to eliminating fifty troublesome words from the 'problem-pack'!

Double trouble

The following pairs of words are frequently confused. Make sure you know the difference in their meaning and how they are used:

advice	advise
affect	effect
appal	appeal
canvas	canvass
complement	compliment
council	counsel
confidant	confident
continuous	continual
dependant	dependent
decent	descent
draft	draught
faint	feint
forward	foreword
farther	further
licence	license
to lie	to lay
lightening	lightning
lose	loose
passed	past
precede	proceed
principal	principle
practice	practise
stationary	stationery
straight	strait
waver	waiver

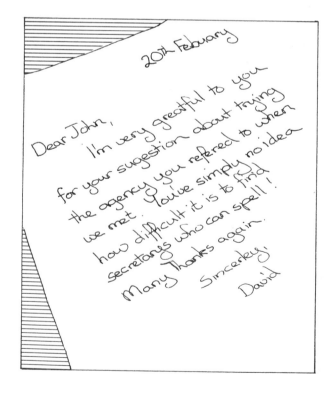

20   Use of English

Reported speech

Reported speech – the system of indirectly conveying what someone has previously said – is frequently used in business and public service organisations.

Many written documents, such as minutes, reports, articles and summaries report for the benefit of the reader what someone has actually said at an earlier time.

Reported speech is easily recognised by the absence of quotation marks and the introductory 'leaders' such as:

Mr Smith replied that . . .
He said that . . .
She hoped it would not . . .

The system for converting direct speech into reported or indirect speech is generally straight-forward, though there are some pitfalls to be avoided.

PERSON		
	Singular	Plural
1st	I	we
2nd	you	you
3rd	he, she	they

Remember that, as a general rule, the first or second persons in direct speech become third persons in reported speech:

'I shall ring you when I reach Bristol.'

He said that he would ring him/her when he reached Bristol.

In addition, it is important to avoid any ambiguities which may result in the change from direct to reported speech:

He thought he ought to resign.

This reported statement could have been as follows in direct speech:

'I think I ought to resign.'
'I think you ought to resign.'
'I think he ought to resign.'

To avoid such ambiguities occurring, it is sometimes necessary to insert a name or an identifying description:

Mr Jones thought Mr Brown ought to resign.
He thought the sales representative ought to resign.
He thought that he, Brown, ought to resign.

Tenses

In reported speech, the tenses of the verbs change as the following table indicates:

Direct speech	Reported speech
I go	He said he . . . went
I am going	he was going
I went	he had gone, he went
I was going	he had been going
I have gone	he had gone
I have been going	he had been going
I had gone	he had gone
I shall go	he would go
I shall be going	he would be going
I shall have gone	he would have gone

Note, however, that sometimes we use the present tense to indicate a customary practice:

'I go to my sports club every Monday.'

He said he was accustomed to going to his sports club every Monday.

The distancing effect

Because the reporting of the direct speech takes place after a lapse of time, some words require to be changed:

'I think this proposal deserves the close attention of everyone here today. I shall be speaking to the staff tomorrow and shall convey to them these suggestions, which have my support.'

He said he thought that proposal deserved the close attention of everyone there that day. He would be speaking to the staff on the following day and would convey to them those suggestions, which had his support.

Note also:
now   becomes   then
yesterday   becomes   the previous day

Using verbs in reported speech

When a lengthy exchange of direct speech is to be converted into reported speech in, say, the minutes of a meeting, it is necessary to avoid the dull repetition of 'he said that' and 'she said that', then 'he said that' . . . More expressive verbs should be used such as: urged that, insisted that, asked whether, to convey the tone of the direct speech.

Style

What is style

One of the often quoted definitions of style is: 'The best words in the best order'. Style involves the making of a number of deliberate choices:

What sort of words shall I use?
What sentence-structure shall I employ?
What tone shall I adopt?

Style in writing, then, is concerned with the conscious selection of an appropriate vocabulary, the construction of apt sentences and the creation of a fitting tone – the total impact of the message in its context.

Yet style is not an artificial branch of writing skills to be grafted on to a written message. It should be an integral part of the composition of the message and should work towards meeting specific objectives.

The first questions which need, therefore, to be answered are:

In what way should a vocabulary be appropriate?
What constitutes an apt sentence-structure?
What makes a tone fitting?

The end to which style is directed begins and ends with the recipient of the written message. Written communications are composed to satisfy specific aims:

the sender seeks
to inform
to persuade
to motivate
to explain to
to confirm to
to reassure
the recipient of the message

When setting out to compose a written message, it is necessary first to ensure that the essential aims of the message have been identified:
Letter of complaint to complain about a defective purchase and obtain its replacement
Letter of adjustment to redress a customer's complaint and retain his goodwill
Sales letter to persuade a customer to stock a new product
Letter of collection to obtain settlement of an overdue account
Sales memorandum to boost sales representatives' morale after a poor sales performance

If the writer has formulated clear and specific aims to be met by his written message, then he will quickly perceive that the style of, say, a letter of complaint, needs to be firm yet not rude, dissatisfied yet not aggressive. Similarly the writer of the letter adjusting the complaint will need to adopt a style which is mollifying and reassuring. The sales letter's author will choose a style which is persuasive and friendly without being unctuous or dishonest, and the sales director's memorandum to his sales force will strive to be positive and encouraging without being complacent or casual. The style, then, of a written message springs directly from its basic aims and is directly concerned with its impact upon the recipient.

In general terms, writers seeking to create a particular style for a given message should ensure that:

The message will be clearly understood.
It will be couched in terms which make its content acceptable.
The recipient will be motivated to act upon the message or to retain its information.

The recipient

If style of writing is primarily concerned with ensuring that a message is understood, accepted and acted upon by its recipient, then it follows that the writer cannot know too much about the person to whom he is writing!

Of course, circumstances frequently occur when letters, leaflets or articles are written for people whom their authors will never meet and therefore cannot know save in broad, general terms. Nevertheless, very many letters, memoranda, and reports are written by authors who have developed relationships with either clients, customers or colleagues.

It is always helpful, therefore, when choosing an appropriate style for a written message to create as full a profile as possible of the message's intended recipient.

Vocabulary

The ability to write effectively – and thus to reach and sway the reader – depends to a very large degree upon making sensitive choices from the stock of words or phrases available to create the desired effect.

The English language is particularly rich in synonyms, idiomatic expressions and patterns of syntax (the ways of constructing sentences), so that the writer is supplied with a large number of permutations through which to convey his meaning. The practised writer is able to impart delicate nuances and shades of meaning, to select at will words which

Choosing a style to suit the recipient's profile

AGE	People's outlooks and attitudes vary according to their age – a factor to be borne in mind when writing to an older or younger recipient.
BACKGROUND	People are moulded by their experiences and lifestyles. The metropolitan city-dweller and the rural farmworker inhabit different worlds, as do the small trader and the chairman of the multinational corporation. It is important, therefore to choose a style and approach in sympathy with the recipient's background.
EDUCATION	In our modern, high-technology society there are many different types of education – practical, technical and academic, and not all are linguistic-based. Every effort should therefore be made to express the message in terms which its recipient will understand and readily accept without being either baffled or patronised.
INTERESTS AND OUTLOOK	It is sometimes helpful to establish a common area of interest with the recipient of the message – not from any sense of seeking to flatter, but rather to establish a rapport. Similarly, knowledge of the recipient's outlook will forestall any tactless observations or remarks.
SPECIALISMS AND RESPONSIBILITIES	The nature and extent of the recipient's specialisms and responsibilities also have a bearing on the style with which he is addressed. Doctors, solicitors, surveyors or civil engineers writing to fellow specialists may well employ language which they would understand but which to the layman might appear to be jargon. It is essential, therefore, to use a specialist or general vocabulary with care, so as to avoid obscurity or unnecessary over-simplification.
RELATIONSHIP OF WRITER AND RECIPIENT	The style of a communication's message may well be affected by the relationship of writer and recipient. What may be recognised as friendly banter between long-established business associates may be regarded as over-familiarity in another context. In addition, the special relationship, for example, between business and customer may require particular care in establishing an appropriately courteous tone.

. . . It is helpful to create as full a profile as possible of the message's intended recipient. . . .

will be either sympathetic or cutting, minutely exact or broadly sweeping, aimed at the intellect or appealing to the heart. The writer must, therefore, constantly monitor his choice of vocabulary to ensure that he creates the desired tone and imparts the required meaning. By asking questions like the following at the point of composition, the writer will become much more sensitive to the power of the words he uses, and thus much more effective:

Will the recipient understand this word or phrase?
Is its meaning specific and unambiguous?
Am I seeking chiefly to inform or to persuade?
Does the word or phrase convey overtones or innuendoes to which the reader may object?
Is the word or phrase tactfully chosen?
Is it the most effective choice or am I being lazy?
Is it sufficiently precise / warm / objective / persuasive / accurate / uplifting etc?

The likely effect of a word or phrase upon the reader will depend upon his ability to comprehend it and upon the associations it has for him. The following table illustrates some of the alternative characteristics which words possess:

Certain combinations reflected in a word – long, polysyllabic, abstract, Latin-rooted – may make strenuous comprehension demands upon the reader, while other combinations – short, monosyllabic, concrete, Old English-rooted – may be much easier to understand. Moreover, this latter combination may also subject the reader to emotional overtones of meaning stemming from the deep associations which the words possess:

residence/house
domicile/home
capitulate/give in
conflagration/fire
extinguish/put out

Word characteristics	
long	short
polysyllabic	monosyllabic
abstract	concrete
objective	subjective
denotative	connotative
informative	persuasive
rational	emotive
old-established	new
formal	familiar, colloquial
indigenous	foreign
Old English roots	Latin/Greek roots
technical	general
abstruse	direct

The appropriate selection of a word or phrase depends very much upon the context of the message and the response sought from the reader:

Document	Context	Tone	Vocabulary bias
report	sales analysis	neutral	objective, informative
unsolicited sales letter	advertising	inducing to buy	subjective, persuasive, emotive
article	publicising company expansion	friendly	direct, persuasive, colloquial

Vocabulary style check
length · syllable count · simple – abstruse · emotive – persuasive · objective – informative · specialist – general · formal – colloquial

Using the Word Characteristics chart as a guide, analyse the following groups of words:

Advertising	Management	Reporting	Selling	Industrial
new	job-appraisal	investigate	discount	strike
wonder	motivate	interpret	special offer	slump
fantastic	enrichment	infer	de luxe	dole
big value	objectives	qualify	sample	lock-out
better	morale	indicate	extras	inflation
magic	aptitude	sample	desirable	bosses
love	target	questionnaire	exclusive	confetti money
warm	deadline	research	family-size	negotiate
cool	efficient	cross-section	fully-guaranteed	unofficial
fresh	effectiveness	value-judgment	personalised	go-slow
sunshine	job-satisfaction	recommendation	custom-built	productivity
tingling	delegate	evaluate	hand-made	piece-work
enjoyment	authorise	analysis	quality	picket
join	accountability	comparatively	performance	provocation
together	enthuse	predominantly	export model	labour
even whiter	analyse	logical	bargain	staff

Study the following extracts and comment upon the vocabulary and its intended effect upon the reader:

Sales report

. . . The effect of the new bonus incentive scheme has been to increase December sales of products generating optimum gross profit by 17% compared with November. . . . The response of sales representatives to the Head Office directive requiring a reduction in days of credit has exceeded expectations. The target of 28 days has been attained. The regional mean average now stands at 26 days. . . .

Unsolicited sales letter advertising perfume

. . . The magic of Michèle, an exquisite new perfume from France has been especially created for women like you. Michèle is the fragrance of a misty morning, the mystery of warm, scented nights. The magic of Michèle tells him you care, when words would break the spell!

Article in a house journal describing a factory construction programme

What is five foot two high, has big, staring eyes and a gaping mouth?
Yours truly! Well, that's how I must have looked when they said, 'Get down to Welborough New Town and find out what the place is like where they're building our brand new factory.'
What is six feet tall and bounces and whistles?
Yes, you've guessed it! Me again, when I'd looked round Welborough. What a place! It's clean, bright as a new pin and already a thriving centre of commerce and culture. . . .

Sentence structure

The ability to transmit a written message effectively to its reader depends not only upon choosing the right words, but also upon constructing suitable sentences.

As a general rule, the shorter the sentence and the fewer the number of syllables per word, the easier it will be to understand. Indeed, some researchers consider that sentences of more than twenty-five words begin to pose comprehension problems for their readers. Much depends, however, upon the clarity and control of the sentence structure.

Composing sentences effectively in continuous prose also relies very much upon using structures which are varied and upon creating a sense of balance within each sentence's design. For example, a succession of very short, simple sentences quickly becomes boring and makes their writer seem immature:

Thank you for your letter of 3rd July 19—. You enquire in it about the cost of Ariel car radios.

There are two models. One is the Ariel Tourist. The other is the Ariel Europa. The Tourist costs £28.00. The Europa costs £42.00. It has the added feature of pre-selected station tuning buttons. The radios are guaranteed for twelve months. The prices include postage and packing costs.

I enclose a catalogue featuring both models. I look forward to hearing from you.

The above example is made up of twelve sentences, the average length of which is about seven words. The reason for its seeming immaturity stems from the shortness of the sentences and the simplicity of much of the vocabulary. Together they demand a reading age of between nine and eleven.

Consider the same message with a more complex sentence structure:

Thank you for your letter of 3rd July 19— enquiring about the cost of Ariel car radios.

I recommend both the Ariel Tourist, which costs £28.00, and the Europa, which has the added feature of pre-selected station tuning buttons, and costs £42.00. Both radios are guaranteed for twelve months and prices include postage and packing costs.

I enclose a catalogue featuring both models and look forward to hearing from you.

The effect of this restructuring is to make the message more interesting and acceptable to the reader. The letter's message is more fluent and the balance of each sentence has improved. Part of the reason for its improved readability is that the reading age has become much more adult.

There are, of course, dangers in allowing sentence structures to run out of control:

As the above facts indicate, the effectiveness of the proposed advertising campaign would depend not only upon the timing of the national press advertisements, where co-ordination would be essential, but also upon the extent of the budget which would be allocated to the commissioning of a series of linked television commercials, both of which would be aimed at securing the interest of the teen-age market as well as the young married couples in their twenties who also share similar tastes in clothing.

The above example is a single sentence of some 82 words! Such a sentence length places undue demands upon the reader in remembering the sense of all its component phrases and clauses. Thus, as another general rule, the longer the sentence, and the more numerous the dependent clauses, the more difficult will it be to understand – especially if there are many long words.

When constructing sentences within paragraphs or a piece of continuous prose, the writer must also aim to create variety and balance in the structure of his sentences. In addition, care must be taken to ensure that the ideas in any passage flow smoothly and easily, so that sentences are linked and the thread of argument remains intact.

As the car radios example illustrates, ideas soon become plodding and boring if expressed in a series of short, simple sentences comprising single main clauses. Many writers therefore try to link two or more ideas in sentences by constructing sentences as follows:

main clause + dependent clause

dependent clause + main clause + dependent clause

Delivery has regrettably been delayed because spare parts are in short supply.

After the automatic key has been depressed, the copier will continue to print copies until the pre-set number has been reached.

Notice that when the dependent clause precedes the main clause, the effect is to emphasise the main clause and especially those words which end the sentence:

Whatever the outcome may be, the board has decided to go ahead with the project.

As your sales record has been outstanding this year, I am pleased to award you a bonus of £500.

Although sales fell last month, total sales to date are 20% up on last year.

Sentence structure style check
length · simple – complex · clause order · variety · balance · linking words

---

One way, therefore, of achieving variety in sentence-structure is to alternate the positioning of clauses in sentences which follow each other.

Whatever the outcome may be, the board has decided to go ahead with the project. Moreover, it wishes to place on record that it has complete trust in the Marketing Department.
Though its development will not be easy, the board is confident that the new product will prove a success.

Notice also in the above example the emphasis placed upon 'prove a success' as the last words in a finishing main clause.

Another means of creating interesting complex sentences is to insert a dependent clause between a subject and its verb:

The merchandiser, which is supplied free of charge, stands approximately two metres high.

If, however, a main clause is followed by one or more dependent phrases or clauses, the effect is for the impact of the sentence to tend to tail off:

The sales target of £50 000 has been reached, although competition was fierce from companies which traditionally trade in our markets.

A sense of anticipation and suspense is created when the order of the clauses in the above example is reversed.
Balance in sentence structure may be achieved in a number of ways and constructions like the following are often helpful:
not only . . . but also, both . . . and, either . . . or, although . . . nevertheless

The colours not only remain fast in the wash, but are also resistant to fading in bright light.
Either we reduce our prices across our whole product range, or we run the risk of becoming uncompetitive.
Our designers have improved both the accuracy and the elegance of our new Chronos wrist watch.

Alternatively, the semi-colon may be used as a pivot upon which to balance a sentence:

The Faragucchi Bullet has been built to last; it has a rust-resistant sub-frame and is meticulously under-sealed.

Tone

The creation of an appropriate tone in a piece of writing is largely cumulative – it is the total effect of the message upon the reader and stems not only from what is transmitted but also from how the message is expressed.
Tone is created by the interaction of a number of factors:

Tone check-list

The context of the message

Choice of vocabulary, terminology

Sentence-structure, syntax, rhythms

Bias of the language: emotive, informative, persuasive, neutral, objective etc.

Relationship of writer and reader: rapport or hostility etc.

The recipient of a message identifies its tone by the way he reacts to it. It is either warm and friendly or cool and distant, formal or informal, terse or reassuring, pompous or modest, rude or courteous. The efficient writer is constantly monitoring the tone of his writing to ensure that he does not inadvertently fail to meet the aim of his message by offending the reader or by evoking a negative response as a result of couching his message in an inappropriate tone.
Consider the following letter of adjustment to a customer who has experienced problems in operating a new cassette-recorder:

Dear Sir,
The problem of operating our Akustik cassette-recorder, of which you complain in your letter of 13th July 19— is simply remedied.
It is merely a matter of depressing the 'Play' and 'Record' buttons simultaneously. Page 2 of the Operating Manual explains the procedure quite straightforwardly.
I trust you will experience no further difficulties.
Yours faithfully,

The writer of the above letter adopts a pompous and condescending tone towards a customer who has experienced difficulty in carrying out what may be a simple operating procedure. As a consequence of the tone of the explanation, the customer is made to feel totally incompetent and the writer's brusque manner does nothing to cement customer relations. How much better would the adjustment letter have been if the writer had created a more helpful and courteous tone:

Dear Mr Gray,

I was sorry to read in your letter of 13th July 19— of the trouble you are experiencing in operating the Akustik cassette-recorder.

Operating an unfamiliar piece of equipment does, I know, sometimes cause initial difficulties. In order to record on the Akustik, it is necessary to depress both the 'Play' and the 'Record' buttons at the same time. You will be able to check that you are recording successfully by noting the movement on the sound level meter's needle. The photographs on page 2 of the Operating Manual are helpful here.

I hope this explanation will enable you to gain much pleasure from your new Akustik. Please let me know if I may be of any further help.

Yours sincerely,

Very often, the choice of an appropriate tone for a particular document springs naturally from its intended use. We expect, for example, that a report will be factual and objective and that the creation of a suitable tone will make use of impersonal and passive verb constructions:

It was evident that . . .
The interviews revealed that . . .
The branch manager, Mr Wilkins, was asked for his views on the reasons for the recent increase in staff turnover. . . .
If the problem is to be resolved, the following action needs to be taken: . . .

We also expect a press-release to be broadly factual, although it seeks to present, say, an insurance company in a good light:

. . The Castle Insurance Company will be moving into the new Castlemount office block during the week-end of 24th–25th March, to ensure a minimum of inconvenience to its customers.

Relays of volunteer staff will be transferring the company's computerised records to their new home in the Computer Centre housed in the basement of the twenty-one storey building. The Castlemount offices are protected by one of the latest thermostatically controlled and smoke-sensitive fire alarm systems . . .

Equally, we expect personal letters from colleagues to be expressed in an appropriately direct and sincere tone:

I was very sorry to learn of your intention to resign. Though I shall miss your help and advice very much, I realise that you are now anxious to take on a post of more responsibility. I sincerely regret that, at this time, I am unable to offer you an appointment which would enable the company to keep your valued services. . . .

Whatever the situation, most recipients of written documents are quick to perceive when a tone is glib, insincere, dishonest or hypocritical:

I was indeed sorry to hear of your intention to resign. The company is particularly fortunate that John Parker is more than ready to take over your department in your stead.

I wish you well in your future post and hope it affords you the satisfaction you have been unable to find here at Marshalls.

If we accept that producing written documents is expensive, time-consuming and essential – both in terms of achieving organisational objectives and fostering human relations – then the creation of a suitable tone in whatever we write is of paramount importance!

Paragraph structures

One further aspect of style concerns the structuring of ideas not only within sentences, but also within paragraphs. Just as the creation of variety is important in sentence structure, so it is in paragraph design. The following diagram illustrates the various effects of structuring paragraphs with the 'key' or 'topic' sentence occurring either at the opening, in the middle or at the close of the paragraph. Each adjacent graph indicates the likely effect of the reader's interest in each case:

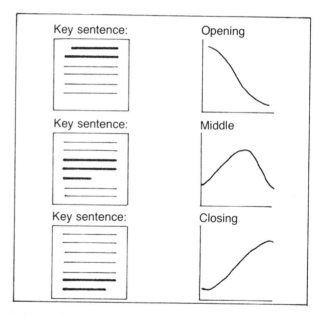

The reader's interest tends to be at its height where the paragraph's most important 'key' sentence makes its impact. Thus opening paragraphs in a passage often start with an arresting key sentence to secure the reader's attention and finishing paragraphs often keep the reader in suspense until a concluding key sentence point is made. Varying paragraph structures helps to create emphasis and to keep the reader's interest alive.

aim for	**Style checks**	avoid

aim for		avoid
clarity precision accuracy		irrelevance vagueness ambiguity
brevity		longwindedness rambling
simplicity directness	**ensure**	obscurity complexity
courtesy helpfulness	**your**	rudeness sarcasm
respect dignity	**style**	pomposity condescension
straightforwardness	**suits**	jargon officialese
freshness caring	**your**	clichés stock responses
appropriate tone	**aims**	over-formality over-familiarity

appropriate
  language
		inappropriate
		  colloquialisms
		slang

honesty integrity		hypocrisy insincerity

lead to		lead to
understanding acceptance action		irritation rejection delay

Keep a constant style check on

vocabulary	is it	obscure? over-simple? accurate? lazy? too abstract? too colloquial? too formal? jargon? precise?
expression	is it	straightforward? pompous? full of clichés? simple? abstruse? stale? ambiguous? clear? fresh?
sentence-structure	is it	too long? rambling? too short? easy to follow? too complex? direct? out of control?
tone	is it	creating the desired effect? warm? aloof? friendly? cold? rude? aggressive? courteous? insincere? honest? not firm enough? hypocritical? over-familiar? too formal?

Your style should reinforce the aims of your message!

Assessment questions

Parts of speech

1 Compose a definition for each of the following: noun, pronoun, verb, adverb, adjective, preposition, conjunction, interjection. Give an example of each.

2 Distinguish between a common, proper and collective noun and supply an example of each.

Syntax

3 How would you define the following: a sentence, a subject, a predicate, a finite verb, an object?
Compose examples of each in suitable sentences and identify them.

4 What is the difference between a transitive and an intransitive verb? Compose two sentences to illustrate your answer.

5 Define: a phrase, a clause.
Supply an example of each.

6 What is the difference between a simple and a complex sentence? Provide an example of each.

7 What is the difference between a main clause and a dependent clause? Compose a sentence containing one of each.

8 Compose two sentences to show the use of a verb, firstly as an adjective and secondly as a noun (gerund).

9 Explain the difference between a verb used actively and passively and design two sentences to show the use of each.

10 What is the effect of using the passive form of the verb in terms of style?

Usage

11 What do you understand by the term 'agreement' in connection with:
subject/verb, pronouns
Illustrate your answer.

12 How would you advise someone wishing to use 'who' or 'whom' correctly in sentences?

13 What is a cliché? Provide two examples.

14 How would you advise someone wishing to avoid writing incomplete sentences?

Punctuation

15 Identify three different uses of the comma. Illustrate your answer.

16 Compose a sentence to illustrate the use of the semi-colon.

17 Explain with illustrations the use of the apostrophe.

18 How is the dash used?

19 What are the conventions governing the use of inverted commas? Illustrate your answer.

20 Provide two examples of the use of brackets.

Spelling

21 How does the addition of a prefix affect the spelling of its base word?

22 What happens to a word ending in a consonant and preceded by a single vowel when an -ing, -er, -ed or -est suffix is added to it?

23 What is a homophone? Illustrate your answer.

24 Provide four prefixes beginning with ph.

25 By what alternative letters might the soft g be followed?

Style

26 What factors do you consider go together to form style?

27 How does an appropriate style help to make a written message effective?

28 What aspects of the recipient's profile should be kept in mind when writing?

29 How many word characteristics can you recall? Compile a list.

30 What factors influence the choice of vocabulary when composing a written document?

31 What advice on sentence structuring would you give someone entering a first job involving drafting written documents?

32 How would you define tone?

33 Identify three different ways of structuring key sentences in paragraphs and explain their effect upon the reader.

34 What do you understand by the terms: jargon, obscurity, ambiguity, condescension?

Discussion topics

1 Is a knowledge of grammar and syntax of any help to a writer?

2 'You can either spell or you can't!'

3 'It's not what you say, it's the way that you say it!'

4 Provided a message gets across, it matters little how.

5 'I write best when I don't think about it'.

Extracts for analysis

What criticisms can you make of the style, tone and use of language in the following extracts? Either discuss or write an account of your findings. Rewrite each extract in what you consider a more appropriate style.

I have to inform you that your enquiry will be dealt with in due course.

I must apologise for the delay in your receiving your vehicle after service.

As you will readily appreciate, motor-vehicle wheels need to be balanced dynamically as well as statically to avoid the transmission of vibration through the steering linkage.

Moreover, the diagnosis of mis-alignment in the near-side front wheel revealed that feathering and premature wear had been caused to the tyre, which as you realise, being assymetrical in tread design is incompatible with tyres of another make.

I trust this explanation will satisfactorily account for the delay.

The reason I am writing to you on a plain piece of notepaper is because of the incompetence of your firm in supplying my order for company stationery, which you may just recall you received last December.

'Mr Johnson said to tell you we seem to have dropped a bit of a clanger over the grinding machine. The drive belt's come adrift and we're up the creek for a spare. He says we're due for a drop next Monday and he'll give you a tinkle, OK?'

It has come to my attention that departmental staff are in breach of their conditions of service as a result of unpunctuality.

Unless a substantial improvement is discerned in the immediate future, disciplinary measures will be taken.

'Thank you for your enquiry, but my company only deals in genuine antiques.'

Our current inability to meet the requirements of your recently remitted order is occasioned by an unanticipated shortage of the spare parts specified.

Due to circumstances beyond our control, there has been a temporary delay in effecting repairs to your lawn-mower, which we hope to rectify as soon as the situation eases.
    Assuring you of our best attention at all times.

Further to your memorandum of 14th June 19—.
    Of course, in normal circumstances my department would be only too pleased to be of assistance with the provision of advertising material for your display on 21st August.
    Regretfully, however, only reference copies of such material are kept centrally. You may care to try Sales.
    Do let me know if I may be of any assistance in any other sphere.

RECOMMENDATIONS

    Any future improvement in com-
    pany turnover is entirely depen-
    dent upon either lowering or
    raising the price or the quality
    of our current product range.

    If the latter option is adopted,
    the prospect of increased compe-
    tition or a reduction in gross
    profits must be faced.

    In such a clear-cut situation,
    the action needed to resolve
    the problem is self-explanatory.

Much as I sympathise with your predicament, I do feel that, I am not in a position to grant you further leave of absence to nurse your sick parent. I am sure you will see the difficult position in which I feel myself to be placed in that I do not consider myself to be entirely unfeeling in such matters, having experienced a similar situation myself. Perhaps if you call in to see me a solution will readily suggest itself, which will prove acceptable to you yourself.